THE
TENNESSEE GAZETTEER,

OR

TOPOGRAPHICAL DICTIONARY;

CONTAINING

A DESCRIPTION OF THE SEVERAL

COUNTIES, TOWNS, VILLAGES, POST OFFICES, RIVERS, CREEKS, MOUNTAINS, VALLEYS, &C.

IN THE STATE OF TENNESSEE,

ALPHABETICALLY ARRANGED.

TO WHICH IS PREFIXED

A GENERAL DESCRIPTION OF THE STATE:

Its Civil Divisions, Resources, Population, &c. and a Condensed History from the Earliest Settlements down to the rise of the Convention in the year 1834.

WITH AN APPENDIX,

Containing a List of the Practising Attorneys at Law in each County; Principal Officers of the General and State Governments; Times of Holding Courts; And other Valuable Tables.

BY EASTIN MORRIS

NASHVILLE:
PUBLISHED BY W. HASELL HUNT & CO.
BANNER AND WHIG OFFICE.

1834.

Notice

In many older books, foxing (or discoloration) occurs and, in some instances, print lightens with wear and age. Reprinted books, such as this, often duplicate these flaws, notwithstanding efforts to reduce or eliminate them. The pages of this reprint have been digitally enhanced and, where possible, the flaws eliminated in order to provide clarity of content and a pleasant reading experience.

Originally published:
Nashville: 1834

Reprinted:
Janaway Publishing, Inc.
Santa Maria, California
2007

Janaway Publishing, Inc.
2412 Nicklaus Dr.
Santa Maria, California 93455
(805) 925-1038
www.janawaygenealogy.com

ISBN 10: 1-59641-120-1
ISBN 13: 978-1-59641-120-3

Made in the United States of America

CONTENTS

The Tennessee Gazetteer 1
General Description of the State of Tennessee 5
    Face of the Country 6
    Minerals, etc. 7
    Climate 8
    Productions, etc. 8
    Antiquities 9
    Natural Curiosities 9
    Rivers 9
    Schools 10
    Civil Divisions 10
    Constitution 12
    Congressional Districts 14
    History 14
    Constitution of the State of Tennessee 70
Tennessee Gazetteer 103
Appendix 285
    A List of Lawyers in the State of Tennessee ...285
    Governors of Tennessee 292
    Government, 1834 293
    Judiciary 293
    Senators and Representatives 297
    Executive Department of the U.S. 300
    Stage Routes in Tennessee 302
    Steam Boat Routes 306
Index 307

PREFACE.

In presenting to the public the "TENNESSEE GAZETTEER," the compiler is not without a hope that it will meet with a favorable reception; as similar publications have been well patronized in many of the States. And as it contains entire, the NEW CONSTITUTION, now pending for ratification or rejection, by the people, he anticipates a speedy sale of the whole edition.

The principal sources from whence the materials have been drawn; are, Haywood's Civil and Political History of Tennessee; Haywood's Natural and Aboriginal History of Tennessee; Flint's Geography and History of the Western States; the Acts of the General Assembly of North Carolina; the Acts and Journals of the General Assembly of the State of Tennessee; Darby's and Morse's Gazetteer; the list of the Post Offices, from the General Post Office; Niles' Weekly Register; National Register; American Almanac; Rhea's large and valuable Map of Tennessee; Lucas' Map of Tennessee; Tanner's latest Maps; J. P. Ayres' Map of Nashville; Mitchell's Map and Tables; Official documents in the office of the Secretary of State; personal observation and research for the last five years; tabular statements furnished by the members of the Legislature, members of the Convention, lawyers, clerks, post-masters, editors of newspapers, clergymen and teachers—and written communications from the following gentlemen, to wit:—Thomas Davis and James T. Byler Esqs., of Bedford county; S. Roberson Esq., of Bledsoe; Nathaniel Cox and John Saffaler Esqs., of Blount; Hugh Graham and Walter R. Evans Esqs., of Claiborne; John C. Roadman Esq., of Cocke; Valerius P. Winchester Esq., of Davidson; James McCombs Esq., of Giles; Asabel Rawlings Esq., of Hamilton; Col. John H. Bills, of Hardeman. J. S. Broyles Esq., of Hardin; William H. Miller Esq., of Humphreys;

Joseph S. Chunn Esq., and Hon. Judge Peck, of Jefferson; Doctor J. G. M. Ramsey of Knox; Samuel M'Connel Esq., of M'Minn; Jas. Chaudoin Esq., of Marion; H. W. K. Myrick Esq., of Maury; William Wray Esq., of Overton; W. Gillenwaters Esq., of Rhea; J. W. Ferguson Esq., of Robertson; John Lynn Jr. and Samuel Rhea Esqrs., of Sullivan; D. A. Deaderick Esq., of Washington; Richard Nixon Esq., of Haywood; Jepthah Gardner Esq., of Weakley; John M. Clemmens Esq., of Fentress; J. Haynes Esq., of Fayette; and J. W. Gibson Esq., of Tipton.

The distances from the post towns and post offices to Washington City, Nashville, &c., are given as received from the post office department, except when they were known to be incorrect. The longitudes of places are given from the meridian of Washington City which is computed at 77 degrees west from London or Greenwich, so that by adding 77 degrees to the given longitudes, you have the distance from the latter place.

The descriptions of the counties, principal towns, rivers, &c., are substantially correct. Many unimportant errors respecting the villages, small creeks, and places of minor note, doubtless exist, but great pains have been taken to prevent them.

The historical sketches from the earliest settlements down to the adoption of the Constitution in 1796, are principally from Haywood's and Flint's, and the chronological memoranda, from thence to the present time, were collated from the journals of state, &c. But as the whole work is confessedly a compilation of historical, geographical, topographical and statistical matter, authors and correspondents consulted, are but seldom credited by marks of quotation.

To a generous public he submits the result of his labors.

EASTIN MORRIS.

GENERAL DESCRIPTION

OF THE

STATE OF TENNESSEE

The State of TENNESSEE is bounded on the east and south east by the State of North Carolina; on the west by the river Mississippi; on the north by the States of Kentucky and Virginia; and on the south by the States of Georgia, Alabama and Mississippi. Mr. Darby in his Gazetteer, traces the lines as follows:

Beginning at the south west angle of the State of Kentucky, on the left bank of the Mississippi river, and running thence east along the south boundary of Kentucky, 64 miles; thence up the Tennessee river, 12 miles; thence by a line a little south of due east along the southern boundary of Kentucky, to the extreme south west angle of Virginia, 250; thence continuing the last mentioned line along the southern boundary of Virginia, to the extreme north east angle of the state, 105; thence south west, along the north west boundary of North Carolina, to the north boundary of Georgia, 174; thence due west, along latitude 35°, the north boundary of Georgia, to the north east angle of Alabama, 100; thence along the north boundary of Alabama, to the Tennessee river, and N.E. angle of the state of Mississippi, 140; thence to the N.W. angle of Mississippi, or S.W. angle of Tennessee, on the Mississippi river, 116; thence up the Mississippi river, to the place of beginning, 150. Total, 1,111 miles.

By this calculation, the area of the state is about 40,900 square miles, or 26,176,000 acres. This estimate is probably too low. A select committee of the legislature in 1833, with

Mr. Nicholson at the head, reported 45,000 square miles, or 28,000,000 acres.[1] The longest line that can be drawn in the state, is from the south west to the north east angle, a distance of near six hundred miles. The medial length is about 430, and medial breadth 104 miles, between 35° and 36° 36′ N. latitude, and 4° 30′ and 13° 20′ W. lon. from Washington City. The extreme north, on the Tennessee river is about 36° 40′.

Face of the Country.—On this subject but few remarks will suffice here, as a minute description of the several counties, towns, rivers, &c. is given under their respective heads in the alphabetical arrangement. It may be proper, however, to observe, that in this respect it presents as great a diversity as that of any state in the Union. The Cumberland Mountains range through the state in an oblique direction from north east to south west, between 7° and 9° west longitude, dividing it into two sections, hitherto designated as East and West Tennessee. Since the purchase in 1818 of all the territory between the Tennessee and Mississippi rivers, all that part of West Tennessee has acquired the name of the 'Western District.' But these three grand divisions are now more appropriately called *East, Middle* and *West* Tennessee.

East Tennessee, including twenty two counties, is generally mountainous. The Alleghanies branch out into a great many ridges; the most lofty of which are Cumberland, Laurel, &c. Stone, Yellow, Iron, Bald, Unica, &c. are different peaks of a continued chain of mountains. There are many other ridges and mountains east of the Cumberland of considerable magnitude, such as Wallen or Walden's Ridge, Copper Ridge, Clinch Mountain, Bays Mountain, &c. &c.

Middle Tennessee, which contains twenty six counties, is comparatively a level country. Parts of the counties of Franklin, Fentress, Jackson, Overton, Smith, Warren and White are somewhat mountainous and broken; and there is a chain

---

[1] The area of Tennessee is 42,244 square miles (*World Almanac*, 1970).

of hills between the Cumberland and Tennessee rivers, and similar elevations between Duck and Elk. But a large proportion of the lands in this middle section, in addition to their acknowledged fertility, lie well for cultivation.

West Tennessee, or Western District has fourteen counties, and presents in the main a gentle undulating surface, and a light sandy soil well adapted to the growth of cotton, which is there the great staple.

All the varieties of soil and scenery to be found in the western country, are exhibited in Tennessee. But with the exception of the numerous mountains, caves, and cataracts to be found in East Tennessee, she has no marked peculiarity among the flourishing states of the great valley of the west.

East Tennessee, although sufficiently fertile for ordinary farming, can never expect to vie with the middle and western sections in profitable agriculture; but she has an inexhaustible water power, which if properly applied, would make it one of the finest manufacturing districts in America. Besides, with the exception perhaps of the single article of cotton, there is scarcely a vegetable product common in the states which could not be advantageously cultivated.

Minerals, &c. Iron ore, of all others the most important to society, is found in great abundance in nearly every county in East and Middle Tennessee. Many of the mines are extensively worked; supplying the country with iron and castings equal if not superior to any in the United States. Lead has been found in several places, but there is no evidence of extensive veins of ore. Fine beds of stone-coal exist in both East and Middle Tennessee. Buhr and other mill stone grit, marble, rock crystals, gypsum, paints and dye stuffs, and salts and nitrous earths may be procured in any quantities in the mountainous districts; and perhaps no state in the Union is so well supplied with fine mineral springs. On the confines of Georgia and North Carolina, the search for gold has become an object of profitable enterprise. A most excellent quarry of variegated marble has been found on the Harpeth, eleven miles from Nashville, and a ware-house for the sale of the polished slabs, has been established in Nashville.

Climate.—In this medial region, between the northern and southern extremities of the country, the climate is, of course, delightful; and may be ranked amongst the healthiest in the world. The summers are not excessively warm for the latitude, and the winters west of the mountains are mild, but rendered somewhat unpleasant by their humidity. Perhaps there are no two contiguous sections of equal extent, and similar latitude in the United States, which differ more in general appearance, and in the temperature of the climate, than do the eastern and western parts of Tennessee. In East Tennessee, the country is too elevated and cold for the culture of cotton; and a sufficiency is not raised for domestic consumption; whilst in Middle and West Tennessee, it is the agricultural staple. The winters in East Tennessee are but little milder than they are in Ohio and Indiana; and deep snows are not unfrequent. In elevated and favourable positions, this state is almost universally healthy. In the valleys adjoining stagnant marshes, and on the alluvions of the large rivers, it is here as elsewhere in similar situations, more or less sickly.

Productions, &c.—All the forest trees common in the western country, are found in this state. Juniper, Red Cedar and Pine exist in various places. Beautiful groves of pine abound in the mountains, and spirits of turpentine, tar, rosin and lampblack, are manufactured in considerable quantities. Apples, pears, and plums, are raised in great perfection. The mulberry tree flourishes as well in this state as any part of the United States. It is to be found in almost every grove, and seems difficult to eradicate. From experiments made, it is evident that at no distant day, the culture of this useful and indigenous tree, will be especially regarded; and that silk will become, as cotton is now, the staple of the country. Some attention has been paid to the cultivation of the vine, and it is found to flourish admirably. Peach trees do well, if they escape the late frosts. Their cultivation has of late, been much neglected, and it is believed there are fewer good peach orchards now, than there were twenty years ago.

Taking the whole produce of the state in one view, cotton is unquestionably the staple article of growth; but as before observed, the diversified soil and climate, rear all the products of the western states, in ample abundance for domestic consumption, at least. Whiskey, hogs, horses, cattle, flour, gun powder, saltpeter, coarse linen, poultry, bacon, lard, butter, apples, pork, tobacco, Irish and sweet potatoes, tar, turpentine, rosin and lampblack, constitute the loading of boats for the southern market.

In East Tennessee, considerable attention is paid to the raising of cattle, horses and hogs, which are driven over the mountains, to the Atlantic country for sale.[3] Middle Tennessee is very celebrated for the raising of fine turf horses; and the farmers have doubtless devoted an undue attention to the rearing of this class, in exclusion of a proportion of saddle and harness horses.

Antiquities.—Mounds and Forts of stone and earth are found in great numbers in this, as well as most of the western states. To describe minutely the various aboriginal remains, would be out of place here. It is sufficient to observe that there is a great similarity in their appearance wherever they are found. Judge Haywood in his 'Natural and Aboriginal History of Tennessee,' has embodied a great variety of interesting facts and ingenuous speculations in relation to them; to which the inquisitive reader is referred for minutiae. See also, articles 'Bledsoe's Lick,' 'Stone Fort,' &c.

Natural Curiosities.—For a description of the mountains, cascades, caves, petrifactions and organic remains, the reader is referred to the articles in the alphabetical arrangement. See 'Bald Mountain,' 'Falling Water,' 'Christian's Creek,' 'Taylor's Creek,' 'Bledsoe's Lick,' 'Bledsoe,' 'White,' 'Warren,' 'Blount,' 'Arch Cave,' 'Haywood,' &c.

Rivers.—The principal rivers are the Mississippi, Tennessee,

---

[3] See "The Great Drives," in Wilma Dykeman, *The French Broad* (Knoxville, 1955), Ch. 9.

Cumberland, Holston, Nolachucky, French Broad, Tellico, Clinch, Big Emmery, Hiwassee, Obid, Caney Fork, Stone's, Harpeth, Red, Powell's, Sequatchee, Elk, Duck, Obion, Forked Deer, Wolf and Hatchee, which, with their principal tributaries, are particularly described under their respective heads.

Schools.—The principal literary seminaries in this state, are the Nashville University, at Nashville; East Tennessee College, at Knoxville; Greenville College, at Greenville; Washington College, in Washington county; Jackson College, in Maury county, and the Southern and Western Theological Seminary at Maryville; and there are one or more incorporated academies in each county, many of which are in a flourishing condition.

CIVIL DIVISIONS.

East Tennessee.

Counties.	*Chief Towns.*	*Situation.*
Anderson,	Clinton,	Clinch river.
Bledsoe,	Pikeville,	Sequatchee river.
Blount,	Maryville,	Little River waters.
Campbell,	Jacksboro,	Cumberland Moun's.
Carter,	Elizabethton,	Watauga river.
Claiborne,	Tazewell,	Russel's creek.
Cocke,	New Port,	French Broad.
Grainger,	Rutledge,	Near Holston.
Greene,	Greenville,	Near Nolachucky.
Hamilton,	Dallas,	Tennessee river.
Hawkins,	Rogersville,	Near Holston.
Jefferson,	Dandridge,	French Broad.
Knox,	Knoxville,	Holston.
M'Minn,	Athens,	Estanalla creek.
Marion,	Jasper,	Sequatchee.
Monroe,	Madisonville,	Bat creek.
Morgan,	Montgomery,	Emmery's river.

TENNESSEE GAZETTEER. 11

Counties.	Chief Towns.	Situation.
Roane,	Kingston,	Clinch
Rhea,	Washington,	Tennessee river.
Sevier,	Sevierville,	Little Pigeon.
Sullivan,	Blountsville,	Watauga waters.
Washington,	Jonesboro',	Limestone creek.

MIDDLE TENNESSEE.

Counties.	Chief Towns.	Situation.
Bedford,	Shelbyville,	Duck river.
Davidson,	Nashville,	Cumberland river.
Dickson,	Charlotte,	Jones' creek.
Franklin,	Winchester,	Elk river.
Giles,	Pulaski,	Richland creek.
Fentress,	Jamestown,	Cumberland Moun't.
Hardin,	Savannah,	Tennessee river.
Hickman,	Centerville,	Duck river.
Humphreys,	Reynoldsburg,	Tennessee river.
Lawrence,	Lawrenceburg,	Shoal creek.
Lincoln,	Fayetteville,	Elk river.
Jackson,	Gainesboro,	Near Cumberland.
Maury,	Columbia,	Duck river.
Montgomery,	Clarksville,	Cumberland river.
Overton,	Livingston,	Branch of Obids river.
Perry,	Perryville,	Tennessee river.
Robertson,	Springfield,	Sulphur Fork.
Rutherford,	Murfreesboro,	Stone's river.
Smith,	Carthage,	Cumberland river.
Stewart,	Dover,	Cumberland river.
Sumner,	Gallatin,	Near Cumberland.
Warren,	M'Minnville,	Branch Caney Fork.
Wayne,	Waynesboro,	Indian creek.
White,	Sparta,	Calf-Killer.
Williamson,	Franklin,	Harpeth.
Wilson,	Lebanon,	Barton's creek.

WEST TENNESSEE.

Counties.	Chief Towns.	Situation.
Carroll,	Huntingdon,	S. Fork of Obion.
Dyer,	Dyersburg,	Forked Deer.
Fayette,	Sommerville,	Loosa Hatchee.
Gibson,	Trenton,	Forked Deer.
Hardeman,	Bolivar,	Big Hatchee.
Haywood,	Brownsville,	Hatchee & F. Deer.
Henderson,	Lexington,	Beech river.
Henry,	Paris,	Near Sandy river.
Madison,	Jackson,	S. Forked Deer.
M'Nairy,	Purdy,	Snake creek.
Obion,	Troy,	Branch of Obion.
Shelby,	Raleigh,	Wolf river.
Tipton,	Covington,	Near Hatchee.
Weakley,	Dresden,	Obion waters.

Constitution.—By the Constitution, which was formed at Knoxville in 1796, the Legislative authority is vested in a General Assembly, consisting of a Senate, and House of Representatives; and the members of both Houses are elected biennially. The number of Representatives bears a given proportion to the number of taxable inhabitants; and the number of Senators must never be more than one half, nor less than one third of the number of Representatives. To be eligible as members of either house, the person must have resided three years in the state, and one in the county, and be possessed of two hundred acres of land.[*]

---

[*] The requirements for membership in the Tennessee General Assembly have been revised and somewhat liberalized in the Constitutions of 1835 and 1870, although certain anachronistic qualifications still apply; e.g., that no minister or priest is eligible to serve in the legislature; that (conversely), no disbeliever in God or the afterlife shall hold *any* civil office in the state; and that no participant in a duel shall sit in the General Assembly. In actual practice, no member of the Assembly is questioned on his belief in the Deity, but each member swears solemnly to his non-participation in duels.

The Executive power is vested in a Governor, who is elected for two years; and is eligible six years out of eight. He must be twenty-five years of age; must have resided in the state four years, and must possess five hundred acres of land, to be eligible to that office.[4]

The elections are held on the first Thursday and Friday in August; and the General Assembly meets at Nashville on the third Monday in September, next following the election: and it may be called together, if necessary, by the Governor.[5]

The right of suffrage is granted to every freeman, white or black, of the age of twenty-one, possessing a free hold in the county where he offers his vote, and to every freeman who has been an inhabitant of any one county in the state, six months immediately preceding the election.

The Judicial power is vested in such superior and inferior courts, as the Legislature may from time to time direct and establish. The Judges are appointed by a joint ballot of both houses and hold their offices during good behaviour.

The Judiciary as now organized, consists of a Supreme court of Errors and Appeals, courts of Chancery, Circuit courts, courts of Pleas and Quarter Sessions, and in Justices of the Peace. There are four Judges of the Supreme court, with a salary of $1,800 each; two Chancellors, with a salary of $1,500 each; and eleven Judges of the Circuit courts, with a salary of $1,300 each. There are two Justices of the Peace in each Captain's company, appointed by the Legislature. They receive no fees for ordinary duties. Whilst sitting as a quorum, in the County courts, they receive from the county a small sum per diem. The Judges of the Circuit courts, are Judges of the state, and they may interchange ridings.

The State is also divided into a number of Solicitorial districts, in each of which there is a Solicitor General or State's Attorney. He receives a small salary, and perquisites.

---

[4] By amendment to the Constitution, in 1953, the governor is elected to a four-year term, without the option of succeeding himself.

[5] These dates have been changed; they are subject to legislative action.

CONGRESSIONAL DISTRICTS.

First.—Carter, Greene, Washington, Cocke and Jefferson.

Second.—Sullivan, Hawkins, Grainger, Claiborne and Campbell.

Third.—Anderson, Knox, Sevier, Blount, and Monroe.

Fourth.—Morgan, Roane, McMinn, Rhea, Hamilton, Bledsoe and Marion.

Fifth.—Fentress, Overton, White, Warren and Franklin.

Sixth.—Jackson, Smith and Sumner.

Seventh.—Wilson and Davidson.

Eighth.—Rutherford and Williamson.

Ninth.—Bedford and Maury.

Tenth.—Lincoln, Giles, Lawrence, Wayne and Hardin.

Eleventh.—Robertson, Montgomery, Stewart, Humphreys, Hickman and Dickson.

Twelfth.—Haywood, Madison, Dyer, Obion, Gibson, Weakley, Henry and Carroll.

Thirteenth.—Perry, Henderson, McNairy, Hardeman, Fayette, Shelby and Tipton.

History.—About the year 1730, a few Indian traders, stationed among the Cherokees, discovered that this beautiful country, was in a manner deserted by the savages, and that the abudance of game, made this a desirable district for the hunter. The information that a fertile country, unoccupied by Indians, thickly clad with cane, and abounding with Buffaloe, Elk, and other choice game, soon allured the daring and enterprising backwoodsmen to her forests. Hunting at that early period, was a lucrative business, and many persons were induced to embark in it, from that consideration alone. But independent of the prospect of gain, there is a fascination in a new country, which will always entice many to emigrate, who if not enriched, are amply compensated by the novelty of the adventure.

The French claimed the whole southern country between the Mississippi and the Alleghany mountains. By a reference to the ancient maps of this country, we discover their early settlements; and the position of their forts, and trading houses. The Holston by these maps is designated Cherokee river. The river to the south of it, occupied the position of the French Broad, and is designated *Tanses* or *Tanasees*. The big Tennessee below that, is called Ho-go-he-chee. Clinch is not laid down, nor is Cumberland, but it is known to have been called Shauvanon, by the French, and Shawanoe by the English. The Indian name of Holston, was Coot-ela. French forts, are represented as standing, one at the mouth of *Cataway*, supposed to be Kentucky; one on the south bank of the Ohio, another at the mouth of the Wabash; one at the junction of the Ohio and Mississippi, one at the Chickasaw Bluffs, and several others farther south and north. The one at the Chickasaw Bluffs was called *Prud home*.[6]

In 1755, the Cherokees were in alliance to the French, and hostile to the English. In 1756 a treaty was made with them, and the Catawbas, by a commissioner appointed by his excellency Arthur Dobbs, the Governor of North Carolina. It was required by the chief of each nation, that a garrison should be established in their respective territories, for the defence of their women and children, should their warriors be called out as allies to the English against the French, and northern Indians. In conformity to the stipulations, Fort Loudon was built, and garrisoned the year following. The Indians, to induce artisans to settle among them, made donations of land.

Shortly after the fall of fort Du Quesne, where Pittsburgh now stands, the Cherokees evinced a hostile spirit. The remembrance of a former war, and instigated by the French of the south, caused the nation to be strongly biassed in their favor.

In 1758, Col. Bird marched with his regiment from Virginia, and built Fort Chissel.[7] He also built a fort on the north bank

---
[6] Properly, Fort Prud'Homme, the site of present-day Memphis.
[7] Fort Chissel refers to Fort Chiswell, in Wythe County, Virginia.

of the Holston, near to Long Island, in which his army wintered. Between forts Chissel and Loudon some settlements were made prior to the breaking out of the war; which commenced in 1759. The principal cause of this war, was, the taking of some horses by the Indians, which belonged to the Virginia settlers; to replace those which the Indians had lost during the preceding war with the French, whilst acting as our allies. The white settlers reseized their horses, and either killed or made prisoners of many who were unconscious of having committed any offence. The impolicy of this step soon became manifest, for an Indian war with all its horrors, was the immediate consequence.

Fort Loudon was established on the north side of Little Tennessee river, about one mile above the mouth of Tellico, in the centre of the Cherokee country. The Garrison was besieged and compelled to surrender for the want of provisions. They were to retreat, agreeably to the terms of capitulation, beyond the Blue Ridge. The whites threw their cannon and small arms into the river, reserving no more guns than were necessary for hunting, and commenced their march. After they had proceeded about twenty miles, the Indians fell upon them and massacred the whole number, except nine, not even sparing the women and children. The number slain, amounted to between two and three hundred. This melancholy disaster happened in 1760.

In 1761, Col. Grant marched against them. Near the battle ground of the last year, the Indians met them, a battle ensued and the whites obtained a victory. After which the Colonel marched his regiment to Etchoe and burnt it, and all the towns in the middle settlements. Their houses and corn-fields were destroyed, and the whole of their country laid waste. The Indians sued for peace, and this war closed in the summer of that year.

The only settlements which had been made in the vicinity of Fort Loudon, were in consequence of this war broken up. But as soon as tranquility was so far restored, as to admit of hunting with safety, 15 or 20 persons, allured by the prospects, formed themselves into a company, and came into the place now called Carter's Valley, in East Tennessee. These men gave names to the chief mountains and rivers. In 1761 the celebrated Daniel Boon, made an excursion from North Carolina, to the waters of Holston. And in 1766, Col. James Smith, late of Bourbon county, Kentucky, traversed a great portion of West and Middle Tennessee. He went in the first place to Holston river, and proceeded in company with Joshua Horton, Uriah Stone and William Baker, who came from Carlisle. They explored the country south of Kentucky, and found no white persons in this region. They also explored Cumberland and Tennessee from Stones' river to the Ohio. In 1768, an exploring party came into the country from Virginia. They traversed the country from Holston to Clinch mountain. In February 1769, they crossed the North Fork of Holston, and proceeded on until they came to Big Creek, now in the county of Hawkins, where they discovered the hunting grounds of a party of Indians. They turned about and went up the river ten or fifteen miles, and concluded to return home. They found on their return, that the country which had so recently been a wilderness, was full of inhabitants; there was a cabin on every spot where the range was good. The first permanent settlements were made in 1768 and 1769. The settlers were chiefly from North Carolina and Virginia. The settlements continued to increase until 1774 and 1775, when an extensive purchase of land from the Indians was made by Henderson and company.

In 1774, the Shawnees and other hostile tribes committed depredations on the Watauga. Capt. Shelby with a company of backwoods riflemen from that section, marched against them, in August of that year, and joined the regiment commanded by Col. Christian, on New River. They then proceeded by way of the Green Briar Levels, and joined Col. Lewis in September. In October the army arrived at the mouth of the Great Kenhawa. A battle was fought on the 10th, in which the citizens of East Tennessee acted a valorous and conspicuous part. Among the distinguished were Gen.

Robertson and Col. Sevier, at that time non commissioned officers. After this memorable engagement, the Indians remained peaceable until 1776. In 1775, the treaty of Henderson with the Cherokees, above alluded to, was brought to a conclusion, and a cession was made; but not without the warm opposition of Chief Occonnostota, who made an animated speech against it. He represented the once flourishing state of his nation, the encroachments of the white people, and their insatiable desire for more land, in a bold and pathetic manner; but he did not prevail.

In 1776, the Indians being instigated by the infernal policy of the British government, commenced their customary depredations. The people of North Carolina and Virginia sent such troops as they could spare, who were aided by the people. In this year a fort was built at Gillespie's, above the mouth of Big Limestone, another called the Wommack fort, east of the Holston, above the mouth of Watauga, ten or twelve miles. The Virginians built a fort at Heaton's station. Evan Shelby erected one on Beaver creek, and John Shelby built one on the Holston. The united settlements elected John Sevier, Carter Wommack and John Hill delegates to the Convention that established the district of Washington.

In June 1776, a battle was fought between the combined forces of the inhabitants and the soldiers from Virginia and the savages, at the Long Island Flats. In this battle we had not a man killed, and only five wounded. The loss of the enemy was upwards of forty. Notwithstanding this lesson, hostilities continued; and not long afterwards Col. Christian, from Virginia, with about 1800 men, marched into the heart of the Cherokee nation. They found no Indians 'til they came to a town called Tamotlee. They then marched to the Great Island town, and tarried there near twenty days; in that time the Indians made overtures for peace, which was granted, but not to take place until the month of May following. Hostilities were to cease in the meantime on both sides, except as to two towns on the Tennessee, which had burnt a prisoner. The excepted towns were burned and the army returned to quarters.

In 1777, an arrangement was brought about between the states of North Carolina, Virginia and the Indians; and a definitive boundary was settled for the Territory, now the state of Tennessee, which was understood, aside from the Indian title, to belong to those states.

This year Washington county was organized, courts established and a land office opened, in which great quantities of land were entered.

In 1779, the combined forces of North Carolina and Virginia, marched against the Indian towns. They came on the Indians by supprise and they fled without giving battle.

The soldiers pursued them, burned their villages and destroyed their crops. This was about the time General Clark took Vincennes. These coincident events restored peace for a time in the western settlements.

During this interval of repose, the territory rapidly increased in population, and the Indians were never after able to break up the settlements. Another county was constituted by the name of Sullivan. In the mean time the Cherokees continued to harrass our borders, and the settlers were compelled to act with great energy and firmness, as well to resist the savages, as the British, who were then scouring the southern frontier.

Middle and West Tennessee.—In the year 1767 Middle Tennessee began to be visited by hunters. In this year Isaac Lindsday, and four others from South Carolina, crossed the Alleghanies and came to Powell's Valley, and passed the Cumberland mountain at Cumberland Gap; thence they came to a place now called Rockcastle, which they so named, from a romantic looking rock.*

They proceeded on until they came to Cumberland, thence down Cumberland to the mouth of Stones river, where they found a dutchman by the name of Micheal Stoner, who had came thither with one Harrod, to hunt. But before this time,

---

* Rockcastle, apparently in Kentucky, is not to be confused with Rock Castle, the home of Daniel Smith, a historic site of the State of Tennessee, at Hendersonville.

some French had settled at the bluff where Nashville now stands.

In 1769 a company from North Carolina and Virginia, consisting of John Rains, Casper Mansker, Abraham Bledsoe, John Baker, Joseph Drake, Obadiah Terril, Uriah Stone, Henry Smith, Ned Cowan, and others, resolved to pass into the Cumberland Valley, for the purpose of hunting. They came to the head of Holston, then down to the Wolf hills, where Abingdon now stands; thence to the north fork of Holston; thence to Clinch river, at Mockason gap; thence to Powells Valley, and thence to the Cumberland mountain and Cumberland river, &c. They thence travelled to Flat Lick; from thence to roaring river, and the Caney Fork of Cumberland. On the head of Roaring river, Robert Crocket, one of the company, was killed. In this excursion they discovered a great many of the caves, so well known at the present day. A great deal of the country they traversed was covered with high grass. By the borders of creeks, they found stones set up, that covered quantities of human bones.

Not long afterwards, ten of the party set out with the proceeds of their hunt, on a trading expedition to the south, intending to go as far as Natchez. They descended the Cumberland, and when they came to the place where Nashville now stands, they discovered the French Lick. At this place they saw immense herds of Buffaloe and other game. They continued their journey, and proceeded as far as the Spanish Natchez, made sale of their skins, &c., and returned.

In 1771, a part of the same company, together with many other persons, again came into West Tennessee to hunt. Amongst the number was an old man by the name of Russell, who was so dim sighted, that he was obliged to tie a piece of white paper to the muzzle of his gun, to direct his sight. In this way he killed a number of deer. He was at one time lost 19 days, in very cold weather. His comrades found him in a perfect state of helplessness, and administered to his wants. He recovered, and resumed his favorite pursuits.

The party continued to hunt through the country until

February, but their ammunition becoming scarce, all of the company, except five, namely, Isaac Bledsoe, William Linch, William Allen, Christopher Stoph and David Linch, returned to procure ammunition, and for other purposes. Linch was taken sick, and Bledsoe came with him into the settlements. The other three were discovered and defeated, before the return of their companions in the ensuing spring. The winter being severe, they did not return to camp until May. The attack upon the three was supposed to have been made by some of the northern Indians. They took Stoph and Allen, but Hughes escaped, and met the rest of the company as they were returning to camp. The party remained from May 1772 until August, hunting and traversing the country. In the meantime they made many important discoveries. Joseph Drake discovered the places now called Drake's Lick, and Drake's Pond; Isaac Bledsoe discovered Bledsoe's Lick, now called *Castalian Springs;* and Mansker discovered the Lick on Mansker's Creek.

In 1775, Mansker renewed his visit to the Cumberland country, and encamped at the lick he had discovered. He remained, and with three others commenced trapping on the Sulphur Fork of Red River.

In 1776, Thomas Sharpe Spencer, and others, came to Cumberland, and built a number of cabins. The greater part of them returned, leaving Spencer and Holiday, who remained until 1779.

They planted a small field of corn at Bledsoe's Lick. Spencer was pleased with his situation, Holiday wished to return, but could not prevail on his friend to accompany him. They had but one butcherknife, between them, and each wanted it. Spencer went with Holiday to the barrens, on the way to Kentucky, and put him on the path, broke his knife in two parts, and gave him *half*. He then returned to Bledsoe's Lick, and for a time lived in a hollow sycamore tree.

In 1779, Captain James Robertson, and others from East Tennessee, crossed the Cumberland mountain. They explored the country to the neighborhood of Nashville, and fixed themselves convenient to the French Lick. They planted corn that season, on the ground where Nashville now stands. They all returned for their families except three, whom they left to keep the Buffaloe's out of their corn. This year a number of families were permanently settled at Mansker's, and Bledsoe's Licks.

In January 1780, about sixty Delaware Indians passed through the Cumberland country. They proceeded to Bear creek, of Tennessee, and continued there during the winter. This is supposed to be the first party which molested the whites on Cumberland. In October 1780, was fought the celebrated battle of Kings mountain. In this action the settlers of Tennessee had a glorious share. Maj. Ferguson commanded the British forces, and Colonels, Campbell, Shelby and Sevier, the intrepid backwoodsmen. The American forces commanded by Col. McDowell, were attacked by Ferguson, near Enoree river, aided by a reinforcement of tories and regulars. The battle was severely fought, but ended in the defeat of the British, who retreated, leaving a number of dead, and more than 200 prisoners. The prisoners equalled one third of the number of the American forces.

Previous to the battle of Kings mountain, Ferguson was at Gilbertstown, N. C., with about 2000 men, and 500 tories ready to join him. In this situation Col. Shelby proposed to attack him with a force of about 900, mounted riflemen. They took up their march, and after pursuing him about thirty six hours without alighting for refreshments, came upon the enemy encamped on Kingsmountain. Col. Sevier commanded the right wing, Colonels Cleveland and Williams the left, and Campbell and Shelby the centre column. After a most furious and bloody contest, the British laid down their arms, and were made prisoners. The commander and one hundred and fifty of the enemy fell on the field, and six hundred and ten were made prisoners. The result of this gallant action animated the drooping spirits of the settlers. It prostrated the hopes of the royalists, and effectually awed and repressed their savage allies. Towards the close of the year 1781, the Cherokees and Chickasaws sued for peace.

The succeeding year the Indians re-commenced hostilities; and for a considerable time it was the custom of the country to place sentinels, to guard the laborers in the field. Many of the inhabitants became disheartened and left the country.

In this year North Carolina passed an act allowing settlers on the Cumberland, *rights of pre-emption.*

Each head of a family, and every single man of the age of twenty-one years was allowed six hundred and forty acres of land, who made actual settlements prior to June, 1780.

In this year also North Carolina established courts of equity in all the districts of the state.

With the close of the war of the revolution, November 30, 1782, the Indians became less troublesome, and emigration increased.

In 1783, North Carolina sent commissioners to examine pre-emption claims, and to lay off the bounty lands given to the soldiers of the regular army; also 25,000 acres given to Gen. Greene for his revolutionary services. In October of this year a land office was opened at Hillsboro' for the sale of western lands. In May following, vast quantities of lands were entered.

In 1784, the legislature of North Carolina passed a law ceding the Territory, now the state of Tennessee, to the Congress of the United States, if they would accept of it within the space of two years from the passage of the act; and North Carolina was to retain her jurisdiction until Congress should make provisions for a Territorial government. After this act, the citizens of Tennessee became fearful, that pending this negociation, they would be deprived of the benefit of the laws of the parent state, and Congress also; and be compelled to contend single-handed with their common enemy, the Indians. They accordingly came to the determination of organizing a Territorial government on their own responsibility. On the 23rd of August, a convention of deputies from the counties of Washington, Sullivan and Green, assembled at Jonesboro.' They appointed John Sevier, President, and Landon Carter, Clerk. They also appointed a committee to take into consideration the state of public affairs, relative to the cession. The committee reported that they had a just and undeniable right to petition Congress to accept the cession made by North Carolina, and for that body to countenance them in forming a separate government. They then drew up a plan of an association, and enacted, that, the laws of North Carolina, so far as was compatible with their new situation, should continue in force; that the management of their affairs should be entrusted to a Convention; and that they should choose a delegate to represent them in Congress. They promised to cultivate dispositions of benevolence, and discountenance every thing opposed to good morals. For the faithful performance, they pledged their lives, fortunes and reputation. After resolving that the public offices withhold the payment of public moneys, until a mode should be prescribed to settle their accounts with the parent state, the Convention adjourned to meet on the 16th of September following.

The Assembly of North Carolina, that fall repealed the act for ceding the Western country to Congress; and in November the Convention again met at Jonesboro', and broke up in confusion. By this time there were three political parties; one, for a Constitution, which had been proposed by a minority; a second, for the plan approved by the committee; and a third, for restoring their allegiance to the State.—After the repeal of the cession act, North Carolina erected the county of Davidson, appointed an assistant-judge, attorney general, &c. They also formed the militia of that district into a brigade, and appointed Col. Sevier brigadier general. Disregarding the repeal of the cession, the organization of courts, &c., a second Convention met at Jonesboro' on the 14th December, 1784. Each county had elected five deputies. John Sevier was made President, and the new State was named *Frankland*. They formed a Constitution, announced to North Carolina that they considered themselves independent of her; and the new government went into immediate operation.

A delegate was sent to Congress with their new Constitution, but he returned without effecting any thing.

A governor in the meantime was elected, courts were organized, and the new state of *Frankland* exercised all the functions of an independent state.

The North Carolina party, though in the minority, commenced legal operations under the authority of that state, and in 1786 Frankland had two conflicting courts within its limits, and each asserting its legitimacy.—Washington county elected members to represent them in the North Carolina legislature, and with them were forwarded the names of all those who wished to secede from the new state of Frankland.

Taxes were imposed by both legislatures, and the people paid tribute to neither. The sheriff of Frankland, with his possee, in some instances went into the other court, seized their papers, and turned their officers out of doors. The North Carolina party, as soon as it had power, retaliated in the same way, and hence it became necessary to appoint the stoutest men in the county to the office of sheriff. In these removals, many valuable papers were lost. Marriage licenses and letters of administration, were granted under the authority of both governments. The members of the two factions became much incensed at each other, and personal combats frequently ensued. It is easy to perceive that such a state of things could not long exist. An Indian war, if possible, was preferable to these intestine broils. Of this, however, they soon had a trial. The Cherokees renewed their attacks upon the settlements. Members of assembly having been elected for the three old counties, went on to Fayetteville, and took their seats in November, 1786. At this critical juncture appeared William Cocke, Esq. on a mission from the western counties, and was permitted to appear at the bar of the House of Commons. In a speech of some hours he depicted in strong colors the misery and helplessness of the inhabitants. His speech was heard with attention, and an act was passed by the legislature pardoning the offenses of all persons, who had returned to their allegiance, and restored them to all the privileges of the other citizens of the state. With regard to decisions respecting property, which were incompatible with justice, they enacted that the persons injured, should have remedy at common law. They continued in office all who held offices in April 1781; but declared vacant the offices of all such persons as had accepted and exercised other offices and appointments; the acceptance and exercise of which were considered to be a resignation of their former offices held under the state of North Carolina.

This measure restored things to their former position, before the formation of the state of *Frankland*; and that little republic fast hastened to a crisis. In the meantime the Governor of Frankland, aware of the tottering situation of his government, used every means in his power to prop it up. He offered the services of his party to the state of Georgia, to prosecute a war against the Creeks. The legislature of that state having deliberated upon the proposition, returned a polite answer, expressing gratitude for the proffered assistance. Sevier also wrote to Dr. Franklin, and obtained his advice. He wrote that he thought that they had better accede to the proposition of the parent state.

Under all these discouraging circumstances, Governor Sevier retained his popularity. He was elected a member of the Cincinnati society, and presented with a flattering address. The common toast in Georgia, was "success to the state of Frankland, his excellency governor Sevier and his virtuous citizens." But all these gratulations proved unavailing. The legislature met for the last time, in September 1787, at Greenville. John Menifee was Speaker of the House of Representatives, and Charles Robinson, Speaker of the Senate. Several bills passed, which were chiefly unimportant amendments of the laws of North Carolina.

At the stated time of election in this year, the western counties elected members of the General Assembly of North Carolina which sat at Tarboro' in November 1787. This assembly extended their former acts of pardon to all who desired to avail themselves of its advantages. They also elected David Campbell, Judge of the Superior Court, for the district of Washington.

In May 1788, Courts were held at Greenville, without interruption, under the authority of North Carolina; at which, were admitted as attorneys, who were licensed by the Judges of North Carolina, Andrew Jackson, John McNairy, David Allison, Archibald Roane and Joseph Hamilton.

To add to the confusion and anarchy in East Tennessee, about this time, a party was getting up, whose object was to attack the Spanish colonies of Louisiana. This was in 1787, when there existed such an excitement in Kentucky upon the subject of the occlusion of the Mississippi against the produce of the west.

The Tennesseeans and Kentuckians felt a strong disposition to take this matter into their own hands. Letters indicative of their designs, were disclosed, and an examination was had by the general government upon the subject. Measures were taken which resulted in the suppression of the project, and our relations with Spain were not materially affected.

In 1789, the legislature of North Carolina authorized and required their Senators in Congress to execute a deed or deeds of conveyance for the territory now the state of Tennessee; and on the 25th day of February 1790 Samuel Johnston and Benjamin Hawkins the senators from that state, executed the same. On the second day of April following, Congress passed an act accepting the ceded territory. A state of repose now followed and the population rapidly advanced.

In May 1790, Congress passed a law for the government of the country south west of Ohio; and William Blount was, by President Washington, appointed the first governor of the territory. He also appointed David Campbell and Joseph Anderson Judges. Governor Blount arrived in the territory in October, 1790, and took up his residence in East Tennessee. He appointed and commissioned the officers both civil and military, for the counties of Washington, Sullivan, Greene and Hawkins, which formed the district of Washington. In November he set off for the district of Mero, which was then composed of the counties of Davidson, Sumner and Tennessee, to appoint the necessary officers there. He could not appoint Brigadier generals, but recommended Col. Sevier for Washington, and Col. Robertson for Mero.

In November 1791, a Mr. Roulstone established a printing office at Rogersville, and issued a paper entitled the 'Knoxville Gazette.' The population of the territory then, amounted to 36,043, including 3,417 slaves. The population of the Cumberland country was 7,042.

Gov. Blount made a treaty with the Cherokees at Knoxville, and they promised perpetual peace. The news of the defeat of Gen. Arthur St. Clair, at Fort Recovery, had been received, and fearing that the northern Indians might join the southern ones, the government was anxious that the latter should join us in a war against the former. Gov. Blount was instructed to invite the Choctaws, Chickasaws and Cherokees, to assemble at Nashville, to make a treaty on the subject. The governor, however, soon discovered that a majority of these Indians felt no disposition to form an alliance, to make war upon the Shawnees. On the contrary, in violation of the treaty of amity, the Cherokees assumed their war dress, declared war against the United States, and became allies to the Shawnees.

Governor Blount ordered out the militia, and Gen. Sevier with a strong force, was stationed at 'South West Point,' in November 1792. Here he laboured to prevent anything that should create new enmities among the Indians. A portion of the Cherokees and Creeks were neutral, and disposed to peace; and the general government acting on the presumption that they were all pacific, ordered a greater part of the troops under Gen. Sevier, to be disbanded. They were accordingly marched to Knoxville, and dismissed on the 8th of January, 1793. The impolicy of this step was soon manifest, by immediate and increased depredations. The people were loud in their complaints against the general government, and declared that they would take measures to defend themselves. The governor had repaired to Philadelphia. Mr. Smith, the governor's secretary, perceived that a war with the Creeks was inevitable, prepared himself to meet it. Troops were ordered to Knoxville where an attack was expected. A number of people had assembled with a determination to march on their own responsibility, into the Cherokee country. Mr. Smith went among them and endeavored to change their purpose. They were inflexible, and marched for the Cherokee towns. Another party followed. Gen. Sevier requested permission to march 150 mounted infantry into the country north of the Tennessee, and into the lower Cherokee towns, which was granted. The expected attack of the Indians was made on the 25th of September, 1793, with 1000 warriors and 100 horses. They crossed the Tennessee below the mouth of Holston, marching all night, for Knoxville. At sun rise they reached a house seven miles below that place, and killed the whole family, 13 in number, except a boy. There were 700 Creeks and 200 Cherokees, who infested the fort. They made little impression on the garrison and retreated. Gen. Sevier lay at this time on the S. bank of Holston, eight miles from Tennessee, with 400 men. He arrived there but a few days before. His force was soon augmented to 1023, with 265 officers. He marched into the Cherokee nation in pursuit of these invaders. He pursued them to Estanaula, on the Coosa, where they arrived on the 25th of October. They took some Cherokee prisoners, who informed them that every Cherokee town had furnished its quota for the late expedition. The Creeks had passed that place on their return from that expedition, anticipating Gen. Sevier's arrival, but a few days. Their rendezvous was at the mouth of Hightower river. On the 17th of October, the army arrived at the forks of Coosa and Hightower rivers. The Creeks and Cherokees had fortified themselves here, to prevent a passage. Col. Kelly with a part of the Knoxville regiment went down the river half a mile, and crossed unperceived.* The Indians discovering them and thinking the whole army had crossed there, ran down upon them. Capt. Evans, who had not crossed, perceiving the mistake, set off with his corps of mounted infantry, up the

* The reference is to Colonel Alexander Kelly.

river to the ford, and began to cross. But few had reached the south bank before the Indians discovered their original error, returned and gave them a warm reception. An engagement took place, and although the Indians outnumbered Evans' four to one, he put them to flight. Spanish guns were found in the encampment. The Americans lost but three. As many of the enemy fell. The army then marched through the Indian country, destroying their towns and laying waste their villages. The Indians fled, leaving almost everything behind them. After this skirmish at Hightower, our troops proceeded without opposition, and the Indians were never after as troublesome. They continued however to steal cattle and horses.

By the ordinance of 1787, whenever the Territory should contain five thousand free male inhabitants, they were to be entitled to a Territorial legislature. Accordingly the grand jury for the district of Hamilton, presented an address to the governor, reminding him of the ordinance, and their rights. They complained in strong terms of the forbearing system of the general government towards the Indians, and of the outrages they were daily committing. They represented themselves and the country, to be in the deepest distress, the public indignation roused, and their vengeance only restrained by respect for the laws. The object of desiring a legislature was that they might protect themselves against the savages.

On the 19th of October, 1793, the governor by an ordinance, authorized the election of persons to represent the people in general assembly, on the third Friday and Saturday in December; two from each of the counties of Washington, Hawkins, Jefferson and Knox; and one from each of the counties of Sullivan, Greene, Tennessee, Davidson and Sumner. The assembly met at Knoxville on the fourth Monday of February, 1794. Members from Knox—Alexander Kelly and John Baird; from Jefferson—Geo. Doherty and Samuel Weir; from Washington—Leroy Taylor and John Tipton; from Sullivan—Geo. Rutledge; from Hawkins—William Cocke and

Joseph McMinn; from Davidson—James White; from Sumner —David Wilson; and from Tennessee—James Ford. David Wilson was chosen speaker and Hopkins Lacy was appointed clerk. When they were assembled, the members walked in procession to the place of worship, where the Rev. Dr. Carrick preached a sermon, from these words, "In the hope of eternal life, which God, that cannot lie, promised before the world began, but hath in due time manifested his word through preaching, which is committed unto me according to the commandment of God our Saviour."[19]

They elected ten persons out of whom Congress were to choose a legislative council. They also presented an address to the governor, recommending an offensive war against the Indians, and the erection of a chain of block-houses, to defend the frontier. They memorialized Congress to declare war against the Creeks and Cherokees, and alleged that since the treaty of Holston they had lost upwards of two hundred citizens, and one hundred thousand dollars worth of property by them.

On the 25th of August 1794, the General Assembly of the Territory commenced their session at Knoxville. The council appointed by the president, consisted of Griffith Rutherford, Gen. John Sevier, Col. James Winchester, Col. Stokely Donelson and Capt. Parmenas Taylor. On the 3d of September, the legislative council, and members of the house of representatives convened, and elected James White Esq. of Davidson, to represent the Territory in Congress.

The Indians still continued their depredations, and on the 6th of September 1794, a negro woman, the property of Peter Turney, was taken off by them, from Sumner, and it became manifest that more effectual measures must be resorted to for suppressing invasions, than those defensive ones, so long relied on, and that recourse must be had, to some striking and decisive blow of retaliation. Sampson Williams,

---

[19] The reference is to the Rev. Samuel Carrick. The quotation is taken, almost verbatim, from J.G.M. Ramsey's *Annals of Tennessee* (Charleston, 1853), 621.

Esq. applied to Col. Whitley of Kentucky, to join him in an expedition against Nickajack, an Indian town on the Tennessee. Col. Ford, between Nashville and Clarksville, raised a captain's company, which was commanded by Capt. Wm. Miles. Gen. Robertson raised volunteers in the neighborhood of Nashville. Col. Montgomery at Clarksville raised troops also, and marched with them in person to the place of rendezvous. Maj. Ore arrived with a body of men from East Tennessee, for the protection of the frontiers of Mero district, and came with them to Nashville, where hearing of what was in agitation, concluded to join the expedition, and it was called his, to give color to the claim of pay for the troops, and the provisions and other articles supplied from the general government. The men under his command having been levied by public authority. He marched his men to the place of rendezvous. Col. Whitley, with his force, soon arrived, and the whole amounted to five hundred and fifty men.—It was agreed that Col. Whitley should have the chief command. The territorial troops were commanded by Col. Montgomery.[11]

All matters being arranged, the whole army took up the line of march. On arriving at Tennessee river, the troops halted in the night, and crossed early in the morning, upon chumps and bundles of dry cane. The whole body landed on the south bank of the river on the fourth day after their march. As soon as the army could be arrayed, they marched up the mountain, penetrated into the heart of the town of Nickajack, before they were discovered, and first alarmed the Indians by the report of their guns. Nickajack was inhabited by about three hundred men, women and children. The army killed in the town a considerable number of warriors. They fired upon the Indians, who took to their canoes to make their escape across the river. Some were killed and some were drowned. Fifteen girls, one squaw, and two boys were taken prisoners; fifty-five warriors were found dead on the field; and the town reduced to ashes. In the town were found two fresh

---

[11] The references are to Colonel William Whitley, Colonel James Ford, Colonel James Montgomery, and Major James Ore.

scalps taken at Cumberland; and several that were hung up as trophies of war. In this place too, they found a quantity of powder and lead, just received from the Spanish government, and a commission to a chief who was killed in the action, by the name of *Breath*. The militia had three men wounded, one of whom died of his wounds. On Friday the 12th of September, they left the river, and encamped on the mountain. The next day they came on to Elk river; the next day to Fennison's Spring; thence to the place now called Purdy's garrison, where a soldier in his sleep climbed a tree, and received a fall, which occasioned his death. Thence they marched to Hart's Spring, and the next day to Nashville, where the troops were discharged.[19]

After this expedition, and the destruction of Nickajack, the Cherokees despaired of preventing the settlement of the whites, and in June 1794 they applied for peace. On the 26th of July, a treaty made with them was ratified at Philadelphia.

This expedition was unauthorized by the general government, and was kept in a manner secret. The constituted authorities, on a partial examination of the matter, were induced to wink at the violation of law, in consequence of the great necessity of the measure.

About this time the settlers were much annoyed by some unprincipled Spaniards, and a war which was waging between the Chickasaws and Creeks. The Chickasaws had then lately evinced their fidelity to the whites, as auxiliaries in Gen. Wayne's army, and public feeling was much in their favor. They appealed to the whites for protection, which could not on principles of gratitude be withheld; and a thousand warriors were supported at Nashville for some time, at the expense of the government.

The Spaniards had built a fort at the Chickasaw Bluffs, where Memphis now stands. It was within the chartered limits of this state, and the territory guaranteed to the Chickasaws; and complaint was made by them to our govern-

---
[19] Purdy's Garrison is the place known as Old Fort Nash, on the Nickajack Trail, in what is now Coffee County.

ment. Boats laden with provisions for them were interdicted, and a war which had lasted some ten years, had reduced them to a state of starvation. Fortunately, however, in October, 1795, Spain acceded to a proposed treaty, which put an end to all controversies between the belligerent parties; —and the boundaries of the United States were definitely settled, as we contended they should be. A treaty was subsequently concluded between those tribes, through the instrumentality of the whites; and in 1796 a treaty was made between the United States and the Creeks.

On the last Monday in June, 1795, the members of the Assembly were convened by the Governor, to take into consideration the expediency of erecting the territorial government into an independent state. A law was passed to take the census, and the number was found to be 77,262, being 17,262 more than the number entitling them to form a constitution. A proclamation was thereupon issued, for the election of five persons in each county to represent them in Convention.

The Territory then contained the following counties:— Blount, Davidson, Sullivan, Greene, Jefferson, Sevier, Hawkins, Sumner, Washington and Tennessee (now Robertson and Montgomery.)

The Convention met at Knoxville on the 11th day of January, 1796. William Blount was chosen President, and William Maclin, Secretary. On the 6th day of February, 1796, in the name of the People south of the river Ohio, they mutually agreed with each other to form themselves into a free and independent state, by the name of TENNESSEE.

A few days afterwards, a copy of the constitution was forwarded by Mr. M'Minn to Timothy Pickering, Esq. the then Secretary of State; and Mr. White, the territorial delegate, procured an act of admission on the 6th day of June, 1796.[13]

---

[13] Tennessee was organized as a state in March, 1796; officially adopted into the Union as the sixteenth state on June 1, 1796. Editor

Writs of election were awarded immediately, to elect representatives to the General Assembly, and a governor of the state. Elections were held pursuant to notice, and Gen. John Sevier was elected the first Governor of Tennessee.

The first General Assembly of the STATE OF TENNESSEE, under the constitution, convened at Knoxville on Monday, the 28th day of March, 1796.

SENATORS.—From the county of *Tennessee*, James Ford; *Sumner*, James Winchester; *Knox*, James White; *Jefferson*, George Doherty; *Greene*, Samuel Frazier; *Washington*, John Tipton; *Sullivan*, George Rutledge; *Blount*, Alexander Kelly; *Davidson*, Joel Lewis; *Hawkins*, Joseph McMinn; And *Sevier*, John Clack.

REPRESENTATIVES.—From the county of *Blount*, Jas. Houston and Joseph Black; *Davidson*, Robert Weakley and Seth Lewis; *Greene*, Joseph Conway and John Guess; *Hawkins*, Thomas Henderson and John Cocke; *Jefferson*, Alexander Outlaw and Adam Peck; *Knox*, John Menifee and John Crawford; *Sullivan*, John Rhea and David Looney; *Sumner*, Stephen Cantrell and William Montgomery; *Sevier*, Spencer Clack and Samuel Newell; *Tennessee*, Thomas Johnson and William Fort; *Washington*, James Stuart and John Blair.

James Winchester was elected Speaker of the Senate, and *Francis A. Ramsey* was chosen first, and *Nathaniel Buckingham* second Clerk. In the House, *James Stuart* was elected Speaker, and *Thomas H. Williams* and *John Sevier* Clerks. On the 30th of March his Excellency John Sevier, the Governor elect, appeared and the oaths of office were administered by the Hon. Judge Anderson. On the next day *William Blount* and *William Cocke* were elected Senators in Congress, and *William Maclin* Secretary of State.

During this session, the state was divided into three judicial districts, Washington, Hamilton and Mero. And the Supreme court of law and equity was made to consist of three Judges, and any one or more authorized to hold the courts. John

---

Morris's date of June 6 is an error; the Fourth Congress adjourned on June 1, 1796.

McNairy, Willie Blount and Archibald Roane, were elected the Judges. The first two declined serving, and their places were filled by William C. C. Claiborne and Howel Tatum. Hopkins Lacy Esq., was appointed Attorney General, for Washington; John Lowry Esq., for Hamilton; And John C. Hamilton Esq., for Mero District. The Treasury department was created, and Landon Carter was elected Treasurer of the districts of Washington and Hamilton, at Knoxville, and William Black Treasurer of the district of Mero, at Nashville. The Assembly adjourned on the 14th of April, after a session of twenty-seven days.

The second General Assembly convened at Knoxville, on Saturday the 30th day of July 1796. It was called to rectify some errors of the preceding session. The Senators had been elected prior to the act of Congress admitting this State into the Union, and the Presidential electors were also improperly chosen. After re-electing William Blount and William Cocke, Senators in Congress, and providing for the election of a Representative to Congress, the election of electors, &c., the Assembly adjourned on the 9th day of August.[14]

During this year the following gentlemen were enrolled as attorney's at law, in the state of Tennessee, to wit: Joseph Anderson, Drury W. Brazeale, John Shields, John Rhea, John Cocke, Alexander Outlaw, Seth Lewis, Thomas Gray, William Charles Cole Claiborne, Charles McClung, Bennet Searcy, Howel Tatum, James Doherty, Isaac McNutt, Samuel Donelson, Robert Knox, Francis Hall, Morgan Brown, Randal McGavock, Andrew Jackson, John Lecory, Hugh L. White, Isham A. Parker, Andrew McNairy and John Wilkinson.

1797. John Sevier was elected Governor and Wm. C. C. Claiborne Representative to Congress. The first session of the second General Assembly commenced at Knoxville, on Monday the 18th day of September. James White was elected

---

[14] Editor Morris refers to the "called" or "extra" session of the 1st General Assembly. It was *not* the second session. The first line of the paragraph should read, "the second session of the first General Assembly. . . ."

Speaker of the Senate, and George Roulstone and N. Buckingham clerks. In the House, James Stuart was chosen Speaker, and Thomas H. Williams and Jesse Wharton Clerks. But few laws of a general nature were enacted this session. Some amendments were made to the poor, registration and revenue laws; and the jurisdiction of slander, actions, indictments or presentments, for assault and battery, &c., were transferred from the Superior to the County courts.

Andrew Jackson was elected a Senator in Congress for six years, and Joseph Anderson for two years. David Campbell was elected Judge of the Superior court, *vice* W. C. C. Claiborne elected Representative to Congress. On the 4th Nov. George Conway was duly commissioned Major General of the Militia of Tennessee.

1798. The second session of the second General Assembly commenced at Knoxville, on the third day of December. William Blount was elected Speaker of the Senate, in the place of James White resigned. And in the House, Edward Scott and Stephen Heard were elected Clerks in the place of Williams and Wharton resigned.

Acts passed, regulating the admission and license of attorney's at law, and providing for the appointment of entry takers, and surveyors, within the several counties. Provision was also made by law, for the appointment of Senators and Representatives of the General Assembly, in conformity to the 1st article of the constitution.

A law was also enacted requiring all judgments in the courts, to be rendered in dollars and cents. Andrew Jackson, who had been appointed *pro tem* Judge *vice* Judge Tatum resigned, was elected by the legislature to that office. Daniel Smith was appointed to fill Mr. Jackson's place in the Senate of the United States, on the 20th September. He served until the 4th March, ensuing, and was succeeded by William Cocke, who was elected by the Legislature. Joseph Anderson, whose time expired on the 4th March, was re-elected a Senator. The session adjourned on the 5th January, 1799, after a session of thirty-five days.

1799. The first session of the third General Assembly, commenced its session at Knoxville on the 16th September. Alexander Outlaw was chosen Speaker of the Senate, and William Dickson Speaker of the House.

Among the general laws passed this session deserving notice, may be included those relating to the jurisdiction of justices of the peace—gaming—the wilful and malicious killing of slaves— horsestealing—partition of lands—executions—divorces, &c. Robert Searcy was re-elected treasurer of Mero district. And the assembly adjourned on the 26th of October. At the preceding August election Wm. C. C. Claiborne was re-elected a member of congress.

1800. By the census taken this year, Tennessee contained a population of 105,602, of which 13,584 were slaves. In July, John Maclin was appointed treasurer of the district of Washington and Hamilton, *vice* Gen. Carter, deceased.

1801. Archibald Roane was elected governor, and William Dickson representative to congress.

The fourth General Assembly commenced its first session at Knoxville, on Monday the 21st day of September. James White was chosen Speaker of the Senate, and William Dickson Speaker of the House of Representatives. Many important laws were enacted this session. Among which may be mentioned, the act regulating North Carolina land warrants, an act relative to the inspection of pork, beef, flour, &c., an act regulating proceedings in the courts of equity, an act defining the jurisdiction of justices of the peace, an act to prevent *frauds* and *purjuries,* an act to empower county courts to emancipate slaves, and an act to prevent duelling. Assembly adjourned 14th November.

1803. John Sevier was elected governor, and John Rhea and George W. Campbell representatives to congress.

The first session of the fifth General Assembly convened at Knoxville on the 19th day of September.—James White was elected Speaker of the Senate, and James Stuart Speaker of the House. No important changes of the then existing laws were made this session. The revenue laws were amended, and the taxes for the year 1804 were imposed as follows, to wit: On each one hundred acres of land, twelve and a half cents; on each free poll and male servant, the same; on each retail store, twenty-five dollars; and on pedlars, the same; billiard tables, one thousand dollars per annum.

Assembly adjourned November the 8th. Previous to which Thomas McCorry was elected treasurer of Washington and Hamilton, and Thomas Crutcher treasurer of Mero district.

1804. The second session of the fifth General Assembly commenced at Knoxville on Monday the 23d of July, and adjourned the 4th of August. Among the general laws passed, was one to regulate the establishment of public roads, &c.

1805. John Sevier was re-elected Governor, and John Rhea and George W. Campbell representatives to Congress.

The sixth General Assembly met at Knoxville on Monday the 16th day of September. Joseph M'Minn was elected Speaker of the Senate, and Robert C. Foster Speaker of the House. No very important alterations or amendments were made to the general laws this session. After the enactment of some fifty or sixty statutes of minor consequence, the Assembly adjourned on the 4th of November.

1806. The second session of the sixth General Assembly commenced at Knoxville on Monday the 28th day of July. During this session an act passed for dividing the state into districts, and providing for the appointment of surveyors, &c. with a view to ascertain the vacant and unappropriated lands, and to adjust the bona fide claims against the state in conformity to an act of Congress passed in the month of April preceding, which authorized the State of Tennessee to issue grants and perfect titles to certain lands. Two land offices were established, one at Knoxville and one at Nashville. The state was divided into six principal districts, exclusive of the district south of French Broad and Holston. In each of which a principal surveyor was appointed, who were required to lay off their districts into subdivisions or sections of six miles square, in those places where the Indian titles were extinguished. And they were moreover required to make distinct mile marks in their lines, and particularly note the prior locations, that the vacant and unappropriated lands might be accurately ascertained.

An act also passed providing for the sale of the lands south of Holston and French Broad, and west of the Big Pigeon rivers.

Some alterations were made in the judicial districts. Mero was divided into three districts. The counties of Robertson, Dickson, Montgomery and Stewart composed one, by the name of Robertson, and the courts were held at Clarksville;— the counties of Jackson, Smith and Wilson composed a second, by the name of *Winchester,* and the courts were held at Carthage;—and the counties of Davidson, Sumner, Williamson and Rutherford formed *Mero,* and the courts were held at Nashville.

The salaries of the judges of the superior courts were fixed at one thousand dollars per annum, and those of the attorneys general at three hundred and fifty.

Twenty-seven academies were established this session, and the academy of Davidson county was incorporated as a college.

After the passage of many important general and local laws, the legislature adjourned on the 13th day of September.

1807. John Sevier was again elected governor, and John Rhea, George W. Campbell and Jesse Wharton were elected members of congress.

The seventh General Assembly convened at Kingston on the 21st September, and adjourned on the 23d to Knoxville. Joseph M'Minn was speaker of the senate, and Joseph M. Anderson principal, and Luke Lea assistant clerk. John Tipton was speaker of the house of representatives, John Lowry principal, and Alexander M. Nelson, assistant clerk.

Governor Sevier, in his message, made some appropriate allusions to the unprovoked attack by the British ship of war Leopard, upon the United States' frigate Chesapeake, and stated that in consequence of this outrage upon the American flag, the President had requested that Tennessee should detail her quota of militia to be ready for any emergency. The executive demand having been signified, a sufficient number of volunteers tendered their services. A revision of the criminal code, and the abolition of sanguinary punishments, education and internal improvement, were recommended as objects worthy of early attention. During the vacation, Hugh L. White, one of the judges, and William Maclin, secretary of state, resigned.

At this session some material amendments were made to the land laws, passed at the preceding general assembly. The punishments for larceny, horse stealing, forgery, purjury, malicious prosecution, arson, maiming, &c. were by law particularly defined. The Nashville Bank, with a capital of $400,000 was incorporated, and East Tennessee college established at Knoxville. The assembly adjourned on the 4th December, after the passage of 104 laws.

Previous to which, Joseph Anderson was elected a senator in congress, Robert Houston was elected secretary of state, Samuel Powell judge *vice* Judge White resigned, Parry W. Humphreys *vice* Judge Emmerson, resigned, Thomas Crutcher and Thomas M'Corry, treasurers of state, and James Winchester and Archibald Roane, commissioners of land claims.

1808. The second session of the seventh General Assembly convened at Knoxville on the 3d day of April, and after providing for the election of representatives in congress, and enacting in all fifty-seven laws, the assembly adjourned *sine die* on the 22d of the same month.

1809. The first session of the eighth General Assembly convened at Knoxville on the 18th September. The state then contained thirty-six counties.

In the senate, Joseph M'Minn was chosen speaker, Joseph M. Anderson principal, and Luke Lea engrossing clerk. In the house of representatives, Joseph Dickson was elected speaker, and Jacob Peck and Alexander M. Nelson clerks. Governor Sevier, in his message, made a favorable representation of the situation of the country. He recommended no alteration of the revenue laws, or the increase of taxes for the ordinary operations of the government. The debtors for lands south of French Broad and Holston were presented as proper objects of legislative relief. Governor Sevier being about to retire from the executive department, and not wishing to anticipate the views of his successor, gave but a brief of general subjects for the early action of the legislature.

A very material alteration in the judiciary system was made this session, by the establishment of circuit in lieu of district courts. The state was divided into five judicial circuits, and five circuit judges were elected. The counties of Greene, Washington, Carter, Sullivan, Hawkins, Grainger, Claiborne and Campbell formed the *first;* in which *William Cocke* was elected judge. The counties of Cocke, Jefferson, Sevier, Blount, Knox, Anderson, Roane, Rhea and Bledsoe formed the *second;* in which *James Trimble* was elected. The counties of Smith, Warren, Franklin, Sumner, Overton, White and Jackson formed the *third;* in which *Nathaniel W. Williams* was elected. The counties of Davidson, Wilson, Rutherford, Williamson, Maury, Giles, Lincoln and Bedford composed the *fourth* in which *Thomas Stuart* was elected. And the counties of Montgomery, Dickson, Hickman, Humphreys, Stewart and Robertson composed the *fifth;* in which *Parry W. Humphreys* was elected judge. The act provided for the holding of semi-annual courts in each county, and gave them original jurisdiction over all matters and causes at common law, and in equity, whereof the superior courts previously had cognizance; and exclusive jurisdiction over all criminal causes; and concurrent jurisdiction with the county courts over all causes then cognizable in the quarter sessions. In each circuit an attorney general was elected. David Yearsly Esq., for the *first;* William Kelly Esq., for the *second;* John H. Bowen Esq., for the *third;* Alfred Balch Esq., for the *fourth;* and George W. L. Marr, for the *fifth.* The superior courts of law and equity were abolished, and a *supreme court of errors and appeals,* established, to be composed of two supreme Judges, and one circuit Judge, and courts to be held annually at Jonesboro',

Knoxville, Carthage, Nashville and Clarksville. The salaries of the supreme Judges were fixed at $1500, and the circuit Judges at $1000, per annum, each. Many other laws but of minor importance, were enacted this session. Among those to which it may be necessary occasionally to refer, is the act to increase the jurisdiction of justices of the peace, and the act concerning the registration of deeds, &c.

Joseph Anderson and Jenkin Whitesides were elected Senators in Congress. The legislature adjourned on the 23d November, having been in session sixty-seven days. Willie Blount was elected governor and Pleasant M. Miller, John Rhea and Robert Weakley, were the representatives in Congress this year.

1810. The population of Tennessee, by the census taken this year, was 261,727, of this number 44,734 were slaves, leaving a free population of 216,983.[16]

The number of Iron works at this time were as follows; 6 bloomeries, valued at $17,000; 7 forges, valued at $10,000; 6 furnaces, valued at $9,800; and 7 naileries, valued at $128,000.

1811. Willie Blount was elected Governor, and Felix Grundy, John Rhea and John Sevier representatives in Congress.

The first session of the ninth general assembly, convened at Knoxville, on Monday the 16th day of September. *Thomas Henderson* was speaker of the senate, and *John Cocke* speaker of the house. The law in relation to the jurisdiction of the courts of record, underwent some amendments this session. The supreme court was vested with exclusive equity jurisdiction, and the circuit Judges were constituted Judges of the state, and authorized to interchange ridings, and were not, from thence, to be associated on the bench with the supreme Judges. The criminal and civil jurisdiction taken from the county courts, at the abolition of the district courts, was

---

[16] The 1810 Census of Tennessee (as well as that of 1800) has been lost. The only counties of Tennessee for which the 1810 Census exists are those of Grainger and Rutherford.

restored, and each county court was allowed to appoint a county solicitor. This session, a bank of the state was established, with branches at Clarksville, Columbia, Jonesboro' and Nashville. John C. McLemore, Esq., of Nashville, having obtained transcript records of all the grants issued by the state of North Carolina founded on military warrants, preemption warrants, Evans' batallions warrants, and service right claims, 4639 in number, a law was enacted, allowing copies certified by him, to be as good and valid as if authenticated by the secretary of the state of North Carolina. After passing near one hundred and thirty local and general statutes, the assembly adjourned on the 22d November.

1812. This being the commencement of the most interesting period in the history of Tennessee, an apology is due for omitting to detail the incidents of the war and the conspicuous part her citizens bore in those memorable conflicts with the British and Indians, in this and the three succeeding years. It was the original design of the compiler to present them, and he had accordingly selected from the archives of the times, many items for that purpose. In attempting to embody them; it was found that justice could not be done the subject, without occupying more space than was allotted for these sketches. And as almost every thing in relation to the late war, is fresh in the recollection of the people, upon reflection, it is deemed advisable to dispense with it altogether and proceed with the legislative and judicial memoranda.

The second session of the 9th general assembly convened at Nashville, on the seventh day of September. Governor Blount delivered a spirited and patriotic message in relation to the declaration of war against Great Britain, and stated that in compliance with the requisition of the war department, he had caused to be detached 2500 men, who were ready to march at the call of their country. In addition to this, he informed the assembly, that thousands of the patriotic citizens had tendered their services to the President, under the act of Congress authorizing him to accept of the services of 50,000 volunteers, and that he had signified his acceptance in terms of the highest approbation. Very few general laws were enacted this session, and both houses adjourned on the 21st October, after a session of eighty-nine days.

1813. The first session of the tenth general assembly convened at Nashville, on the 21st September, 1813. Willie Blount, governor, Wm. G. Blount, secretary of State, Robert C. Foster, speaker of the senate, and Thomas Claiborne, speaker of the house.

During this session an act passed, authorizing the governor to march 3,500 men against the Creek Indians. And all proceedings at law were suspended against militia men, until the expiration of their term of service.

A law was enacted to prevent the prosecuting of separate suits against joint, or joint and several obligors. Again there was an alteration in the judiciary. The circuit courts were vested with concurrent jurisdiction with the courts of pleas and quarter sessions in all civil causes, except appeals from justices of the peace, and original equity jurisdiction, concurrent with the supreme court. Appeals from the county courts to the supreme court in the nature of writs of error, were in future to be allowed, &c.

The legislature after passing one hundred and thirty-nine acts, adjourned on the 20th November. The number of militia returned from this state, to the war department, and laid before Congress in February of this year, amounted to but 29,183. If this statement be correct, Tennessee had frequently, during the war, one third of her whole military force in actual service.

The representatives in Congress this year, were John H. Bowen, Felix Grundy, Thomas K. Harris, Parry W. Humphreys and John Sevier.

Bennet Searcy and William Kelly, were commissioned circuit Judges, and Henry Minor and James C. Mitchell, were appointed solicitors general.

1815. This year Joseph McMinn was elected governor. There were 32,969 votes given. McMinn had 14,980; Robert Weakley 6,028; Jesse Wharton 5,918; Robert C. Foster 3,626;

and Gen. Johnson 2,417 votes. Willie Blount, Newton Cannon, Bennet H. Henderson, Samuel Powell, James B. Reynolds and Isaac Thomas, were elected representatives in Congress.

The first session of the eleventh general assembly, convened at Nashville, on Monday the 18th day of September. Col. Edward Ward was elected speaker, Joseph M. Anderson principal clerk, and Thomas Jefferson Campbell, assistant clerk of the senate.

In the House of Representatives, James Fentress was elected speaker, and William Alexander and Jacob Tipton, clerks. Governor Blount delivered his last message to the General Assembly, and congratulated the country on the termination of the war in a manner so honorable to the American character, &c. He was waited on by a committee of the legislature, and presented with a complimentary address, to which he responded in an appropriate manner. On the 27th September, Governor M'Minn took the oaths of office, and delivered his inaugural address. During the vacation, Governor Blount appointed *pro tempore* the following officers—William Cooke, judge *vice* judge White, resigned; James P. Taylor, attorney general *vice* Mr. Yearsly, deceased; Francis Jones, attorney general, *vice* Isaac Thomas, resigned; William R. Hess, attorney general *vice* Alfred Balch, resigned; and William L. Brown, attorney general *vice* Henry Minor, resigned.

No very important alterations in the general laws were made this session. Three banks were incorporated; one at Jonesboro,' one at Fayetteville, and one at Franklin.

William Alexander, Esq. was elected secretary of state, George W. Campbell and John Williams, senators in Congress, and Matthew Nelson, treasurer of East Tennessee. The assembly adjourned on the 17th November.

1817. The first session of the twelfth general assembly, convened at Knoxville, on Monday the 15th day of September. Edward Ward was chosen speaker, and Joseph M. Anderson and Daniel Graham, were elected clerks of the Senate. In the house, James Fentress was elected speaker, and Thomas

J. Campbell and Jacob Tipton clerks. They continued in session until the 25th November, and about two hundred acts were passed; of those deserving notice, may be included the act more effectively to suppress the vice of gaming, and the act authorizing the justices of the quarter sessions, to elect a quorum from their own body, to hold the county courts.

The sixth judicial district was established, composed of the counties of Lincoln, Giles, Maury, Bedford and Lawrence, and Alfred M. Harris was elected Judge. The state was divided into ten solicitorial districts, and ten solicitors general were elected. The first district was composed of the counties of Greene, Washington, Carter and Sullivan, and J. P. Taylor was elected solicitor general; the second was composed of the counties of Hawkins, Grainger and Campbell, in which Sterling Cocke was elected; the third was composed of the counties of Cocke, Jefferson, Sevier and Blount, in which John Wilkinson was elected; the fourth was composed of the counties of Knox, Morgan, Roane and Rhea, in which Wm. E. Anderson was elected; the fifth was composed of the counties of Bledsoe, Warren, White, Overton and Jackson, in which Thos. J. Campbell was elected; the sixth was composed of the counties of Smith, Wilson and Rutherford, in which Samuel H. Laughlin was elected; the seventh was composed of the counties of Davidson, Williamson and Sumner, in which Thomas Washington was elected; the eighth was composed of the counties of Franklin, Bedford and Lincoln, in which William B. Martin was elected; the ninth was composed of the counties of Giles, Maury, Lawrence and Hickman, in which Robert L. Cobbs was elected; and the tenth was composed of the counties of Dickson, Stewart, Humphreys, Montgomery and Robertson, in which Cave Johnson was elected.

Ten banks were incorporated this session, to wit: at Gallatin, Carthage, Rogersville, Nashville, Kingston, Winchester, Fayetteville, Maryville, Shelbyville and Murfreesboro'.

Joseph McMinn was this year re-elected governor. Thirty-three thousand eight hundred and sixty-two votes were given.

McMinn had 28,402, Robert C. Foster 15,460.

Robert Whyte was appointed Judge of the supreme court, *vice* Judge Overton resigned, and John Haywood *vice* Judge Cooke deceased. Thomas Emmerson was appointed Circuit Judge *vice* William Kelly resigned.

William G. Blount, Thomas Claiborne, Dr. Samuel Hogg, Francis Jones, George W. L. Marr and John Rhea, were elected members of the fifteenth Congress.

1818. The returns of the militia this year, in December, makes the number only 29,183, one third at least, below the real strength, as more than 40,000 votes were given the next year.

1819. The thirteenth general assembly convened at *Murfreesboro'*, on Monday the 20th day of September. Robert Weakley was speaker, and James K. Polk and Alexander B. Bradford clerks of the senate. In the house James Fentress was speaker and Thomas J. Campbell and Jacob Tipton clerks. Governor McMinn in his message, strongly urged the propriety of revising the criminal code and establishing a penitentiary. In relation to capital offences, he mentions a fact, which may be worthy of future consideration, and that is "that during a lapse of nearly four years, only three sentences of death had occurred in the state, and only one execution."

During the vacation John H. Eaton was appointed senator in Congress in the place of G. W. Campbell resigned. Thomas Emmerson Judge of the supreme court, *vice* Archibald Roane deceased; Samuel Powell circuit Judge *vice* Judge Emmerson resigned; Parry W. Humphreys circuit Judge *vice* Bennet Searcy deceased. Jacob C. Isaacs circuit judge *vice* Nathaniel W. Williams resigned; and Daniel Graham secretary of state *vice* William Alexander deceased. Joseph McMinn was re-elected Governor, he received 33,524 votes, and his opponent, Enoch Parsons, 8,079.

Among the public acts of this session deserving notice, may be included an amendatory law respecting North Carolina land claims, and an act limiting the time of prosecuting of actions, either in law or equity, for the recovery of real estate, to seven years from the time the right accrued. This act has been very justly appreciated by the farmers of the country. It has almost driven from the courts an expensive and harrassing species of litigation, and has had a most salutary effect in quieting the citizens in their landed possessions.

A law was enacted requiring depositions in chancery to be in writing, and allowing appeals in chancery, from the circuit to the supreme court. The seventh judicial circuit was established, composed of the counties of Roane, Rhea, Bledsoe, Marion, McMinn, Hamilton and Monroe.

The governor's salary was raised to $2,000, and the secretary of state's to $750 per annum.

John H. Eaton was elected senator in Congress. On the last balloting Eaton had 31, and P. W. Humphreys 29 votes. Thomas Emmerson was elected supreme Judge, and Samuel Powell, Parry W. Humphreys and Nathaniel W. Williams circuit Judges. Sam. Houston, James Rogers and John A. Montgomery, were elected solicitors general. Daniel Graham Esq., was elected secretary of state.

After the enactment of 242 laws, the legislature adjourned on the 30th November.

The representatives in Congress, elected this year, were Robert Allen, Henry H. Bryan, Newton Cannon, John Cocke, Francis Jones and John Rhea.

1820. By the census taken this year, Tennessee contained a population of 422,813, of which 80,097 were slaves, and 2,739 were free persons of color.

The twenty-two counties east of the mountains, and comprising East Tennessee, contained 121,734 whites, 12,413 slaves, and 1,165 free persons of color. Total 135,312.[10]

The twenty-six counties west of the mountains, and comprising what is now called Middle Tennessee and the Western District, contained 218,191 whites; 67,684 slaves; and 1,574 free persons of color. Total 287,501.

---

[10] The 1820 Census for the "twenty-two counties east of the mountains" has been lost.

In the whole state there were

Free white males under ten years of age,	67,746
" " of ten and under sixteen	28,497
" " between sixteen and eighteen	7,472
" " of sixteen and under twenty-six,	31,028
" " between twenty-six and forty-five,	27,349
" " of forty-five and upwards,	18,780
Free white females, under ten years of age,	63,419
" " of ten and under sixteen,	27,770
" " of sixteen and under twenty-six,	31,569
" " of twenty-six and under forty-five,	27,931
" " of forty-five and upwards.	15,638

Number of persons engaged in agriculture, 101,717, in commerce, 892.

The second session of the 13th General Assembly convened at Murfreesboro' on the 26th June. The governor in his message, drew a doleful picture of the finances, and the distresses of the great mass of the people in consequence of the scarcity of a sound circulating medium. Like many of the western statesmen of that day, he seemed to think that all their misfortunes were occasioned by defective legislation. Accordingly he recommended the establishment of a loan office on the credit of the state, and a variety of other schemes then prevalent, to increase the currency and give a temporary relief to the debtor part of the community. Fortunately for the country, the loan office bill was rejected, but it was succeeded by an institution scarcely less exceptionable in its character. On the 25th of July, an act passed to establish 'The Bank of the State of Tennessee, in Nashville, with a branch at Knoxville, with a capital not to exceed one million of dollars. The Treasury deposites arising from the ordinary revenue of the state, and the proceeds of the sales of Hiwassee lands &c., &c. formed the basis for the issuance of paper. The bank was placed under the government of a President and ten Directors. And they were required to establish an agency in each county, and to forward to the agents a due proportion of money, to be loaned out in small sums to the good people, upon a credit of 90 days, with the privilege of a renewal upon the payment of ten per cent, &c. The directors were appointed by the legislature, the capital belonged to the state, and the great body of the people were to be borrowers. At the end of the first year, the directory reported the capital to be $200,000 in bank; due from the purchasers of Hiwassee lands $450,000, and $20,000 in the old State Bank, making 670,000. Sundry amendments to the charter were made from time to time, and some additional investments. In 1827 the sum of $531,711.73 had been received from the sales of the Hiwassee lands, and the whole capital of the bank, except the one half of that sum was appropriated to common schools —*which see* 1827. An act concerning the registration of deeds; an act to regulate executions and providing for the redemption of slaves and real estate, and an act respecting endorsers of promissory notes, bills &c., passed this session. And the assembly adjourned on the 31st July.

1821. William Carroll, who had distinguished himself as a general officer in the late war, was this year elected governor of the state by an overwhelming majority. His competitor was Col. Edward Ward, who was in 1815-17 speaker of the senate. Gen. Carroll had 31.029, and Col. Ward 7.294 votes. Messrs. Allen, Bryan, Cannon, Cocke, Jones and Rhea were re-elected to congress.

The fourteenth General Assembly met at Murfreesboro' on the 17th September. Sterling Brewer was chosen speaker of the senate, and James K. Polk, clerk. In the house, James Fentress was elected speaker, and Thomas J. Campbell and Jacob Tipton, clerks. Gov. M'Minn again recommended the enactment of relief laws. He also recommended a revision of the financial system, and the appointment of an auditor general, or some comptrolling officer in the treasury department. And it is much to be regretted that the assembly did not profit by the suggestion. He made also some commendable allusions to the subjects of education and internal improvement.

On the first of October, General Carroll, the governor elect, appeared and took the oaths of office. In his first communication to the legislature, he satisfied the public that the confidence reposed in his ability to administer the affairs of the state had not been misplaced. The relief, replevin and stay laws, and all other temporising expedients hitherto so much relied upon for the restoration of a sound currency, and the agricultural and commercial prosperity of the country, he opposed with his accustomed firmness; and earnestly recommended to the people to seek a relief from their embarrassments, not by a legislative interposition between the debtor and the creditor, but by a rigid system of economy and retrenchment in their domestic relations. He brought to the view of the legislature the inefficiency of the judiciary as then organized, and the confused and uncertain administration of the law by distinct tribunals having concurrent jurisdiction. To remedy which, he recommended the establishment of a separate court of chancery, and the repeal of the law giving concurrent jurisdiction to the circuit and county courts. He also recommended the establishment of a penitentiary, and the abolition of the pillory, whipping, branding, and other barbarous and sanguinary punishments. Proper suggestions were also made for improving the militia, the dissemination of learning, and extending the benefits of internal improvement.

An act to regulate the mode of proceeding for a forcible entry and detainer, and an act to prescribe the punishment for counterfeiting, passed this session.

An eighth judicial circuit was established, composed of the counties of Henry, Carroll, Henderson, Madison, Shelby, Wayne, Hardin and Perry; and Joshua Haskill, Esq. was elected judge. Two additional solicitorial districts were also created: Humphreys, Henry and Carroll, composed the 13th; and Hardin, Madison and Perry, the 14th.—Assembly adjourned 17th November, after a session of sixty-two days.

1822. The second session of the fourteenth General Assembly convened at Murfreesboro' on the 22d July, for the purpose of laying off the state into nine congressional districts.

The counties of Carter, Washington, Sullivan, Hawkins and Greene, formed the *first;* Grainger, Claiborne, Cocke, Jefferson, Knox, Sevier and Blount, the *second;* Campbell, Anderson, Morgan, Roane, Rhea, Bledsoe, Marion, Hamilton, M'Minn and Monroe, the *third;* Franklin, Warren, White, Fentress, Overton and Jackson, the *fourth;* Smith, Sumner and Wilson, the *fifth;* Davidson, Williamson and Rutherford, the *sixth;* Bedford, Lincoln, Giles and Maury, the *seventh;* Robertson, Montgomery, Dickson, Stewart, Humphreys and Hickman, the *eighth;* and Wayne, Hardin, Perry, Lawrence, Henry, Carroll, Henderson, M'Nairy, Fayette, Tipton, Dyer, Obion, Weakley, Gibson and Haywood, the *ninth;* under the census of 1820.

The judiciary was amended this session by adding another judge to the supreme court bench, and requiring the judges to hold distinct chancery sessions, and they were invested with original equity jurisdiction.

William L. Brown, Esq. was the additional judge elected, and Jacob Peck Esq. was elected supreme judge *vice* judge Emmerson, resigned. Thomas J. Campbell was elected solicitor general for the 11th, and Thomas H. Fletcher for the 8th solicitorial district. Several other acts of importance were passed, and previous to the adjournment which took place on the 25th of August, swords were voted to Generals Jackson and Gaines for their gallantry in the late war.

1823. This year, Gen. Carroll was re-elected governor without opposition. He received 32,597 votes. John Blair, John Cocke, James Standifer, Jacob C. Isaacs, Robert Allen, Samuel Houston, James T. Sanford, James B. Reynolds and Adam R. Alexander were elected to represent this state in the 18th congress.

The fifteenth General Assembly convened at Murfreesboro' on the 15th day of September, 1823. Col. Robert Weakley was chosen speaker of the senate, and Joseph M. Anderson and Russel Dance, clerks.—In the house, James Fentress was elected speaker, and Robert L. Caruthers and John D. Martin, clerks. The governor again recommended the establishment of a penitentiary, and the revision of the criminal code. He moreover stated that he had not changed his views of *relief laws;* and in confirmation of their impolicy, he cited a late opinion of the supreme court declaring the endorsement law of 1820 unconstitutional.

Not many general statutes were enacted this session. The ninth judicial district was established, composed of the counties of Perry, Henderson, Carroll and Henry; and John C. Hamilton was elected judge. The counties of M'Nairy, Hardeman and Shelby were formed into the 15th solicitorial district; and Valentine D. Barry was elected solicitor general; and the counties of Obion, Weakley and Dyer, were formed into the 16th; and James R. Chalmers was elected solicitor general.

On the 1st of October came on the election for a senator in congress for six years from the 4th March, 1823. Andrew Jackson had 35, and John Williams 25 votes. On the 12th of October, Joseph M. Anderson, Esq., the first clerk in the senate, died, and the usual tribute of respect was paid to his memory by the members of both houses. Daniel Graham was re-elected secretary of state, and the Hon. Joseph Phillips was elected president of the state bank. The Hon. William L. Brown, one of the judges of the supreme court, resigned. The assembly adjourned on the 29th November, after a session of seventy-six days.

1824. The second session of the fifteenth General Assembly convened at Murfreesboro' on the 20th September, 1824, by order of the governor, principally to correct a mistake in the act providing for the election of president and vice president.

Governor Carroll again recommended a reform in the judiciary, and the establishment of separate chancery courts. The circulating medium he represented as greatly improved. He alluded to the visit of La Fayette to the United States, and recommended an expression of the legislature upon the subject. A joint committee was appointed and resolutions were adopted, that the governor be requested, in the name and on behalf of the citizens of Tennessee, to welcome the arrival of the brave and good La Fayette, and to request him to visit the state at as early a day as convenient. And that it might be the act of the whole state, his Excellency was authorised to make suitable arrangements for his reception at the public expense. An amendment was made to the judiciary by adding judges to the supreme bench; and an act was passed more effectually to suppress the vice of gaming, &c. The assembly adjourned on the 22d of October, after a session of thirty-three days.

1825. This year Gen. Carroll was re-elected governor without opposition; and Adam R. Alexander, John Blair, Jacob C. Isaacs, John H. Marable, James C. Mitchell, Samuel Houston and James K. Polk were elected representatives in congress.

The first session of the sixteenth General Assembly began at Murfreesboro' on the 19th September. Robert C. Foster was chosen speaker of the senate, and Russel Dance and Benj. M. Bradford were elected clerks. In the house, William Brady was chosen speaker, and John P. Erwin and William F. Brown were elected clerks.

The assembly consisted of 38 farmers, 12 lawyers, 5 doctors and 5 merchants. Of these, 21 were natives of Virginia, 16 of North Carolina, 14 of Tennessee, 3 of Kentucky, 2 of Pennsylvania, 2 of Maryland, 1 of South Carolina, and 1 of Ireland.

Governor Carroll in his message, after alluding to the improved state of the currency, &c. recommended some improvement in the militia, and a classification, with a view to their better instruction and discipline. He again pressed the subject of amending the judiciary, by constituting but one tribunal for the trial of jury causes, the establishment of an able supreme court, and the erection of a distinct court of chancery. A revision of the penal code and the establishment of a penitentiary was again most earnestly suggested. The welcome reception of La Fayette in May preceding by the patriotic citizens of Tennessee, he noticed in appropriate terms, and highly commended the citizens of Nashville for their liberality and kind attention to the volunteer companies encamped some ten or twelve days awaiting La Fayette's arrival. In consequence of which, the public expenditures had fallen short of $3,500. The governor expressed his belief that the time had arrived for Tennessee to do something in the way of internal improvements.

On the 2nd October, a resolution passed both houses again recommending Gen. Andrew Jackson as a suitable candidate for the presidency, Mr. Reneau of the House only dissenting, and that on the ground that it was not the province of a legislative body, and was an useless waste of time. On the 14th Oct'r. both houses in convention, agreeably to a previous resolution, received Gen. Jackson with ceremonious form, and four days after, he resigned his seat in the senate of the United States.

This session the secretary of state was made ex-officio commissioner of North Carolina land claims, and acts passed to revise the statutes, &c., and John Haywood and Robt. L. Cobbs, Esqs. were appointed for that purpose. Hugh L. White was elected senator in Congress *vice* Andrew Jackson resigned; Thomas B. Craighead was elected solicitor of the 9th district *vice* Mr. Cobbs resigned, and Joseph Philips was re-elected president of the State Bank. A resolution was adopted to remove the seat of government to Nashville, and the assembly adjourned on the 7th Dec., after a session of 80 days.

1826. The second session of the 16th General Assembly convened at Nashville, on Monday the 16th day of October. Thomas J. Campbell was chosen clerk of the House in the place of John P. Erwin resigned. The governor, after alluding to the ordinary duties of the session again urged a revision of the criminal laws, the establishment of a penitentiary, and the reorganization of the courts. During the vacation William E. Keneday was appointed judge of the 6th circuit, and Hugh Dunlap Attorney General for the 13th district, and their appointments were confirmed by election. Henry Nixon was elected Attorney General of the 12th district *vice* James Scott resigned. The legislature passed 47 general and 199 local acts, amongst which was an act to apportion the senators and representatives agreeably to the enumeration of the free male inhabitants taken this year.

During this session a sword was voted to General William Carroll, for his distinguished services during the war. And on the 4th November John H. Eaton was re-elected to a seat in the United States Senate. The legislature adjourned on the 11th December.

The cotton crop was estimated this year at 50,000 bales being 10,000 more than the estimate of the preceding year.

1827. Samuel Houston was elected Governor, and John Bell, John Blair, Robert Desha, Jacob C. Isaacs, Pryor Lee, John H. Marable, James C. Mitchell, James K. Polk and David Crockett were elected representatives in Congress.

The first session of the 17th General Assembly convened at Nashville on Monday the 17th day of September. William Hall was elected Speaker of the Senate and Russel Dance clerk. In the House John H. Camp was elected Speaker and Thomas J. Campbell and James A. Whitesides Clerks.

Governor Carroll again recommended the establishment of a penitentiary and an amendment of the judiciary. He also suggested the propriety of erecting a monument to the memory of General James Robertson. During the vacation H. Crabbe was appointed judge of the Supreme Court and Abraham Martin attorney general of the 8th district.

This session a material amendment was made in the judiciary by the creation of a distinct Chancery court. The Supreme court was made to consist of three judges, and two chancellors were appointed, one for East and one for West Tennessee, who were required to hold chancery courts at Rogersville, Kingston, Carthage, M'Minnville, Frankin, Columbia, Charlotte, Jackson and Paris; and the Supreme court was divested of original equity jurisdiction.

One the 1st October 1827 Samuel Houston, the governor elect took the oaths of office and a committee was appointed to wait on his predecessor, Gen. William Carroll and express to him the high sense which the general assembly entertained of his services. William E. Anderson and Nathan Green were elected the first Chancellors, Hugh L. White was re-elected Senator, receiving 57 votes, Thomas Crutcher was re-elected Treasurer of Middle Tennessee and Miller Francis of East Tennessee. The Western District was formed into a treasury division, and James Caruthers was elected Treasurer. Leonard P. Cheatham was elected President of the State Bank, Robert L. Caruthers Attorney General for the 6th, Erwin Frierson for the 8th and James P. Lowry for the 11th solicitorial district. The assembly adjourned on 15th December, after a session of ninety days.

1829. On the 16th April, Samuel Houston, governor of the state resigned his office, and Gen. William Hall of Sumner, the Speaker of the Senate became the governor ex officio until the meeting of the legislature. At the August election, Gen. William Carroll was again elected governor without opposition, receiving 57,551 votes. John Bell, John Blair, David Crockett, Robt. Desha, Jacob C. Isaacs, Cave Johnson, Pryor Lea, J. K. Polk and James Standifer were elected members of the 21st Congress.

The first session of the 18th general assembly convened at Nashville on Monday the 21st September 1829. In the senate Joel Walker was elected Speaker and William K. Hill and William Martin clerks. In the house of representatives Ephraim H. Foster was elected Speaker, and Thomas J. Campbell and Edmund Tipton Clerks.

Governor Hall in his message in a delicate manner, alluded to the sudden and unexpected resignation of Governor Houston, and by reason of which, as Speaker of the Senate, it had become his duty to exercise the executive functions.[17] He warmly recommended a revision of the penal code—the establishment of a penitentiary, and a modification of punishments in accordance with the march of intellectual improvement, and the chastened spirit of christianity. The subjects

---

[17] Sam Houston was the first of three governors of Tennessee to resign from the office (the others were William G. Brownlow in 1869 and James B. Frazier in 1905). The reasons for Houston's action have been exhaustively examined, but never satisfactorily explained.

of internal improvement and education, were properly noticed, as also the unstable state of the currency, and the destructive effects of usury upon the commerce of the country.

On the 1st of October, William Carroll, the Governor elect, took the oaths of office, and a joint select committee was appointed to tender to General William Hall the thanks of the General Assembly, for the able and efficient manner in which he had discharged the duties of chief magistrate.

On the fifth of October, Governor Carroll delivered his message, and in addition to the suggestions of his predecessor, he recommended the closing of the concerns of the Bank of the State. And he once more pressed the subjects of an amendment of the criminal laws—the establishment of a penitentiary—systems of general education, internal improvements, &c.

This session was marked with a spirit of liberal and enlightened legislation. The great interest of education and internal improvement were thoroughly investigated and many important laws were enacted.

Early in the session, Mr. Greene of the Senate introduced resolutions on the subject of internal improvement, and General Dunlap of the House, in a number of reports and resolutions, very ably advocated an immediate adoption of the policy. Mr. Huntsman of the Senate, and Mr. Huling of the House, from their respective judiciary committees, made detailed reports on the propriety of reform in the judicial department; and Mr. Campbell of the Senate brought forward and sustained with signal ability, his several bills for a revision of the penal code, the establishment of a state prison, &c.[19]

To the honor of the state, a penitentiary was established, and an act was passed to reform and amend the penal laws, whereby a multitude of barbarous and sanguinary punishments were erased from the statute book. Murder in the second degree, manslaughter, arson, rape, bigamy, sodomy,

---

[19] The men referred to are Adam Huntsman, Frederick W. Huling, and Thomas J. Campbell.

incest, burglary, robbery, stealing negroes, larceny over ten dollars, house breaking, receiving stolen goods, stealing notes or bills, counterfeiting, receiving and passing base notes with an evil intent, passing counterfeit money, forgery, perjury, bribery, horse stealing and a variety of other offences were made punishable by confinement at hard labor in the penitentiary.

Among the other important acts this session, were the adoption of a system of common schools—organizing a board of internal improvement and the appropriation of $150,000; sixty thousand in East Tennessee, sixty thousand in Middle Tennessee and thirty thousand in West Tennessee, and the incorporation of a medical society.

John A. Aiken Esq. was elected Attorney General for the third, and George W. Terrel Esq. for the thirteenth solicitorial district. On the 16th of October, Felix Grundy Esq. was elected a Senator in Congress to fill the vacancy occasioned by the resignation of John H. Eaton, appointed Secretary of War. Joseph Philips Esq. was elected President and Nicholas Hobson Esq. Cashier of the Bank of the State of Tennessee. James A. Whitesides Esq. was appointed to incorporate the acts of this session in the revised code of Haywood and Cobbs. The Assembly adjourned on the 14th January 1830, after a session of 115 days.

1830. By the census taken this year under the authority of the United States, the population was upwards of six hundred and eighty four thousand, to wit:[19]

EAST TENNESSEE.

	Free White Males.	F. White Females.	F. People of color.	Slaves.	Total.
Anderson,	2,497	2,336	26	471	5,312
Bledsoe,	2,118	2,147	64	419	4,748

[19] The Census of 1830 is the first complete extant census of Tennessee. In 1830, Tennessee was the fifth most populous state of the Union. Under the reapportionment after the census, the state had thirteen representatives in the House of Representatives, the largest ever. It is of interest to note that several counties of the state had a larger population in 1830 than in 1970, 140 years later.

TENNESSEE GAZETTEER. 61

	Free White Males.	F. White Females.	F. People of color.	Slaves.	Total.
Blount,	4,994	4,921	90	1,022	11,027
Campbell,	2,444	2,350	71	245	5,110
Carter,	3,064	2,879	14	461	6,418
Claiborne,	3,952	3,811	92	615	8,470
Cocke,	2,636	2,679	95	638	6,048
Grainger,	4,396	4,498	263	909	10,066
Greene,	6,665	6,578	97	1,070	14,410
Hamilton,	1,089	1,045	25	115	2,274
Hawkins,	5,905	5,733	386	1,659	13,683
Jefferson,	5,300	5,194	83	1,222	11,799
Knox,	6,148	6,208	108	2,034	14,498
M'Minn,	6,732	6,487	21	1,257	14,497
Marion,	2,758	2,483	6	269	5,516
Monroe,	6,363	6,256	37	1,053	13,709
Morgan,	1,297	1,219	6	60	2,582
Roane,	5,069	5,060	94	1,117	11,340
Rhea,	3,828	3,709	3	642	8,182
Sevier,	2,650	2,672	13	382	5,777
Sullivan,	4,435	4,247	204	1,187	10,073
Washington,	4,911	4,899	145	1,040	10,995
Total E. Tenn.	89,233	87,411	1,943	17,887	196,474

MIDDLE TENNESSEE.

	Free White Males.	F. White Females.	F. People of color.	Slaves.	Total.
Bedford,	12,755	11,941	86	5,662	30,444
Davidson,	8,432	7,556	472	11,629	28,089
Dickson,	2,862	2,709	32	1,658	7,261
Franklin,	6,122	5,893	39	3,590	15,644
Fentress,	1,343	1,297	1	119	2,760
Giles,	6,808	6,061	16	6,035	18,920
Hardin,	2,278	2,111	62	416	4,867
Hickman,	3,509	3,382	15	1,226	8,132
Humphreys,	2,751	2,682	31	725	6,189
Jackson,	4,407	4,222	138	1,135	9,902
Lawrence,	2,492	2,360	5	555	5,412
Lincoln,	9,196	8,738	64	4,088	22,086

	Free White Males.	F. White Females.	F. People of color.	Slaves.	Total.
Maury,	9,293	8,871	28	9,961	28,153
Montgomery,	4,412	4,087	63	5,803	14,363
Overton,	3,695	3,637	67	847	8,246
Perry,	3,645	2,980	5	408	7,038
Robertson,	4,888	4,696	95	3,623	13,302
Rutherford,	8,831	8,490	155	8,654	26,130
Smith,	9,391	7,723	83	4,294	21,492
Stewart,	2,864	2,644	85	1,395	6,988
Sumner,	6,702	6,477	133	7,247	20,559
Warren,	6,986	6,669	40	1,656	15,351
Wayne,	2,937	2,783	14	279	6,013
White,	4,576	4,402	67	922	9,967
Williamson,	8,236	7,770	129	10,473	26,608
Wilson,	9,853	9,399	302	5,923	25,477
Total in M. T.	149,264	139,580	2,227	98,324	389,395

WEST TENNESSEE.

	Free White Males.	F. White Females.	F. People of color.	Slaves.	Total.
Carroll,	4,004	3,681	31	1,662	9,378
Dyer,	690	598	15	601	1,904
Fayette,	2,948	2,465	48	3,193	8,654
Gibson,	2,388	2,109	23	1,281	5,801
Hardeman,	4,197	3,761	23	3,647	11,628
Haywood,	1,915	1,595	9	1,853	5,354
Henderson,	3,894	3,400	5	1,442	8,741
Henry,	4,824	4,401	55	2,950	12,230
M'Nairy,	2,755	2,561	4	377	5,697
Madison,	3,975	3,529	43	4,203	11,750
Obion,	907	854	1	337	2,099
Shelby,	1,974	1,563	62	2,053	5,652
Tipton,	2,002	1,566	17	1,732	5,317
Weakley,	2,048	1,895	5	848	4,796
W. Tennessee,	38,521	33,978	341	26,161	99,001
M. Tennessee,	149,264	139,580	2,227	98,324	389,395
E. Tennessee,	89,233	87,411	1,943	17,887	196,474
Total	277,018	260,969	4,511	142,372	684,870

1831. William Carroll was elected governor without opposition, and John Blair, Thos. D. Arnold, James Standifer, Jacob C. Isaacs, William Hall, John Bell, James K. Polk, Cave Johnson and William Fitzgerald were elected members of Congress.

The 19th General Assembly convened at Nashville on the 19th day of September, Burchet Douglass was elected Speaker of the Senate, and William K. Hill and Luke Lea jr. Clerks. In the House, Frederick W. Huling was chosen Speaker, and Thomas J. Campbell and James A. Whitesides, Clerks. The Governor in his message recommended the winding up of the State Bank, and the application of part of the stock for the improvement of the roads, &c. He informed the general assembly that the penitentiary, which had been commenced on the first day of April, 1830, was so far completed on the first day of January, 1831, as to admit of the reception of convicts, and that the expense fell short of $50,000. A reform in the judiciary system was again recommended. During the vacation, the governor made the following temporary appointments, to wit: Thomas H. Fletcher, Secretary of State, *vice* Daniel Graham resigned, William A. Cooke, Chancellor, *vice* William E. Anderson resigned, Bromfield L. Ridley, Solicitor, *vice* John B. Rodgers resigned, and Gideon J. Pillow, Solicitor, *vice* Thomas B. Craighead resigned.

Some important amendments were made in the judiciary system this session. The supreme court was made to consist of a chief justice and three associate judges, and provision was made for the appointment of a reporter. A law also passed to abolish imprisonment for debt, except in cases of fraud, on all debts contracted subsequent to the first of March 1831. A material alteration was also made in the registration laws, making the instrument to take effect from the date of its registration instead of the day of its execution. The insurrection of the Negroes in Virginia, gave rise to a rigorous statute in relation to the slaves and free persons of color. Free persons of color were prohibited from emigrating to this state under a penalty of fine and imprisonment in the penitentiary, and the owners of slaves were not permitted to emancipate them except upon the express condition that they should be immediately removed from the state. The Hon. John Catron was elected chief justice, and Nathan Greene associate judge of the supreme court. William A. Cook was elected chancellor, Roger Barton was elected attorney general for the 15th district, Edward Dillahunty for the 9th, and Wm. B. Campbell for the 5th.

Eastin Morris was elected president and Nicholas Hobson cashier of the State bank. The legislature adjourned on the 21st December after a session of 94 days. The number of justices of peace in the state this year were reported to be 2,366. The number of public arms were reported to be 7538 stand of muskets, 360 brace of pistols, 60 swords, and 3 six pounders.

1832. The second session of the 19th general assembly convened at Nashville on Monday, the 3d day of September, agreeably to the governor's proclamation, for the purpose of laying off the state into congressional districts, and providing for the election of electors for President and Vice President. Governor Carroll, in a brief message, expressed his belief that it was not his duty under the constitution to present for the consideration of the members any other subjects than those for which they were specially called. They however remained in session fifty days, and enacted a number of general and local statutes. The state was divided into 13 congressional districts, for which see (*ante. page* 14). For the election of electors 15 districts were created; an elector to reside in each district, and the whole to be elected by a general ticket. A very salutary act was passed in relation to the sale of lottery tickets. The Union bank of the state of Tennessee, with a capital of three millions of dollars, was chartered. The principal bank established at Nashville, with branches at Knoxville and Jackson. A lunatic hospital was also established at Nashville, and ten thousand dollars appropriated to purchase a site and commence the building.

Robert L. Caruthers Esq. solicitor general of the sixth district, resigned, and Samuel Yerger, Esq. was elected in his stead. The assembly adjourned on the 22d of October.

1833. William Carroll was elected governor without opposition, and the following persons were elected members of Congress: For the first district, John Blair; second, Samuel Bunch; third, Luke Lea; fourth, James Standifer; fifth, John B. Forrester; sixth, Balie Peyton; seventh, John Bell; eighth, David W. Dickenson; ninth, James K. Polk; tenth, William M. Inge; eleventh, Cave Johnson; twelfth, David Crockett, and thirteenth, William C. Dunlap.

This year a vote was taken upon calling a convention to revise the Constitution of the state. There were 90,781 votes given for members of the General Assembly, and 53,639 for a convention, being a majority of 8,122 of all the votes given. A census of the free white male inhabitants above the age of twenty one years was also taken, which with the enumeration of 1805, 1812, 1819 and 1826, is here given.

Free Male Inhabitants.

Counties	1805	1812	1819	1826	1833	Total in 1833.
E. T.						
Anderson	671	488		727	892	
Bledsoe		570	336	904	942	
Blount	907	1,336		1,774	1,909	
Carter	550	607	696	904	1,357	
Claiborne	714	720	818	1,074	1,379	
Campbell		494	534	742	902	
Cocke	611	804	699	864	974	
Greene	996	1,437	1,523	1,937	2,481	
Grainger	932	986	910	1,951	1,508	
Hawkins	1,425	1,193	1,483	2,113	2,208	
Hamilton				255	402	
Jefferson	1,012	1,073	1,193	1,705	1,754	
Knox	1,626	1,589		2,103	2,431	

Counties	1805	1812	1819	1826	1833	Total in 1833.
Monroe				1,707	2,369	
McMinn				2,164	2,403	
Marion				880	903	
Morgan			233	316	487	
Rhea		680		1,083	1,436	
Roane	560	738	855	1,627	1,823	
Sullivan		1,072		1,534	1,821	
Sevier	702	744	730	898	988	
Washgt'n	1,163	1,315	1,317	737	2,004	
M. T.						33,373
Bedford		1,731	2,519	3,195	4,277	
Davidson	1,855	2,235	1,882	2,965	3,668	
Dickson		683	740	857	1,038	
Fentress				460	643	
Franklin		1,180	1,516	2,025	2,230	
Giles		1,056	1,383	2,013	2,485	
Hickman		539	602	1,021	1,316	
Humphr's		282	594	796	1,153	
Jackson		957	999	1,398	1,742	
Lawr'nce			458	601	1,014	
Lincoln		1,391		2,825	3,379	
Maury		1,864	2,311	3,418	4,093	
Montg'ry	675	993	1,245	1,670	1,879	
Overton		882		953	1,430	
Rob'rtson		852	1,210	1,726	1,968	
Ruth'ford		1,543	2,076	3,038	3,541	
Sumner		1,754	1,781	2,684	2,648	
Smith		1,640	1,769	2,510	3,267	
Stewart		625	915	879	1,325	
Wilson		1,947		2,930	3,516	
W'mson.	1,051	1,759	1,948	2,398	3,368	
Wayne		1,030		752	1,276	
Warren			1,591	2,148	2,495	
White			1,087	1,478	1,873	55,624

Counties	1805	1812	1819	1826	1833	Total in 1833.
W. T.						
Carroll				1,187	2,038	
Dyer				181	453	
Fayette				265	1,659	
Gibson				429	1,613	
Hard'man				980	1,922	
Hen'rson				868	1,621	
Henry				1,651	2,241	
Hardin				638	1,152	
Haywood				265	1,094	
McNairy				373	1,246	
Madison				1,175	2,028	
Obion					481	
Perry				714	1,297	
Shelby				260	1,152	
Tipton				139	1,010	
Weakley				562	1,005	22,012
	15,450	40,677	37,963	82,426		111,009

The first session of the twentieth General Assembly was held at Nashville, on Monday the 16th day of September. David Burford of Smith was elected Speaker of the Senate, and William K. Hill and Luke Lea Jr. were appointed clerks. In the House, Frederick W. Huling was chosen speaker and James A. Whitesides and James M. Howry clerks.

The next day the Governor delivered his message, in which among other things he alluded to the vote of the people in favor of a Convention and the consequent inexpediency of presenting many subjects for the consideration of the legislature. As the adoption of a new Constitution would doubtless change the fundamental principles of the government, all general laws should be founded upon, and controlled by its provisions.—He gave a favorable report of the penitentiary experiment, and the apparent moral reformation of the convicts; and that they had enjoyed good health until the 2nd of June, when the cholera commenced its dreadful ravages. Of the 83 then in prison, not one escaped the disease, and nineteen fell victims to the scourge. He suggested the propriety of closing the concerns of the Bank of the State of Tennessee, and expressed a desire that the General Assembly should not authorize the executive to subscribe for the additional five thousand shares of the capital stock of the Union Bank of the State of Tennessee, reserved to the State by the charter, &c.

During the vacation the following temporary appointments were made, John W. Cooke Esq., Judge of the ninth circuit, in the room of the Hon. John W. Hamilton deceased; Abraham Caruthers Esq., Judge of the third circuit, in the place of the Hon. Nathaniel W. Williams deceased; Lunsford M. Bramlett, Judge of the sixth circuit *vice* the Hon. William E. Kennedy resigned; and Thomas A. R. Nelson, Solicitor General for the first district, in the room of James P. Taylor Esq. deceased. All of whom were afterwards elected by the legislature.

Amongst the general laws enacted this session, was an act to extend the laws and jurisdiction of the State over that tract of country now in the occupancy of the Cherokee Indians—an act to regulate and simplify the distribution and division of the estates of persons dying insolvent—an act to amend the registration laws, and regulating probate of deeds and other instruments, and an act for calling a Convention, &c. Several important rail road companies were incorporated. The Planters' Bank, at Nashville, the Farmers and Merchants' Bank, of Memphis, and the Tennessee Marine and Fire Insurance Company, at Nashville, were also incorporated. The Assembly adjourned on the second day of December.

1834. On the first Thursday and Friday in March, an election was held for sixty delegates in pursuance of an act of the General Assembly of the State, entitled "An act to provide for the calling of a Convention," passed the 27th day of November 1833, and the following persons were elected: For the county of *Carter*, William B. Carter; *Washington*, Mathew Stephenson; *Sullivan*, Abram M'Clellan; *Greene*, Robert J. M'Kinney; *Hawkins*, John A. M'Kinney; *Jefferson, Grainger, Claiborne and Campbell*, Calloway Hodges, Richard Bradshaw and Gray Garrett; *Cocke and Sevier*, William C. Roadman; *Knox*, Joseph A. Mabry; *Blount*, James Gillespy; *Monroe*, Bradley Kimbrough; *McMinn*, John Neal; *Roane*, James I. Greene; *Anderson and Morgan*, John Whitson; *Rhea and Hamilton*, William T. Senter; *Bledsoe and Marion*, John Kelly; *Washington, Greene, Sevier, Cocke, Blount, Monroe and M'Minn*, John M'Gaughey; *Overton and Fentress*, Hugh C. Armstrong; *Jackson*, James W. Smith; *White*, Richard Nelson; *Warren*, Isaac Hill; *Franklin*, George W. Richardson; *Warren and Franklin*, William C. Smartt; *Smith and Sumner*, John J. White, Robert Allen and Isaac Walton; *Wilson*, Burchett Douglass and Robert M. Burton; *Rutherford*, William Ledbetter and Henry Ridley; *Bedford*, Jos. Kincaid and Jonathan Webster; *Lincoln and Giles*, James Fulton, A. A. Kincannon and Thomas C. Porter; *Davidson*, Francis B. Fogg and Robert Weakley; *Williamson*, Newton Cannon and William G. Childress; *Maury*, Terry H. Cahal and Robert L. Cobbs; *Robertson*, Richard Cheatham; *Dickson, Stewart and Humphreys*, James Gray and John Montgomery; *Hickman, Wayne and Lawrence*, Boling Gordon and Henry Sharp; *Henry*, Peter Kendall; *Carroll*, Ennis Ury; *Henderson*, John Purdy; *Perry, Hardin and M'Nairy*, James Scott and Maclin Cross; *Hardeman*, Julius C. N. Robertson; *Fayette*, West H. Humphreys; *Shelby*, Adam R. Alexander; *Gibson and Dyer*, Nelson I. Hess; *Weakley and Obion*, George W. L. Marr; *Haywood and Tipton*, William H. Loving.

The delegates assembled at Nashville on Monday the 19th day of May. Gen. William B. Carter was elected President, Col. William K. Hill Secretary, and Doctor Wm. I. I. Morrow Assistant Secretary, and the Convention was opened with prayer with the Rev. James Smith. After a laborious session of one hundred and four days, the following Constitution was adopted and submitted to the people.[20]

CONSTITUTION
OF THE
STATE OF TENNESSEE.

WHEREAS, THE PEOPLE OF THE TERRITORY OF THE UNITED STATES, SOUTH OF THE RIVER OHIO, *having the right of admission into the General Government as a Member State thereof, consistent with the Constitution of the United States, and the act of cession of the State of North Carolina, recognizing the ordinance for the government of the territory of the United States, north west of the river Ohio, by their Delegates and Representatives in Convention assembled, did, on the sixth of February, in the year of our Lord one thousand seven hundred and ninety-six,* ORDAIN AND ESTABLISH A CONSTITUTION OR FORM OF GOVERNMENT; *and mutually agreed with each other to form themselves into a* FREE AND INDEPENDENT STATE, *by the name of* "THE STATE OF TENNESSEE;" *and whereas the General Assembly of said* STATE OF TENNESSEE, *(pursuant to the third section of the tenth article of the Constitution) by an act passed on the twenty-seventh day of November, in the year of our Lord one thousand eight hundred and thirty-three entitled "An act to provide for the calling of a Convention," did authorize and provide for the election,* BY THE PEOPLE, *of Delegates and Representatives, to meet at Nashville, in Davidson county, on the third Monday in May, in the year of our Lord one thousand eight hundred and thirty-four,*

---

[20] Tennessee has had three constitutions. The text of the 1796 Constitution can be found in Robert H. White, *Messages of the Governors of Tennessee* (7 vols.; Nashville, 1952-67), I, 663-73; the second Constitution (1835) in *ibid.*, III, 951-65; and the third (1870), in *ibid.*, VI, 731-53. Thomas Jefferson referred to Tennessee's original Constitution as the "least imperfect and most republican" of any state's articles of government, said Ramsey in *Annals*, 657.

"FOR THE PURPOSE OF REVISING, AND AMENDING *(or changing)* THE CONSTITUTION:"
WE, *therefore*, THE DELEGATES AND REPRESENTATIVES OF THE PEOPLE OF THE STATE OF TENNESSEE, *elected and in Convention assembled, in pursuance of the said Act of Assembly,* HAVE ORDAINED AND ESTABLISHED *the following* AMENDED CONSTITUTION AND FORM OF GOVERNMENT FOR THIS STATE, *which we recommend to* THE PEOPLE OF TENNESSEE *for their ratification; that is to say:*

ARTICLE I.
DECLARATION OF RIGHTS.

SECTION 1. That all power is inherent in the people, and all free governments are founded on their authority, and instituted for their peace, safety and happiness; for the advancement of those ends, they have, at all times, an unalienable and undefeasible right to alter, reform or abolish the government in such manner as they may think proper.

SEC. 2. That government being instituted for the common benefit, the doctrine of non-resistance against arbitrary power and oppression, is absurd, slavish and destructive of the good and happiness of mankind.

SEC. 3. That all men have a natural and indefeasible right to worship Almighty God according to the dictates of their own conscience; that no man can, of right, be compelled to attend, erect or support any place of worship, or to maintain any Minister against his consent; that no human authority can, in any case whatever, control or interfere with the rights of conscience; and that no preference shall ever be given, by law, to any religious establishment or mode of worship.

SEC. 4. That no religious test shall ever be required as a qualification to any office or public trust under this State.

SEC. 5. That elections shall be free and equal.

SEC. 6. That the right of trial by jury shall remain inviolate.

Sec. 7. That the people shall be secure in their persons, houses, papers and possessions, from unreasonable searches and seizures; and that general warrants, whereby an officer may be commanded to search suspected places, without evidence of the fact committed, or to seize any person or persons not named, whose offences are not particularly described and supported by evidence, are dangerous to liberty and ought not to be granted.

Sec. 8. That no free man shall be taken or imprisoned, or disseized of his freehold, liberties or privileges, or outlawed, or exiled, or in any manner destroyed or deprived of his life, liberty or property, but by the judgment of his peers, or the law of the land.

Sec. 9. That in all criminal prosecutions, the accused hath a right to be heard by himself and his counsel; to demand the nature and cause of the accusation against him, and to have a copy thereof; to meet the witnesses face to face; to have compulsory process for obtaining witnesses in his favor; and in prosecutions by indictment or presentment, a speedy public trial, by an impartial jury of the county or district in which the crime shall have been committed; and shall not be compelled to give evidence against himself.

Sec. 10. That no person shall, for the same offence, be twice put in jeopardy of life or limb.

Sec. 11 That laws made for the punishment of facts committed previous to the existence of such laws, and by them only declared criminal, are contrary to the principles of a free government; wherefore no *ex post facto law* shall be made.

Sec. 12. That no conviction shall work corruption of blood or forfeiture of estate. The estate of such persons as shall destroy their own lives, shall descend or vest as in case of natural death. If any person be killed by casualty, there shall be no forfeiture in consequence thereof.

Sec. 13. That no person arrested or confined in jail, shall be treated with unnecessary rigor.

Sec. 14. That no freeman shall be put to answer any criminal charge but by presentment, indictment or impeachment.

SEC. 15. That all prisoners shall be bailable by sufficient sureties unless for capital offences when the proof is evident or the presumption great. And the privilege of the writ of *habeas corpus* shall not be suspended, unless when in case of rebellion or invasion the public safety may require it.

SEC. 16. That excessive bail shall not be required, nor excessive fines imposed, nor cruel and unusual punishments inflicted.

SEC. 17. That all courts shall be open; and every man, for an injury done him in his lands, goods, person, or reputation, shall have remedy by due course of law and right and justice administered without sale, denial, or delay. Suits may be brought against the State in such manner, and in such courts, as the Legislature may by law direct.

SEC. 18. That the person of a debtor, where there is not strong presumption of fraud, shall not be continued in prison after delivering up his estate for the benefit of his creditor or creditors, in such manner as shall be prescribed by law.

SEC. 19. That the printing presses shall be free to every person who undertakes to examine the proceedings of the Legislature, or of any branch or Officer of Government; and no law shall ever be made to restrain the right thereof. The free communication of thoughts and opinions is one of the invaluable rights of man, and every citizen may freely speak, write and print on any subject, being responsible for the abuse of that liberty. But in prosecutions for the publication of papers investigating the official conduct of officers or men in public capacity, the truth thereof may be given in evidence; and in all indictments for libels, the jury shall have a right to determine the law and the facts, under the direction of the Court, as in other criminal cases.

SEC. 20. That no retrospective law, or law impairing the obligation of contracts, shall be made.

SEC. 21. That no man's particular services shall be demanded, or property taken, or applied to public use, without the consent of his representatives or without just compensation being made therefor.

SEC. 22. That perpetuities and monopolies are contrary to the genius of a free State, and shall not be allowed.

SEC. 23. That the citizens have a right, in a peaceable manner, to assemble together, for their common good, to instruct their representatives, and to apply to those invested with the powers of government for redress of grievances or other proper purposes, by address or remonstrance.

SEC. 21. That the sure and certain defence of a free people, is a well regulated militia: and, as standing armies in time of peace are dangerous to freedom, they ought to be avoided, as far as the circumstances and safety of the community will admit; and that in all cases the military shall be kept in strict subordination to the civil authority.

SEC. 25. That no citizen of this State, except such as are employed in the army of the United States, or militia in actual service, shall be subjected to corporeal punishment under the martial law.

SEC. 26. That the free white men of this State have a right to keep and to bear arms for their common defence.

SEC. 27. That no soldier shall, in time of peace, be quartered in any house without the consent of the owner; nor in time of war, but in a manner prescribed by law.

SEC. 28. That no citizen of this State shall be compelled to bear arms, provided he will pay an equivalent, to be ascertained by law.

SEC. 29. That an equal participation of the free navigation of the Mississippi, is one of the inherent rights of the citizens of this State: it cannot, therefore, be conceded to any prince, potentate, power, person or persons whatever.

SEC. 30. That no hereditary emoluments, privileges, or honors, shall ever be granted or conferred in this State.

SEC. 31. That the limits and boundaries of this State be ascertained, it is declared they are as hereafter mentioned, that is to say: Beginning on the extreme height of the Stone mountain, at the place where the line of Virginia intersects it, in latitude thirty-six degrees and thirty minutes north; running thence along the extreme height of the said mountain to the place where Watauga river breaks through it; thence a direct course to the top of the Yellow mountain, where Bright's road crosses the same; thence along the ridge of said mountain between the waters of Doe river and the waters of Rock creek, to the place where the road crosses the Iron mountain; from thence along the extreme height of said mountain, to the place where Nolichucky river runs through the same; thence to the top of the Bald mountain; thence along the extreme height of said mountain, to the Painted Rock, on French Broad river; thence along the highest ridge of said mountain, to the place where it is called the Great Iron or Smoky mountains; thence along the extreme height of said mountain, to the place where it is called Unicoi or Unaka mountain, between the Indian towns of Cowee and Old Chota; thence along the main ridge of the said mountain, to the southern boundary of this State, as described in the act of cession of North Carolina to the United States of America: and that all the territory, lands and waters lying west of the said line, as before mentioned, and contained within the chartered limits of the State of North Carolina, are within the boundaries and limits of this State, over which the people have the right of exercising sovereignty and the right of soil, so far as is consistent with the constitution of the United States, recognizing the articles of confederation, the bill of rights, and constitution of North Carolina, the cession act of the said State, and the ordinance of Congress for the government of the territory north west of the Ohio: *provided,* nothing herein contained shall extend to affect the claim or claims of individuals, to any part of the soil which is recognized to them by the aforesaid cession act: *and provided also,* that the limits and jurisdiction of this State shall extend to any other land and territory now acquired, or that may hereafter be acquired by compact or agreement with other States or otherwise, although such land and territory are not included within the boundaries herein before designated.

Sec. 32. The people residing south of French Broad and Holston between the rivers Tennessee and Big Pigeon, are entitled to the right of pre-emption and occupancy in that tract.

ARTICLE II.

Section 1. The powers of the Government shall be divided into three distinct departments; the Legislative, Executive and Judicial.

Sec. 2. No person or persons belonging to one of these departments, shall exercise any of the powers properly belonging to either of the others, except in the cases herein directed or permitted.

Sec. 3. The Legislative authority of this State shall be vested in a General Assembly, which shall consist of a Senate and House of Representatives, both dependent on the people.

Sec. 4. An enumeration of the qualified voters and an apportionment of the Representatives in the General Assembly, shall be made in the year 1842, and within every subsequent term of ten years.

Sec. 5. The number of Representatives shall, at the several periods of making the enumeration, be apportioned among the several counties or districts according to the number of qualified voters in each, and shall not exceed seventy-five, until the population of the State shall be one million and a half; and shall never thereafter exceed ninety-nine, *provided*, that any county having two-thirds of the ratio, shall be entitled to one member.

Sec. 6. *The number of Senators shall, at the several* periods of making the enumeration, be apportioned among the several counties or districts, according to the number of qualified electors in each, and shall not exceed one third the number of Representatives. In apportioning the Senators among the different counties, the fraction that may be lost by any county or counties, in the apportionment of members to the House of Representatives, shall be made up to such county or counties in the Senate, as near as may be practicable: when a district is composed of two or more counties, they shall be adjoining; and no county shall be divided in forming a district.

SEC. 7. The first election for Senators and Representatives shall be held on the first Thursday in August 1835; and forever thereafter elections for members of the General Assembly shall be held once in two years, on the first Thursday in August, and shall terminate the same day.

SEC. 8. The first session of the General Assembly shall commence on the first Monday in October 1835; and forever thereafter, the General Assembly shall meet on the first Monday in October next ensuing the election.

SEC. 9. No person shall be a Representative, unless he shall be a citizen of the United States, of the age of twenty-one years, and shall have been a citizen of this State for three years, and a resident in the County he represents, one year immediately preceding the election.

SEC. 10. No person shall be a Senator, unless he shall be a citizen of the United States, of the age of thirty years, and shall have resided three years in this State, and one year in the county or district, immediately preceding the election. No Senator or Representative shall, during the time for which he was elected, be eligible to any office or place of trust, the appointment to which is vested in the Executive or the General Assembly, except to the office of trustee of a literary institution.

SEC. 11. The Senate and House of Representatives, when assembled, shall each choose a speaker and its other officers, be judges of the qualifications and election of its members, and sit upon its own adjournments from day to day. Two thirds of each House shall constitute a quorum to do business, but a smaller number may adjourn from day to day, and may be authorized by law to compel the attendance of absent members.

SEC. 12. Each House may determine the rules of its proceedings, punish its members for disorderly behaviour; and, with the concurrence of two thirds, expel a member, but not a second time for the same offence; and shall have all other powers necessary for a breach of the Legislature of a free State.

Sec. 13. Senators and Representatives shall in all cases, except treason, felony or breach of the peace, be privileged from arrest during the session of the General Assembly, and in going to and returning from the same; and, for any speech or debate in either House, they shall not be questioned in any other place.

Sec. 14. Each House may punish by imprisonment, during its session, any person not a member, who shall be guilty of disrespect to the House, by any disorderly or contemptuous behaviour in its presence.

Sec. 15. When vacancies happen in either House, the Governor for the time being, shall issue writs of election to fill such vacancies.

Sec. 16. Neither House shall, during its session, adjourn without the consent of the other, for more than three days; nor to any other place than that in which the two Houses shall be sitting.

Sec. 17. Bills may originate in either House, but may be amended, altered or rejected, by the other.

Sec. 18. Every bill shall be read once, on three different days, and be passed each time in the House where it originated, before transmission to the other. No bill shall become a law, until it shall be read and passed on three different days in each House, and be signed by the respective Speakers.

Sec. 19. After a bill has been rejected no bill containing the same substance, shall be passed into a law during the same session.

Sec. 20. The style of the laws of this State shall be, *"Be it enacted by the General Assembly of the State of Tennessee."*

Sec. 21. Each House shall keep a journal of its proceedings, and publish it, except such parts as the welfare of the State may require to be kept secret; the ayes and noes shall be taken in each House upon the final passage of every bill of a general character, and bills making appropriations of public moneys; and the ayes and noes of the members on any question, shall at the request of any two of them be entered on the journal.

SEC. 22. The doors of each House, and of Committees of the Whole, shall be kept open, unless when the business shall be such as ought to be kept secret.

SEC. 23. The sum of four dollars per day, and four dollars for every twenty-five miles travelling to and from the Seat of Government, shall be allowed to the Members of the first General Assembly, as a compensation for their services. The compensation of the Members of the succeeding Legislatures, shall be ascertained by law; but no law increasing the compensation of the members, shall take effect until the commencement of the next regular session after such law shall have been enacted.

SEC. 24. No money shall be drawn from the treasury, but in consequence of appropriations made by law: and an accurate statement of the receipts and expenditures of the public money, shall be attached to and published with the laws, at the rise of each stated session of the General Assembly.

SEC. 25. No person, who heretofore hath been, or may hereafter be, a collector or holder of public moneys, shall have a seat in either House of the General Assembly, until such person shall have accounted for and paid into the treasury, all sums for which he may be accountable or liable.

SEC. 26. No judge of any court of law or equity, Secretary of State, Attorney General, Register, Clerk of any court of record, or person holding any office under the authority of the United States, shall have a seat in the General Assembly; nor shall any person in this State hold more than one lucrative office at the same time: *provided*, that no appointment in the Militia, or to the office of Justice of the Peace, shall be considered a lucrative office, or operate as a disqualification to a seat in either House of the General Assembly.

SEC. 27. Any Member of either House of the General

Assembly, shall have liberty to dissent from, and protest against, any act or resolve which he may think injurious to the public or to any individual, and to have the reasons for his dissent entered on the journals.

Sec. 28. All lands liable to taxation, held by deed, grant or entry, town lots, bank stock, slaves between the ages of twelve and fifty years, and such other property as the Legislature may from time to time deem expedient, shall be taxable. All property shall be taxed according to its value; that value to be ascertained in such manner as the Legislature shall direct, so that the same shall be equal and uniform throughout the State. No one species of property from which a tax may be collected, shall be taxed higher than any other species of property of equal value. But the Legislature shall have power to tax merchants, pedlars, and privileges, in such manner as they may, from time to time, direct. A tax on white polls shall be laid, in such manner and of such an amount, as may be prescribed by law.

Sec. 29. The General Assembly shall have power to authorize the several Counties and incorporated Towns in this State, to impose taxes for county and corporation purposes respectively, in such manner as shall be prescribed by law; and all property shall be taxed according to its value, upon the principles established in regard to State taxation.

Sec. 30. No article manufactured of the produce of this State, shall be taxed otherwise than to pay inspection fees.

Sec. 31. The General Assembly shall have no power to pass laws for the emancipation of slaves, without the consent of their owner or owners.

ARTICLE III.

Section 1. The Supreme Executive power of this State, shall be vested in a Governor.

Sec. 2. The Governor shall be chosen by the electors of the Members of the General Assembly, at the times and places where they shall respectively vote for the members thereof. The returns of every election for Governor shall be sealed up, and transmitted to the seat of government, by the returning officers, directed to the Speaker of the Senate, who shall open and publish them in the presence of a majority of the members of each House of the General Assembly. The person having the highest number of votes, shall be Governor; but if two or more shall be equal and highest in votes, one of them shall be chosen Governor by joint vote of both Houses of the General Assembly. Contested elections for Governor, shall be determined by both Houses of General Assembly, in such manner as shall be prescribed by law.

SEC. 3. He shall be at least thirty years of age, shall be a citizen of the United States, and shall have been a citizen of this State seven years next before his election.

SEC. 4. The Governor shall hold his office for two years and until his successor shall be elected and qualified. He shall not be eligible more than six years in any term of eight.

SEC. 5. He shall be commander-in-chief of the army and navy of this State and of the militia, except when they shall be called into the service of the United States.

SEC. 6. He shall have power to grant reprieves and pardons, after conviction, except in cases of impeachment.

SEC. 7. He shall, at stated times, receive a compensation for his services, which shall not be increased or diminished during the period for which he shall have been elected.

SEC. 8. He may require information in writing, from the officers in the executive department, upon any subject relating to the duties of their respective offices.

SEC. 9. He may, on extraordinary occasions, convene the General Assembly by proclamation; and shall state to them, when assembled, the purposes for which they shall have been convened: but they shall enter on no legislative business except that for which they were specially called together.

SEC. 10. He shall take care that the laws be faithfully executed.

SEC. 11. He shall, from time to time, give to the General

Assembly, information of the state of the Government, and recommend to their consideration such measures as he shall judge expedient.

SEC. 12. In case of the removal of the Governor from office, or of his death, or resignation, the powers and duties of the office shall devolve on the Speaker of the Senate; and in case of the death, removal, from office, or resignation of the Speaker of the Senate, the powers and duties of the office shall devolve on the Speaker of the House of Representatives.

SEC. 13. No member of Congress, or person holding any office under the United States, or this State, shall execute the office of Governor.

SEC. 14. When any officer, the right of whose appointment is by this Constitution vested in the General Assembly, shall, during the recess, die, or the office, by the expiration of the term or by other means, become vacant, the Governor shall have the power to fill such vacancy, by granting a temporary commission, which shall expire at the end of the next session of the Legislature.

SEC. 15. There shall be a seal of this State, which shall be kept by the Governor, and used by him officially, and shall be called the *Great Seal of the State of Tennessee.*

SEC. 16. All grants and commissions shall be in the name and by the authority of the State of Tennessee, be sealed with the State seal, and signed by the Governor.

SEC. 17. A Secretary of State shall be appointed by joint vote of the General Assembly, and commissioned during the term of four years; he shall keep a fair register of all the official acts and proceedings of the Governor; and shall, when required, lay the same, and all papers, minutes and vouchers relative thereto, before the General Assembly: and shall perform such other duties as shall be enjoined by law.

ARTICLE IV.

SECTION 1. Every free white man of the age of twenty-one years, being a citizen of the United States, and a citizen of the County wherein he may offer his vote, six months next preceding the day of election, shall be entitled to vote for Members of the General Assembly, and other civil officers, for the County or District in which he resides: *provided*, that no person shall be disqualified from voting in any election on account of color, who is now by the laws of this State, a competent witness in a court of justice against a white man. All free men of color, shall be exempt from military duty in time of peace, and also from paying a free poll tax.

SEC. 2. Laws may be passed excluding from the right of suffrage, persons who may be convicted of infamous crimes.

SEC. 3. Electors shall in all cases, except treason, felony or breach of the peace, be privileged from arrest or summons, during their attendance at elections, and in going to and returning from them.

SEC. 4. In all elections to be made by the General Assembly, the Members thereof shall vote *viva voce*; and their votes shall be entered on the journal. All other elections shall be by ballot.

ARTICLE V.

SECTION 1. The House of Representatives shall have the sole power of impeachment.

SEC. 2. All impeachments shall be tried by the Senate; when sitting for that purpose, the Senators shall be upon oath or affirmation. No person shall be convicted without the concurrence of two-thirds of the Senators sworn to try the officer impeached.

SEC. 3. The House of Representatives shall elect, from their own body, three Members, whose duty it shall be to prosecute impeachments. No impeachment shall be tried until the Legislature shall have adjourned *sine die*, when the Senate shall proceed to try such impeachment.

SEC. 4. The Governor, Judges of the Supreme Court, Judges of Inferior Courts, Chancellors, Attorneys for the State, and Secretary of State, shall be liable to impeachment, whenever they may, in the opinion of the House of Representatives, commit any crime in their official capacity, which may require disqualification; but judgment shall only extend to removal from office, and disqualification to fill any office thereafter. The party shall, nevertheless, be liable to indictment, trial, judgment and punishment, according to law.

Sec. 5. Justices of the Peace, and other civil officers, not hereinbefore mentioned, for crimes or misdemeanors in office, shall be liable to indictment in such courts as the Legislature may direct; and upon conviction, shall be removed from office, by said court, as if found guilty on impeachment; and shall be subject to such other punishment as may be prescribed by law.

ARTICLE VI.

Section 1. The Judicial power of this State, shall be vested in one Supreme Court, in such Inferior Courts as the Legislature shall from time to time ordain and establish, and the Judges thereof and in Justices of the Peace: The Legislature may also vest such jurisdiction as may be deemed necessary in Corporation Courts.

Sec. 2. The Supreme Court shall be composed of three Judges, one of whom shall reside in each of the grand divisions of the State; the concurrence of two of said Judges, shall in every case be necessary to a decision. The jurisdiction of this Court shall be appellate only, under such restrictions and regulations as may from time to time be prescribed by law; but it may possess such other jurisdiction as is now conferred by law on the present Supreme Court. Said Courts shall be held at one place, and at one place only, in each of the three grand divisions in the State.

Sec. 3. The General Assembly shall, by joint vote of both Houses, appoint Judges of the several Courts of law and equity; but courts may be established to be holden by Justices of the Peace. Judges of the Supreme Court shall be thirty-five years of age, and shall be elected for the term of twelve years.

SEC. 4. The Judges of such Inferior Courts as the Legislature may establish, shall be thirty years of age, and shall be elected for the term of eight years.

SEC. 5. The Legislature shall elect Attorneys for the State, by joint vote of both Houses, of the General Assembly, who shall hold their offices for the term of six years. In all cases where an Attorney for any district fails or refuses to attend, and prosecute according to law, the court shall have power to appoint an attorney *pro tempore*.

SEC. 6. Judges and Attorneys for the State, may be removed from office by a concurrent vote of both Houses of the General Assembly, each House voting separately; but two-thirds of all the Members elected to each House must concur in such vote: the vote shall be determined by ayes and noes, and the names of the Members voting for or against the Judge or Attorney for the State, together with the cause or causes of removal, shall be entered on the journals of each House respectively. The Judge or Attorney for the State, against whom the Legislature may be about to proceed, shall receive notice thereof, accompanied with a copy of the causes alleged for his removal, at least ten days before the day on which either House of the General Assembly shall act thereupon.

SEC. 7. The Judges of the Supreme and Inferior Court, shall, at stated times, receive a compensation for their services, to be ascertained by law, which shall not be increased or diminished, during the time for which they are elected. They shall not be allowed any fees or perquisites of office, nor hold any other office of trust or profit under this State, or the United States.

SEC. 8. The jurisdiction of such Inferior Courts, as the Legislature may from time to time establish, shall be regulated by law.

SEC. 9. Judges shall not charge Juries with respect to

matters of fact, but may state the testimony and declare the law.

Sec. 10. The Judges or Justices of such Inferior Courts of law as the Legislature may establish, shall have power, in all civil cases, to issue writs of *certiorari* to remove any cause or transcript thereof, from any inferior jurisdiction, into said court on sufficient cause supported by oath or affirmation.

Sec. 11. No Judge of the Supreme or Inferior Courts, shall preside on the trial of any cause, in the event of which he may be interested or where either of the parties shall be connected with him by affinity or consanguinity, within such degrees as may be prescribed by law, or in which he may have been of counsel, or in which he may have presided in any Inferior Court, except by consent of all the parties. In case all or any of the Judges of the Supreme Court, shall be thus disqualified from presiding on the trial of any cause or causes, the Court, or the Judges thereof, shall certify the same to the Governor of the State, and he shall forthwith specially commission the requisite number of men of law knowledge, for the trial and determination thereof. In case of sickness of any of the Judges of the Supreme or Inferior Courts, so that they or any of them are unable to attend, the Legislature shall be authorized to make provision by general laws, that special Judges may be appointed to attend said Courts.

Sec. 12. All writs and other process shall run in the name of the State of Tennessee; and bear test and be signed by the respective clerks. Indictments shall conclude, *"against the peace and dignity of the State."*

Sec. 13. Judges of the Supreme Court shall appoint their Clerks, who shall hold their offices for the period of six years. Chancellors (if Courts of Chancery shall be established) shall appoint their Clerks and Masters, who shall hold their offices for the period of six years. Clerks of such Inferior Courts as may be hereafter established, which shall be required to be holden in the respective counties of this State, shall be elected by the qualified voters thereof, for the term of four years; they shall be removed from office for malfeasance, incompetency or neglect of duty, in such manner as may be prescribed by law.

SEC. 14. No fine shall be laid on any citizen of this State, that shall exceed fifty dollars; unless it shall be assessed by a jury of his peers, who shall assess the fine at the time they find the fact, if they think the fine should be more than fifty dollars.

SEC. 15. The different counties in this state shall be laid off as the General Assembly may direct, into districts of convenient size, so that the whole number in each County shall not be more than twenty-five, or four for every one hundred square miles. There shall be two Justices of the Peace and one Constable elected in each district, by the qualified voters therein, except districts including county towns, which shall elect three Justices and two Constables. The jurisdiction of said officers shall be co-extensive with the County. Justices of the Peace shall be elected for the term of six, and Constables for the term of two years. Upon the removal of either of said officers from the district in which he was elected, his office shall become vacant from the time of such removal. Justices of the Peace shall be commissioned by the Governor. The Legislature shall have power to provide for the appointment of an additional number of Justices of the Peace in incorporated towns.

ARTICLE VII.

SECTION 1. There shall be elected in each County, by the qualified voters therein, one Sheriff, one Trustee, and one Register; the Sheriff and Trustee for two years, and the Register for four years: *provided,* that no person shall be eligible to the office of Sheriff more than six years in any terms of eight years. There shall be elected for each County, by the Justices of the Peace, one Coroner and one Ranger, who shall hold their offices for two years. Said officers shall be removed for malfeasance, or neglect of duty, in such manner as may be prescribed by law.

SEC. 2. Should a vacancy occur, subsequent to an election, in the office of sheriff, trustee, or register, it shall be filled by the justices; if in that of the clerks to be elected by the people, it shall be filled by the courts; and the person so appointed, shall continue in office until his successor shall be elected and qualified; and such office shall be filled by the qualified voters at the first election for any of the county officers.

SEC. 3. There shall be a Treasurer or Treasurers appointed for the State, by the joint vote of both Houses of the General Assembly, who shall hold his or their offices for two years.

SEC. 4. The election of all officers, and the filling of all vacancies that may happen, by death, resignation or removal, not otherwise directed or provided for by this Constitution, shall be made in such manner as the Legislature shall direct.

SEC. 5. The Legislature shall provide, that the election of the county and other officers by the people, shall not take place at the same time that the general elections are held for Members of Congress, Members of the Legislature, and Governor. The elections shall commence and terminate on the same day.

ARTICLE VIII.

SECTION 1. All Militia officers shall be elected by persons subject to military duty, within the bounds of their several companies, battalions, regiments, brigades and divisions, under such rules and regulations as the Legislature may, from time to time, direct and establish.

SEC. 2. The Governor shall appoint the Adjutant General and his other Staff Officers; the Majors General, Brigadiers General and commanding officers of regiments, shall respectively appoint their Staff Officers.

SEC. 3. The Legislature shall pass laws, exempting citizens belonging to any sect or denomination of religion, the tenets of which are known to be opposed to the bearing of arms, from attending private and general musters.

ARTICLE IX.

SECTION 1. Whereas, Ministers of the Gospel are, by their profession, dedicated to God and the care of souls, and ought not to be diverted from the great duties of their functions; therefore, no Minister of the Gospel or Priest of any denomination whatever, shall be eligible to a seat in either House of the Legislature.

SEC. 2. No person who denies the being of God, or a future state of rewards and punishments, shall hold any office in the civil department of this State.

SEC. 3. Any person who shall, after the adoption of this Constitution, fight a duel, or knowingly be the bearer of a challenge to fight a duel, or send or accept a challenge for that purpose, or be an aider or abettor in fighting a duel, shall be deprived of the right to hold any office of honor or profit in this State, and shall be punished otherwise, in such manner as the Legislature may prescribe.

ARTICLE X.

SECTION 1. Every person who shall be chosen or appointed to any office of trust or profit, under this Constitution, or any law made in pursuance thereof, shall, before entering on the duties thereof, take an oath to support the Constitution of this State, and of the United States, and an oath of office.

SEC. 2. Each Member of the Senate and House of Representatives, shall, before they proceed to business, take an oath or affirmation, to support the Constitution of this State, and of the United States, and also the following oath: "I, ———————, do solemnly swear, (or affirm,) that, as a Member of this General Assembly, I will, in all appointments, vote without favor, affection, partiality, or prejudice; and that I will not propose or assent to any bill, vote or resolution, which shall appear to me injurious to the people, or consent to any act or thing whatever, that shall have a tendency to lessen or abridge their rights and privileges, as declared by the Constitution of this State.

SEC. 3. Any elector who shall receive any gift or reward for his vote, in meat, drink, money, or otherwise, shall suffer such punishment as the laws shall direct. And any person who shall directly or indirectly give, promise or bestow, any such reward to be elected, shall thereby be rendered incapable for six years, to serve in the office for which he was elected, and be subject to such further punishment, as the Legislature shall direct.

SEC. 4. New Counties may be established by the Legislature, to consist of not less than three hundred and fifty square miles, and which shall contain a population of four hundred and fifty qualified voters. No line of such county shall approach the court house of any old County from which it may be taken, nearer than twelve miles. No part of a county shall be taken off to form a new County or a part thereof, without the consent of a majority of the qualified voters in such part taken off. And in all cases where an old County may be reduced for the purpose of forming a new one, the seat of justice in said old county shall not be removed without the concurrence of two thirds of both branches of the Legislature, nor shall said old County be reduced to less than six hundred and twenty-five square miles: *provided*, however that the County of Bedford may be reduced to four hundred and seventy-five square miles; and there shall not be laid off more than one new county on the West, and one on the East, adjoining the County of Bedford, and no new County line shall run nearer than eleven and a half miles of the seat of justice of said County. The line of a new County may run within eleven miles of the seat of justice of Franklin County; *provided*, it does not reduce said County to less contents than six hundred and twenty five square miles. The Counties of Carter, Rhea, Tipton, Dyer and Sullivan are excepted out of the provisions of this section: the County of Humphreys may be divided, at such time as may be prescribed by the Legislature, making the Tennessee river the dividing line; a majority of the qualified voters of said County voting in favor of said division: the Counties of Carter, Rhea and Humphreys, shall not be divided into more than two Counties each; nor shall more than one new County be taken out of the Territory now composing the Counties of Tipton and Dyer; nor shall the seats of justice in the Counties of Rhea, Carter, Tipton, and Dyer be removed, without the concurrence of two thirds of both branches of the Legislature. The County of Sullivan may be reduced below the contents of six hundred and twenty-five square miles, but the line of any new County which may hereafter be laid off shall not approach the County seat of said County nearer than ten miles. The counties of Marion and Bledsoe shall not be reduced below one thousand qualified voters each, in forming a new County or Counties.

SEC. 5. The citizens who may be included in any new county, shall vote with the county or counties from which they may have been stricken off, for members of Congress, for Governor and for members of the General Assembly, until the next apportionment of members to the General Assembly after the establishment of such new County.

ARTICLE XI.

SECTION 1. All laws and ordinances now in force and use in this State, not inconsistent with this Constitution, shall continue in force and use, until they shall expire, be altered or repealed by the Legislature.

SEC. 2. Nothing contained in this Constitution, shall impair the validity of any debts or contracts, or affect any rights of property, or any suits, actions, rights of action, or other proceedings in courts of justice.

SEC. 3. Any amendment or amendments to this Constitution may be proposed in the Senate or House of Representatives; and if the same shall be agreed to by a majority of all the members elected to each of the two Houses, such proposed amendment or amendments shall be entered on their journals, with the yeas and nays thereon, and referred to the General Assembly then next to be chosen: and shall be published for six months previous to the time of making such choice. And if in the General Assembly next chosen as aforesaid, such proposed amendment or amendments shall be agreed to by two-thirds of all the members elected to each House, then it shall be the duty of the General Assembly to submit such proposed amendment or amendments to the people, in such manner, and at such time, as the General Assembly shall prescribe. And if the people shall approve and ratify such amendment or amendments, by a majority of all the citizens of the State, voting for Representatives, voting in their favor, such amendment or amendments shall become part of this Constitution. When any amendment or amendments to the Constitution shall be proposed in pursuance of the foregoing provisions, the same shall at each of the said sessions be read three times on three several days in each House. The Legislature shall not propose amendments to the Constitution, oftener than once in six years.

SEC. 4. The Legislature shall have no power to grant divorces, but many authorize the courts of justice to grant them for such causes as may be specified by law: *provided,* that such laws be general and uniform in their operation throughout the State.

SEC. 5. The Legislature shall have no power to authorize lotteries for any purpose, and shall pass laws to prohibit the sale of lottery tickets in this State.

SEC. 6. The Legislature shall fix the rate of interest—and the rate so established shall be equal and uniform throughout the State.

SEC. 7. The Legislature shall have no power to suspend any general law for the benefit of any particular individual, nor to pass any law for the benefit of individuals inconsistent with the general laws of the land; nor to pass any law granting to any individual or individuals, rights, privileges, immunities, or exemptions, other than such as may be, by the same law extended to any member of the community, who may be able to bring himself within the provisions of such law: *provided always,* the Legislature shall have power to grant such charters of corporation as they may deem expedient for the public good.

SEC. 8. The Legislature shall have the right to vest such powers in the courts of justice, with regard to private and local affairs, as may be deemed expedient.

SEC. 9. A well regulated system of internal improvement is calculated to develop the resources of the State, and promote the happiness and prosperity of her citizens; therefore it ought to be encouraged by the General Assembly.

SEC. 10. Knowledge, learning, and virtue, being essential to the preservation of republican institutions, and the diffusion of the opportunities and advantages of education throughout the different portions of the State, being highly conducive to the promotion of this end; it shall be the duty of the General Assembly in all future periods of this government, to cherish literature and science. And the fund called the *common school fund,* and all the lands and proceeds thereof, dividends, stocks, and other property of every description whatever, heretofore by law appropriated by the General Assembly of this State for the use of common schools, and all such as shall hereafter be appropriated, shall remain a *perpetual fund,* the principal of which shall never be diminished by legislative appropriation, and the interest thereof shall be inviolably appropriated to the support and encouragement of common schools throughout the State, and for the equal benefit of all the people thereof; and no law shall be made authorizing said fund, or any part thereof, to be diverted to any other use than the support and encouragement of common schools: and it shall be the duty of the General Assembly, to appoint a Board of Commissioners, for such term of time as they may think proper, who shall have the general superintendence of said fund, and who shall make a report of the condition of the same, from time to time, under such rules, regulations and restrictions as may be required by law; *provided,* that if at any time hereafter a division of the public lands of the United States, or of the money arising from the sales of such lands, shall be made among the individual States, the part of such lands, or money, coming to this State, shall be devoted to the purposes of education and internal improvement; and shall never be applied to any other purpose.

SEC. 11. The above provisions shall not be construed to prevent the legislature from carrying into effect any laws that have been passed in favor of the colleges, universities or academies, or from authorizing heirs or distributees to receive and enjoy escheated property, under such rules and regulations as from time to time may be prescribed by law.

SEC. 12. The Declaration of Rights hereto prefixed is declared to be a part of the Constitution of this State, and shall never be violated on any pretence whatever. And to guard against transgression of the high powers we have delegated, we declare that every thing in the Bill of Rights contained is excepted out of the general powers of government, and shall forever remain inviolate.

SCHEDULE.

SECTION. 1. That no inconvenience may arise from a change of the Constitution, it is declared, that all officers, civil and military, shall continue to hold their offices; and all the functions appertaining to the same shall be exercised and performed according to the existing laws and Constitution, until the end of the first session of the General Assembly, which shall sit under this Constitution, and until the government can be reorganized and put into operation under this Constitution, in such manner as the first General Assembly aforesaid shall prescribe, and no longer.

SEC. 2. The General Assembly which shall sit after the first apportionment of Representation under the New Constitution, to wit: in the year one thousand eight hundred and forty-three, shall, within the first week after the commencement of the session, designate and fix the Seat of Government; and when so fixed, it shall not be removed, except by the consent of two-thirds of the members of both Houses of the General Assembly. The first and second sessions of the General Assembly under this Constitution shall be held in Nashville.

SEC. 3. Until a land office shall be opened, so as to enable the citizens south and west of the congressional reservation line, to obtain titles upon their claims of occupancy, those who hold lands by virtue of such claims, shall be eligible to serve in all capacities where a freehold is, by the laws of the State, made a requisite qualification.

Done in Convention at Nashville, this thirtieth day of August, one thousand eight hundred and thirty-four, and of the Independence of the United States of America the fifty-ninth.

In testimony whereof, we have hereunto subscribed our names.

WILLIAM B. CARTER, President.

Robert Allen,
Hugh C. Armstrong,
Adam R. Alexander,
Richard Bradshaw,
Robert M. Burton,
Willie Blount,
Maclin Cross,
James Gray,
Newton Cannon,
William G. Childress,
Terry H. Cahal,
Robert L. Cobbs,
Richard Cheatham,
Burchett Douglass,
Francis B. Fogg,
Gray Garrett,
James Gillespy,
Bolling Gordon,
Callaway Hodges,
Isaac Hill,
Adam Huntsman,
West H. Humphreys,
Nelson I. Hess,
John Kelly,
Andrew A. Kincannon,
Joseph Kincaid,
Peter Kendall,
Bradley Kimbrough,
William Ledbetter,
William H. Loving,
Abraham McClellan,
Robert J. McKinney,

Joseph A. Mabry,
John McGaughey,
John Montgomery,
George W. L. Marr,
John Neil,
Richard Nelson,
Thomas C. Porter,
John Purdy,
William C. Roadman,
George W. Richardson,
Henry Ridley,
Julius C. N. Robertson,

Matthew Stephenson,
William T. Senter,
James W. Smith,
William C. Smartt,
Henry Sharp,
James Scott,
Ennis Ury,
John Whitson,
Isaac Walton,
John J. White,
Jonathan Webster,
Robert Weakley.

WILLIAM K. HILL, Secretary.

ORDINANCE.

I. *Ordered,* That it shall be the duty of the several officers of this State, authorized by law to hold elections for members of the General Assembly, to open and hold an election, at the places of holding elections for members to the General Assembly, in their respective counties, on the first Thursday and Friday in March next, for the purpose of receiving the votes of such qualified voters as may desire to vote for the adoption or rejection of this amended Constitution: *provided,* that no person shall be deemed a qualified voter in said election, except such as are included within the provisions of the first section of the fourth article of this amended Constitution.

II. *Ordered,* That it shall be the duty of said return-officers in each county in this State, to prepare polling books, which shall be opened on said days of election, and in which shall be enrolled the name of each voter by the assistance of clerks, who shall be appointed and sworn as clerks in other elections. Said officers shall prepare a ballot box in which shall be placed the ticket of each voter. Each ticket shall have written thereon the words, "I ratify the amended Constitution:" or if the voter is opposed to it: "I reject the amended Constitution," or the words "Ratification" or "Rejection," or some such words as will distinctly convey the intention of the voter. The justices of the several county courts in this State, at some term previous to the day of said election, shall appoint three inspectors for each precinct; and in case of failure of the courts to appoint inspectors, then said returning officers shall appoint them. It shall be the duty of said returning officers, in presence of the said inspectors, to count the votes given for the ratification and rejection of the Constitution, of which they shall keep a true and correct estimate in said poll book. Said returning officer shall deposit the original poll books of said election with the clerk of the County Court in their respective counties, and shall within five days after said election, make out duplicate statements of the number of votes in their respective counties for ratifying and rejecting the Constitution; and shall forward by mail one of said certificates to the Governor, one to the Secretary of State, and shall likewise deposit one with the clerk of the county court. It shall be the duty of said several clerks, carefully to examine the said poll books, and forthwith to certify to the Secretary of State, a full, true and perfect statement of the number of votes taken for and against the Constitution as appears from the poll books, filed in their office. Should said returning officers, or any of them, fail to make returns, in due time as above directed, the Secretary of State shall then be authorized to dispatch a special messenger for the purpose of obtaining a certified copy of the result of said elections.

* III. *Ordered,* That upon the receipt of the said returns, it shall be the duty of the Governor, Secretary of State and any one of the Judges of the Supreme Court, or any two of the said named officers, to compare the votes given in said election for the ratification and rejection of the amended Constitution; and if it shall appear from said returns, that a majority of all the votes given in said election, is for ratifying the amended Constitution, then it shall be the duty of the Governor forthwith to make proclamation of that fact, and thenceforth this amended Constitution shall be ordained and established as the Constitution of the State of Tennessee. It shall moreover be the duty of the Governor, in and by said proclamation, to command the sheriffs and other officers directed by law to hold and superintend elections, to open the polls of elections at the places of holding elections for members of the General Assembly in their respective counties, on the first Thursday in August one thousand eight hundred and thirty five, for the purpose of electing a Governor, and for the election of Senators and Representatives to the General Assembly of this State from the several districts and counties as mentioned and described in this ordinance; at which time and places elections shall also be held for members of Congress; and said officers shall make returns of said elections under the same rules and regulations as are now required by the existing laws. And it shall be the duty of the Secretary of State to record the returns made from each county or district, and the result of said election in a bound book to be preserved in his office.

IV. *Be it further Ordered,* That if any sheriff or other acting officer, shall fail, within the time prescribed by this ordinance, to discharge any of the duties hereby required, such sheriff or other returning officer so failing as aforesaid, shall forfeit and pay the sum of five thousand dollars, to be recovered by action of debt in any of the courts of record in this State; to be sued for in the name of the Governor, for the use and benefit of Common Schools.

V. *Be it further Ordered,* That until the first enumeration and apportionment of representation in one thousand eight hundred and forty-one, as directed by the amended Constitution, the following districts shall be formed, each of which shall elect one Senator, and the polls of election shall be compared at the several places herein mentioned, on the first Monday succeeding the day of election; to wit:

The Counties of Carter, Sullivan and Washington shall form one District; and the polls shall be compared in the town of Jonesborough. The Counties of Greene and Hawkins, shall compose one district; and the polls shall be compared in the town of Greenville.

The Counties of Cocke, Sevier, Jefferson and Blount, shall form one District; and the polls shall be compared in the town of Sevierville. The Counties of Grainger, Claiborne, Campbell, Anderson and Morgan, shall compose one District; and the polls shall be compared at the house of Robert Glenn Esq., in Campbell County.

The Counties of Knox and Roane, shall form one District; and the polls shall be compared at Campbell's Station.

The Counties of Monroe and McMinn, shall compose one District and the polls shall be compared in the town of Athens.

The Counties of Rhea, Bledsoe, Marion and Hamilton, shall compose one District; and the polls shall be compared at the town of Dallas.

The Counties of Warren and Franklin, shall compose one District; and the polls shall be compared at Hillsborough.

The Counties of Overton, Jackson, Fentress and White, shall compose one District; and the polls shall be compared at Livingston.

The Counties of Lincoln and Giles, shall compose one District; and the polls shall be compared at the House of John Kennedy.

The Counties of Smith and Sumner shall compose one District; and the polls shall be compared at Hartsville.

The County of Bedford, shall compose one District; and the polls shall be compared in Shelbyville.

The County of Maury, shall compose one District; and the polls shall be compared in Columbia.

The County of Rutherford, shall compose one District; and the polls shall be compared in Murfreesborough.

The County of Davidson, shall compose one District; and the polls shall be compared in the city of Nashville.

The County of Williamson, shall compose one District; and the polls shall be compared in the town of Franklin.

The Counties of Lawrence, Wayne and Hickman, shall compose one District; and the polls shall be compared at Catron and Napier's Furnace.

The Counties of Dickson, Stewart and Humphreys, shall compose one District; and the polls shall be compared at Simmons' old place on Yellow creek.

The Counties of Robertson and Montgomery, shall compose one District; and the polls shall be compared at Port Royal.

The County of Wilson, shall compose one District; and the polls shall be compared in Lebanon.

The Counties of Hardeman, Fayette and Shelby, shall compose one District; and the polls shall be compared in Sommerville.

The Counties of Madison, Haywood and Tipton, shall compose one District; and the polls shall be compared in Brownsville.

The Counties of Carroll, Gibson and Dyer, shall compose one District; and the polls shall be compared in Trenton.

The Counties of Henry, Weakley and Obion, shall compose one District; and the polls shall be compared in Dresden.

The Counties of Henderson, Perry, McNairy and Hardin, shall compose one District; and the polls shall be compared at the house of James Wright, in Hardin County.

And until said enumeration and apportionment of one thousand eight hundred and forty-one, the Counties of Carter, Sullivan, Washington, Greene, Hawkins, Cocke, Sevier, Jefferson, Blount, Grainger, Claiborne, Knox, Roane, Monroe, M'Minn, Rhea and Bledsoe, shall each elect one Representative; and the polls shall be compared at their respective Court Houses.

The Counties of Sullivan and Hawkins, shall jointly elect one Representative; and shall compare the polls at Kingsport.

The Counties of Greene and Washington shall jointly elect one Representative; and the polls shall be compared at the house of Joshua Royston, Esq.

The Counties of Knox and Roane, shall jointly elect one

Representative; and the polls shall be compared at Campbell's Station.

The Counties of Monroe and M'Minn shall jointly relect one Representative, and the polls shall be compared at Athens.

The Counties of Campbell, Anderson and Morgan, shall jointly elect two Representatives; and the polls shall he compared at the house of James Ross Esq., in Anderson County.

The Counties of Marion and Hamilton, shall jointly elect one Representative; and the polls shall be compared at Dallas.

The Counties of Warren, Franklin, Bedford, Lincoln, Giles, Maury, Rutherford, Williamson, Davidson, Wilson, Smith and Sumner, shall each elect two Representatives; and the polls shall be compared at their respective Court-Houses.

The Counties of Lawrence, Wayne, Hickman, Dickson, Humphreys, Montgomery, Stewart, Robertson, Overton, Jackson, Fentress, White, Hardin, McNairy, Hardeman, Fayette, Shelby, Perry, Henderson, Madison, Haywood, Tipton, Carroll, Gibson, Henry and Weakley, shall each elect one Representative; and the polls shall be compared at their respective Court-Houses.

The Counties of Obion and Dyer, shall jointly elect one Representative; and the polls shall be compared at the house of William Terrell Esq., in Dyer County.

The returns of the elections for Representatives, shall be made at the several places herein pointed out, on the first Saturday succeeding the day of election.

WILLIAM B. CARTER, *President.*

Attest:
WILLIAM K. HILL, *Secretary.*

TENNESSEE GAZETTEER.

A

Abingdon, a town laid off on the land of Jacob Moore, in the county of McMinn, and established by the Legislature, December 1st, 1827.

Adamsville, a post office in McNairy county.

Alexander's Creek, a north branch of Holston, in Hawkins county.

Alexandria, a post town in Smith county, established in 1820, on the land of Daniel Alexander; it is 30 miles N.E. from Murfreesboro', 44 miles E. from Nashville, and 15 miles S.W. from Carthage. It contains about 250 inhabitants, one doctor, five stores, three groceries, two taverns, two tailors' shops, two blacksmiths' shops, one shoe shop, two saddlers' shops, two carpenters, one tanyard and two churches.[21]

Alpin's Fork, a creek in Haywood county, which heads near Brownsville, and running north a few miles, joins Nixon's Fork; forming Indian Camp creek, a branch of Forked Deer.

Amoee River, a south branch of the Hiwassee river in the Cherokee nation, on which there is a Post Office by the same name.[22]

Anderson, a county in East Tennessee, bounded on the N.W. by Morgan, on the S.W. by Roane, on the N.E. by Campbell and on the S.E. by Knox. It is about 30 miles long with a mean breadth of 25, extending over 750 square miles. Cumberland mountain traverses this county, and protrudes several spurs from the main ridge. It is therefore considerably broken, though possessing much good soil; it is also well watered by Clinch and its tributaries on the S.E., and the head waters of the Cumberland on the North. This county

---

[21] Alexandria is now in DeKalb County (established in 1837).

[22] The Amoee River, properly Ocoee, rises in Georgia and flows through Polk County, emptying into the Hiwassee River.

was erected in 1801, and contained a population in 1820, of 4,668, of which 349 were slaves. Seat of Justice, Clinton. Central Latitude 36° 10′ N., Longtitude, 7° 30′ W. from Washington City. Population in 1830, was 5,312.

Anderson's X Roads, a post office in Morgan county, established in 1833.[23]

Anderson's Creek, rises in Anderson county, and running south, empties into Embree's river, east of Spencer's Hill, in the county of Morgan. See *Crooked Fork.*

Angelica Creek, rises in Campbell county, and running north, empties into the South Fork of Cumberland, in Wayne county, Kentucky, at the junction of Mountain Branch.

Annsville, a Post Office in Madison county.[24]

Arch Cave and Big-bone Cave. Two celebrated caves on the dividing line between White and Warren counties, on the Cumberland Mountain. They are six or eight hundred yards apart, or rather their mouths are, for they unite. They were discovered in 1806, and were sold out in shares to 40 or 50 persons for sixty thousand dollars; and were afterwards purchased by Col. Ross of Virginia. About twenty thousand pounds of salt petre were made from the Arch Cave. There are several branches to the Big-bone cave; from one of which the dirt has been collected for upwards of half a mile. Three men are said to have explored this cave, a distance of ten or twelve miles; they were doubtless mistaken as to the distance. The bones of a large animal, supposed to belong to the cat species, were found in this cave. "The ribs were placed on

---

[23] Discontinued as a post office. It will be observed that a great number of post offices were established about the year 1833. The names of many of them are unfamiliar and cannot be identified. Some of them continued under other names; others were soon discontinued. The explanation can only be that proliferation of "cross-roads" post offices was a feature of the "spoils system" of the Jackson administration. In the following years many of them were discontinued as economy measures in tighter times. The communities they represented continued, of course, often under other names, without the identity of the post office.

[24] Discontinued as a post office.

the back bone, the lower end in the ground, Jacob Drake five feet nine inches high, walked erect in the hollow. The width of the ribs was between four and five inches. The hollow of the back bone was between two and three inches in diameter. The socket of the bone, working in the shoulder blade, six inches. The tusk, between four and fives inches in diameter, similar to a dog's. The claw, twelve inches in the round, from point to point; straight, nine inches hollow, one inch in diameter; weight one pound and three quarters. There was also a scoop net made of bark thread; a mockason made of the like materials; a mat of the same material enveloping human bones, were found in salt petre dirt six feet below the surface."—*Haywood.*

Arnoldam, a post office in Humphreys county.[25]

Arrington's Creek, a north branch of Harpeth, in Williamson county.

Athens, the seat of justice of McMinn county; situated on Estannallee creek, 165 miles south-east from Nashville. It contains about 500 inhabitants, four lawyers, four divines, two churches, four doctors, a male and female academy, one common school, ten stores, one tavern, one printing office, one painter, two hatters, two tailors, two shoemakers, two blacksmiths, ten carpenters, five cabinet makers, three tanners, two silversmiths, one wagon-maker, two mills, one factory, and one carding machine. Courts were removed from Calhoun to this place in 1823. In 1834, a branch of the 'Planters' Bank' was located here. It is 50 miles S.W. from Knoxville and 572 from Washington City. Lat. 35° 30′. N., long. 7° 35′ W.

---

[25] Discontinued as a post office.

B

Baker's Fork, a south branch of the Nolachucky, on which there is a paper mill. Its mouth is a few miles south of Greenville College, in Greene county.

Baker's Creek, a north-east branch of Tennessee river, emptying in at Morganton, Blount county.

Bald Mountain, a mountain lying between French Broad and Nolachucky rivers; on the line between this state and North Carolina. The bald spot, which gives name to the mountain, lies south of Jonesboro', Washington county. It arises to a beautiful cone, much higher than the surrounding mountains, and in summer is luxuriantly clothed, with grass and herbage, thickly set with flowers, and is entirely clear of trees and shrubs; and the comb or ridge approaching the cone, presents the same appearance for about three hundred yards. The whole has the appearance of a beautiful meadow, and the soil although so high, is rich and black, and what is more remarkable, on the north side, where the bald part joins the woods, it is in as straight a line as if it had been cleared for the purpose of cultivation, but it is doubtless one of nature's fantasies.

Barrel's Creek, a south branch of Cumberland, in Stewart county.

Barren Creek, a branch of Collin's river in Warren county, flowing east past the town of McMinnville.

Barretsburg, a post office in Washington county, established in 1833.[28]

Barton's Creek, a south branch of Cumberland, in Wilson county; a considerable branch of which arises near the court house in the town of Lebanon; it then winds its way through beautiful cedar groves, some twelve or fifteen miles, and falls into the river above Cairo, and below the mouth of Spring creek.

Barton's Creek, a south branch of Cumberland, in Dickson

---

[28] Discontinued as a post office.

and Montgomery counties, on which are several iron works and forges.

Batson's, a post office in Dickson county.[27]

Bat Creek, a south branch of the Tennessee river, in Monroe county, between Island and Wendel's creeks. It rises near Madisonville, the seat of justice.

Batavia, a town in Carroll county, established in 1831, on the land of James C. Brown.[28]

Battle Creek, rises in Marion county, and running southeast, empties into the Tennessee river, below the mouth of Sequatchee, N.W. of Nickajack, and immediately below Lowrey's Island.

Battle Creek, a post office in Marion county.[29]

Bay's Mountain, on the line between Hawkins and Greene counties, extending from the Chucky bend N.E. between Lick creek, (a branch of the Nolachucky) and Holston river.

Bean's Creek, a south branch of Elk river, in the S.W. part of Franklin county, between Roaring and Cave spring creeks.

Bean's Creek, a small stream in Franklin county. It joins Elk river between Caldwell's and Tallassee creeks.[30]

Bean's Station, a post office in Grainger county, 30 miles N.E. from Knoxville.

Bear Creek, a north branch of Elk river, which it joins a few miles above Winchester in Franklin county.—Also a west branch of Cumberland, in the county of Stewart.

Beaver Creek, a branch of Clinch river, in the N.E. corner of Roane county.

Beaver Creek, one of the head branches of Obion river. It rises in the east end of Carroll county, and flows past the town of Huntingdon, the seat of justice, and after receiving Gaines' and Reedy creeks, is from thence called *Obion.*

Beaver-dam Creek, a south branch of Holston river, in the east angle of Sullivan county.

[27-29] Discontinued as a post office.

[30] This and the preceding entry apparently refer to the same stream, Bean's Creek, near Huntland and Falls Mill in southwestern Franklin County; the community is served by the Huntland post office.

BEE 109

Beaver-dam Creek, a south branch of Duck river, in Hickman county.

Bedford, a county in Middle Tennessee, bounded on the west by Maury, north west by Williamson, north by Rutherford, north east by Warren, south east by Franklin, and south by Lincoln. This county is thirty-five miles in length, with a mean width of twenty-five, and contains an area of about 875 square miles. Its surface is rolling and exceedingly well watered. The fine stream of Duck river flows from east to west, a little south of the centre, and receives on the *north*, the united streams of East, Middle and Wartrace forks, also Jones', Fall, North Fork, Wilson's and Cane Spring creeks; on the *south*, Powell's, Sinking creek, &c. Bedford was erected Dec. 3, 1807, and receives its name in memory of Thomas Bedford. Its population in 1820 was 12,336 whites, 3,558 slaves, and 88 free persons of colour, total 16,012. Population in 1830, 30,449.—There are five towns in the county, viz. Shelbyville (the seat of justice) Farmington, Gideonsville and Davisville. There are post offices named, Civil-Order, Chapel Hill, Beech Grove and Davis' Mills. Iron ore is said to exist in great abundance in this county. Cotton and grain are the staples. Cen. lat. 35° 30′ N., lon. 9° 30′ W.

Beech Creek, an east branch of Tennessee, in Wayne county, below Carrollville.

Beech Creek, a south branch of Holston, in the east part of Hawkins county, and it joins the river opposite to Rogersville.

Beech Grove, a post office in Bedford county, on the route from Shelbyville to McMinnville, 48 miles S.E. from Nashville.[31]

Beech Hill, a post office in Jackson county, 68 miles N.E. from Nashville. It is the present residence of Col. Smith.[32]

Beech Plains, a post office, lately established, in Bedford county—*changed to Macon*.[33]

---

[31] Beechgrove is a town and post office, now in Coffee County (established in 1836).

[32-33] Discontinued as a post office.

Beech River, a small navigable stream, which takes its rise near the west end of Henderson county, and running nearly due east near the town of Lexington, empties into the Tennessee, in Perry county, just below the town of Perryville.

Belboro, a post office lately established in Williamson county.[34]

Belmont, a post office in Fayette county.[35]

Belmontaine, a post office in Haywood county.[36]

Belknap's, a post office, lately established in Stewart county.[37]

Bellville, a village in Davidson county, on the west bank of Harpeth.[38]

Bend Creek, a north east branch of the Caney Fork of Cumberland, and runs in, opposite the Caney Bend in White county.

Bent Creek, a north branch of the Nolachucky river, and empties in at the Chucky Bend, in Jefferson county.[39]

Beoison's Creek, a western branch of the Tennessee, and empties in at the town of Coffee, in Hardin county.[40]

Bigby Creek, a south branch of Duck river on the W. side of Maury county.

Bigbyville, a village in Maury county, south of Columbia.

Big Bone Cave, on the line of White and Warren counties: See *"Arch Cave."*

Big Butt, a mountain on the south line of Washington county.

Big Barren Creek, a small northern branch of Clinch river, which rises near Tazewell, in Claiborne county, and joins the river about a mile below the Knoxville road.[41]

Big Barren Creek, a post office, in Claiborne county.[42]

Big Creek, a north branch of Holston, in Hawkins county.

[34-37] Discontinued as a post office.

[38] The community of Bellevue, west of Nashville.

[39] Now in Hamblen County (established in 1870).

[40] Properly, Beason's Creek, near Crump, in Hardin County.

[41] Listed today as "Barren Creek."

[42] Discontinued as a post office.

BIR   111

Big Creek, a branch of the Loosa Hatchie, in Shelby county; on this creek there is a post office bearing the same name; 240 miles S.W. by W. from Nashville.⁴³

Big Creek, a north branch of Holston, opposite the mouth of French Broad, in Knox county.

Big Hatchee, a river which rises in the state of Mississippi, and enters this state in the south east corner of M'Nairy county, thence through Hardeman in a north west direction, enters the south west corner of Haywood, and bearing north west, runs into Tipton ten miles north of the south east corner, thence by a slight northern curve, passes through Tipton and enters the Mississippi, at the bend above the second Chickasaw Bluffs, in lat. 35° 32′ N. It is navigable for large keel boats eight or nine months in the year, and for smaller ones all the year, as high as the town of Bolivar.— Steam boats of 150 tons ascend without much difficulty in a good stage of water. Its general width at low water is about sixty yards, and depth from three to twelve feet.

Big Honeycut, a south branch of Holston in Hawkins county.

Big Muddy, a branch of Big Hatchee, rises in Fayette county and falls into the river below M'Guire's Bluff, Haywood county. It is a never failing stream, and contains sufficient water to propel machinery at any season of the year.

Big Pigeon River, a south branch of French Broad river. It runs a N.W. direction through Cocke county and falls into the river below New Port, south of the Chucky Bend.

Big Sycamore, a branch of Clinch river, taking its rise at the foot of Newman's Ridge, and running in a south west direction, joins the river on the north, between Raven hill and Lone mountain, in Claiborne county.

Big War Creek, a south east branch of Clinch in Hawkins county.⁴⁴

Birdsong Creek, a west branch of Tennessee river in Humphreys county, between Cypress and Eagle creeks.

---

⁴³ The post office of the same name has been discontinued.
⁴⁴ Big War Creek is in Hancock County (established in 1844).

Black Water, a post office in Hawkins county, 252 miles east from Nashville—[discontinued.]

Blair's X Roads, a post office in Grainger county, 191 miles east from Nashville.[45]

Blair's Ferry, a post office in Roane county, 144 miles S.E. from Nashville.[46]

Bledsoe, a county in East Tennessee, erected Nov. 30, 1807, bounded on the south by Marion, on the south west by Franklin, on the west by White, on the north by Morgan, on the east by Rhea; and south east by Hamilton. This county is mountainous, and is watered on the south by the Sequatchee river, and on the north by the head waters of Embree's river. The soil in some parts is highly productive, particularly in the Sequatchee Valley, where corn, cotton, wheat and rye are raised in great abundance. It area has not been obtained; it extends from S. to N. with the Cumberland mountains some fifty miles, with a mean width of 12 or 15. It contained in 1820 a population of 4,005. In 1830, 4,648. That part of the Sequatchee Valley lying in this county, is estimated to contain 2,500 souls. Perhaps no county in the State exceeds Bledsoe for sublime and picturesque scenery. The Sequatchee river sinks under a mountain some eight or ten miles—a fountain spring, about ten miles from its head contains an area of an acre; and Christian's creek another branch of Sequatchee, falls over a bluff of Walden's ridge, covered with spruce pine, something like three hundred feet. Pikeville is the seat of justice and there are post offices at High Plains, Crab Orchard, and Mount Airy. Cen. lat. 35° 45′ N., long. W. C. 8° 15′ W. *See Sequatchee.*

Bledsoe's Creek, a beautiful and bold running stream, which rises in the north part of Sumner county and flowing south, empties into the Cumberland, above the town of Cairo. It is the largest creek in the county, and waters a great body of rich land under a high state of cultivation, and it has many

---

[45] Discontinued as a post office.

[46] The village of Blair, in Roane County, is served by the Harriman post office.

excellent mills erected on it. Its principal branch is Desha's creek.

Bledsoe's Lick, a very noted sulphur spring, situated eight miles east, from Gallatin, in the county of Sumner; on the road leading to Carthage. It is noted as being one of the first places settled in the state, west of the mountains. Experience has proved that its waters are highly medicinal, and that they are equal if not superior to any in the state. Judge Haywood, in his history of Tennessee, gives the following description of this place, which is substantially correct.

"About 200 yards from the lick, in a circular enclosure between Bledsoe's lick creek and Bledsoe's spring branch, upon level ground, is a wall fifteen or eighteen inches in height, with projecting angular elevations, of the same height as the wall: and within it are about sixteen acres of land. In the interior is a raised platform, from 13 to 15 feet above the common surface, about 200 yards from the wall to the south, and about fifty from the northern part of it. The platform is sixty yards in breadth, and is level on top, and is, to the east of a mound, to which it joins, of seven or eight feet higher elevation, or eighteen feet from the common surface, about twenty feet square. On the eastern side of the latter mound is a small cavity, indicating that steps were once there, for the purpose of ascending from the platform to the top of the mound. In the year 1785, there grew on the top of the mound a black oak, three feet through. There is no water in the circular inclosure, or court. Upon the top of the mound was ploughed up, some years ago, an *image*, made of sand stone. On one cheek was a mark resembling a wrinkle, passing perpendicularly up and down the cheek. On the other cheek were two similar marks. The breast was that of a female, and prominent. The face was turned obliquely up, towards the heavens. The palms of the hands were turned upwards before the face, and at some distance from it, in the same direction that the face was. The knees were drawn near together and the feet with the toes towards the ground, were separated wide enough to admit of the body being seated;

between them. The attitude seemed to be that of adoration. The head and upper part of the forehead, were represented as covered with *a cap, or mitre, or bonnet*, from the lower part of which came horizontally a brim, from the extremities of which the cap extended upwards conically." ° ° ° °

"Near to this mound is a cave, which contained at the time of the first settlements by the whites, a great number of human skulls, without any other appearance of human bones near them." Mr. Earle has lately made another and more scrutinizing examination of this mound, by which have been brought to light several particulars of great consequence—His report follows. "This mound is situated in a plane, and is surrounded by hills which enclose from seventy-five to eighty acres of flat land with *three* fine sulphur springs; and at the junction of four roads leading to different parts of the state and considerably traveled; and about two miles from *Cragfont*, the residence of General Winchester. This is the place where Spencer and his friend Mr. Drake, spent the winter of 1779 and 1780. The trunk of the tree which they inhabited during this hard winter is just visible above the ground. The diameter is twelve feet. The mound measures, beginning at the northeast corner running *east*, four and a half poles, to the *north-east corner;* then the horizontal projection from the principal mound, with one pole, then *east* eleven poles to the south-east corner; then *west* eleven poles to the original mound; thence with the original mound west four and a half poles, thence north four and a half poles to the north-west corner, before mentioned. The elevation to the top of the chief mound is two and a half poles; its diameter two poles in the centre and from three to four feet. The declivity of the mound is an angle of about forty-five degrees. A tree of considerable size is yet growing on the mound; and a decayed stump two and a half feet in diameter, but too much decayed to count the annual rings or circles in it. An intrenchment and circumvallation enclosing forty acres, encircles this mound and others of lesser size. There is a circumvallatory parapet five feet high. On the parapet are small tumuli, like water towers, about ninety-five feet distant from one to the other. In the line of circumvallation and from each fifth tumulus, there is an average distance of forty-five or from thence to 180 feet to the next one. It thus continues around the whole breast work."

"Mr. Earle dug into the parapet in several places from two to three feet in depth and found ashes, pottery ware, flint, muscle shells, coal &c., on the out side of the intrenchment, and a number of graves. In several different places flat stones are set up edge-wise, enclosing skeletons buried from twelve to eighteen inches under the surface. Three hundred yards from the great mound on the south-east side of the intrenchment, is a mound of fifty yards in circumference, and six in height. In the opposite direction from this to the *north-east*, stands another smaller mound, and of the same dimensions of the one last mentioned. So that the three stand upon a line from north-east to south-east. * * * * * * * *"

"The next principal mound in size within the entrenchment, is in a south east course from the great mound, and about 170 yards distant; circumference, 90 yards; elevation, 10 feet. Thirty five yards distant in a south west course, is a small tumulus two thirds as large as the one just mentioned. At the same distance, on the north east corner of the great mound, is another of the same size of the last mentioned. Each of these tumuli hath a small one of about half its size in the centre between them and the great mound."

The earth with which this mound was constructed, appears to have been taken not from one place, leaving a cavity in the earth, but evenly from all the surface around the mound. In about two hundred yards distant, extending from the mound, the soil hath been taken off to a considerable depth. Mr. Earle made an excavation in the principal mound twenty two feet, commencing ten feet from the common surface.— At two feet from the summit was found a stratum of ashes fourteen inches through, to a stratum of earth.—The layers of ashes were counted, and amounted to twenty eight. At eight feet, the diggers came to the skelton of a child, lying on three cedar piles, five feet and a half in length, and considerably decayed, but sound at the head. The head of the child lay towards the east facing the west, with a jug made of sand stone lying at its feet. At nineteen feet they dug up part of a corn cob. Various other bones were found, amongst which was the jaw-bone with the tusk attached to it, of some unknown animal. From these facts, it is evident that this lick has been a great place of resort as well by the various animals as the aborigines of the country.—In digging into the earth to sink a gum for the collection of water, the workmen came to the tusk of some huge animal, between two and three feet in length.—Also, grinders eight or nine inches wide. The tusk was bent like that of a hog, but not so much so in proportion to its size." It is thirty three miles N. of E. from Nashville, and 674 miles S.W. from Washington City in lat. 36° 20′, N., lon 9° 12′ W. The name of this place has been changed to *Castalian Springs,* which see.

Blooming Grove Creek, a north branch of Cumberland river, which empties above New York, in Montgomery county, about forty eight miles from Nashville.

Blount, a county in East Tennessee, erected by the Territorial Legislature, July 11, 1795, and was represented in the Convention that formed the constitution by David Craig, James Greenaway, Joseph Black, James Houston and Samuel Glass. It is bounded on the south by Monroe, on the north by Knox and Sevier, east by the state of North Carolina, and on the west by part of Roane. It is thirty eight miles long with a mean width of 18, and contains an area of about 625 square miles. The surface is hilly and varied. Staples grain, flour and salted provisions. Blount contained in 1820, a population of 11,368, of which 1,011 were slaves. Little and Holston rivers on the north and north west, and Little Tennessee on the south west, are its principal waters.

"Eight miles west of Maryville, is a spring, to the south of which is a bridge; at the base of which is a sink hole. One standing on the side of the bridge and looking through a fissure into the rocks, may see water nearly upon a level with his breast, in which are fish.—The spring is fifteen feet lower, and one hundred and fifty feet from the spot, where the water is seen in the interior of the cave. This spring is unfathomable.—The water is clear and of a bluish cast. Near the base of the bridge is a sinkhole, in which there is no water." Gold is found in this county on the east border. The towns in this county are Maryville, (the seat of justice) Louisville, Unitia and Morganton. There are also post offices at Chota, Mount Pisgah, Nine Mile Creek and Cloverhill. Cent. lat. 35° 40′ N., long. WC. 7° W. It contained in 1830 a population of 11,027.

Blountsville, a post town and seat of justice of Sullivan county; established, July 10, 1795. It is situated on Muddy creek, a north branch of Holston river. It contained in July 1829, a population of 209, twenty eight houses, one Presbyterian and one Methodist church, one lawyer, one doctor, six stores, two taverns, and ten mechanics. It is 320 miles east from Nashville, 109 N.E. from Knoxville, 20 north from Jonesborough, 23 S.W. from Abingdon, Va. and 434 from Washington City, in lat. 36° 30′ N., lon. 5° 20′ W.

Blue Creek, an east branch of Tennessee, in Perry county.

Blue Creek, a small stream which rises in the edge of Dickson county, and running in a south west direction, empties into Duck river, at the Big bend, in Humphreys County. It is about ten miles in length, and affords a sufficient quantity of water to turn a grist mill half the year, but there are no good sites. The land along this creek is second rate, on which are many excellent farms.

Blue Creek, a small branch of Tennessee river, in Humphreys county.

Blue Spring Creek, an east branch of the Calf-killer, in White county.

Bluff Creek, a south branch of Cumberland, in Davidson county.[47]

---
[47] This stream, properly Big Bluff Creek, enters the Cumberland River west of Asland City, in Cheatham County (established in 1856).

Boat Yard, at the mouth of the S. branch of Holston—see 'Kingsport.'

Boiling Fork, a south east branch of Elk river, which empties in below the town of Winchester, in Franklin county. It might be rendered navigable for small boats.

Bolivar, a flourishing post town, and seat of justice of Hardeman county; pleasantly situated on the south west bank of the Big Hatchee river, below the mouth of Spring creek. In December 1828, it contained a splendid brick court house and jail, ten stores, three taverns, one grocery, one printing office, five doctors, five lawyers, one commission house, and mechanics of almost every description. Since which time, it has increased with almost unexampled rapidity. This town being at the head of steam boat navigation on the Hatchee, it must become a place of commercial importance. It is 174 miles S.W. from Nashville, and 916 from Washington City, in lat. 35° 12' N., lon. 11° 55' W.

Boon's Creek, a south branch of Wataga in Washington county.

Boon's Hill, a post office in Lincoln.[48]

Bowers', a post office in Weakley county.[49]

Bowlinggreen, a town established in 1817, on the land of Samuel Chapman, near M'Carty's landing, in Stewart county. The post office here is now called 'Branson's.'[50]

Boyd's Creek, a south branch of French Broad, in Sevier county, west of Sevierville.

Boyd's Creek, a post office in Sevier county, 194 miles east from Nashville.[51]

Bradshaw's Creek, a north branch of Elk river, in Giles county, S.E. of Pulaski and below Carr's creek, on the line of Lincoln county.

Brainard Mission, a missionary station within the chartered

---

[48] No longer a post office; the community, Boonshill, is in the northwest section of Lincoln County.

[49-50] Discontinued as a post office.

[51] The post office is discontinued; the community, in the northwest section of Sevier County, still bears the name.

limits of the county of Hamilton, on south Chickamaga creek, in the Cherokee nation, 15 miles south of the temporary seat of justice, and five miles north of the Georgia state line. At this station the Cherokee children are correctly instructed in the minor branches of English literature. There is a male and female academy supported principally by donations from charitable societies, and individuals of the eastern and northern states. The number of scholars in each academy varies from 25 to 30. President Monroe made a donation of one thousand dollars to aid in the erection of the *female* academy. This institution was founded in the year 1816, by the Rev. Cyrus Kingsbury, a gentleman of indefatigable industry in the missionary cause. In June 1829, the establishment was under the general superintendance of Mr. John C. Elsworth. Miss Ames principal of the female academy.

Branson's, a post office in Stewart county, on the left bank of Cumberand river; formerly called *Bowlinggreen.*

Bratton's, a post office in the county of Smith.[52]

Bridge Creek, an east branch of Calf-killer, in White county.

Brick Academy, a place of some note, seven miles south of west from Columbia, in Maury county, at which there are three families, one store and one physician.[53]

Brimstone Creek, a west branch of Cumberland, in Jackson county. Also, a branch of Newriver, in Morgan county, west of Brimstone mountain.[54]

Brookhill, a post office in Montgomery county, 54 miles N.W. from Nashville.[55]

Brown's Cove, a post office in Franklin county, 75 miles S.E. from Nashville.[56]

Brownham, a post office in Lincoln county, 100 miles E. of S. from Nashville.[57]

---

[52] Now Brattontown, in Macon County; served by Lafayette post office.

[53] Discontinued as a post office.

[54] Brimstone Creek, a tributary of the Cumberland, is in Clay County (established in 1870); the New River tributary of the same name is in Scott County (established in 1849).

[55-57] Discontinued as a post office.

Brownsboro', a town on the Nolachucky river, S.W. of Washington college, in Washington county, at Mitchell's Mills, 18 miles below Bumpass' Cove Iron Works.[58]

Brownsville, a post town and seat of justice of Haywood county; established in 1824, and named in honor of Major General Jacob Brown. It is situated on the dividing ridge, between the Forked Deer and Big Hatchee rivers, and contained in January 1829, 30 or 40 families, about 400 inhabitants, a temporary court house, jail and academy, four lawyers, three doctors, six stores, two taverns, four house carpenters, one blacksmith, two shoe makers, one hatter, one tailor and one wagon and carriage maker. It is 174 miles S.W. from Nashville, and 980 from Washington City. Lat. 35° 35' N., lon. 11° 15'W.

Brunsonville, a town, established in 1819, on the Cumberland river, at the mouth of Saline creek, on the land of Reed Luton, Stokely Vinton and John Acre, in Stewart county.[59]

Brush Creek, a north branch of Cumberland river.[60]

Brush Creek, an east branch of Calf-killer, in White county.

Brush Creek, a north branch of Sequatchee river, which rises in the Cumberland mountains, in White, and running about twenty miles, joins the river on the line between Bledsoe and Marion counties.[61]

Buchanan's Creek, a branch of Richland, in Giles county, below Pulaski.

Budd's Creek, a south branch of Cumberland river, in Montgomery county, above Palmyra.

Bud Creek, a south branch of Tennessee river, in Roane county.

Buffalo Ironworks, in section 2, range 6, Lawrence county, belonging to Judge Catron.

---

[58] The present Limestone, in Washington County, on the border of Greene County.

[59] Properly, Tobacco Port, in Stewart County.

[60] In Montgomery County.

[61] The mouth of Brush Creek is in Sequatchie County (established in 1857).

BUT 121

Buffalo River, takes its rise in Lawrence and Hickman counties, touches the N. E. corner of Wayne, passes through the E. side of Perry and joins Duck river, in the N. E. corner of the latter county, in lat. 35° 50′, lon. 10° 43′ W.

Buffalo Creek, a north branch of New river, in Campbell county.[a2]

Buffalo Mountain, on the line between Carter and Washington counties.

Buffalo Port, a post office, in Perry county, established in 1833.[a3]

Buffalo Creek, a south branch of Wataga, in Carter county, which heads near the foot of Buffalo mountain.

Bull Run, an east branch of Clinch, W. of Copper ridge, in Anderson county.

Butler's Ferry, a post office in Jackson county, 75 miles east from Nashville.[a4]

Bumpass' Creek, a west branch of Nolachucky, in Washington county, on which are Embree's iron works.

Bumpass' Cove, the valley north of Bumpass' creek. The soil is of the class denominated mulatto land.

Bush Creek, a south branch of Cumberland, in Davidson county.[a5]

Bush Creek, a north branch of Cumberland, in Davidson county.

Butler, a post office, in Obion county, established in 1833.

[a2] Buffalo Creek is in Scott County (established in 1849).
[a3] Discontinued as a post office.
[a4] The community of Butler's Ferry, no longer a post office, is in Clay County (established in 1870); mail service through Celina.
[a5] This entry probably refers to Brush Creek, in Cheatham County (established in 1856).

C

Cade's Cove, a post office, in Blount county.⁶⁶

Cairo, a post town, in Sumner, situated on the north bank of Cumberland river, about three quarters of a mile below the mouth of Bledsoe's creek. It was incorporated in 1815, and contains thirty families, two physicians, an academy and church, one tavern, one cabinet maker, one machine maker, one cotton and wool factory, one rope walk, two tailors, two blacksmiths, one gunsmith, and two shoemakers. It is five miles E. from Gallatin, 30 from Nashville and 12 from Lebanon.

Cainsville, a town in Wilson county, fourteen miles south from Lebanon, established in 1829.

Caldwell's Creek, one of the head branches of Elk river, in the N. E. corner of Franklin county.⁶⁷

Caledonia, a post town, in Henry county, ten miles S. W. from Paris, and 120 N. of W. from Nashville; established in 1832, on the land of Wm. C. Rogers, Esq.⁶⁸

Calf-killer river, a north east branch of the Caney Fork of Cumberland, which rises in the Cumberland mountains N. E. of Sparta. It interlocks with the head streams of the Caney Fork, is rapid in its descent, shaping its course generally to south and south west, and is 30 or 40 miles in length. Its confluence with the Caney Fork, is about eight miles south of Sparta. Its principal tributary streams on the east side, are, Bridge, Brush, Bluespring and Wildcat creeks. On the west side, Plum, Cherry and Town Creek. The latter forms a junction with the Calf-killer. About half a mile below Sparta, on the Calf-killer, is a fall of about fifteen feet nearly perpendicular, at which place there are mills and iron works. This is thought to be one of the most eligible sites in the western country for a national armory. In the neighborhood

---
⁶⁶ Cade's Cove is a part of the Great Smoky Mountains National Park; post office is Townsend.
⁶⁷ Now in Grundy County (established in 1844).
⁶⁸ No longer identifiable.

of these falls are found inexhaustible mines of iron ore of good quality. Upon this river, above Sparta, are six or seven salt springs, at which considerable quantities of salt have been made.

Calhoun, a post town, in M'Minn county, on the Hiwassee river, ten miles below Columbus, and fourteen miles south from Athens, below the mouth of Estannallee creek. It contains about a dozen families, one store, one tavern and five or six mechanics. It is 169 miles S. E. from Nashville, 70 S. W. from Knoxville and 611 from Washington City, in lat. 35° 15' N., lon. 7° 34' W.

Calhoun's Creek, a branch of Calf-killer, and forms a junction on the line of White and Warren counties, S. W. of Sparta, called on modern maps, *Rocky river*.

Camp Creek, a south branch of the Nolachucky, in Green county, between Horse and Cove creeks, on which are iron works.

Camp Creek, a post office in Green county, established in 1833.[59]

Camp Creek, a branch of Hardin's creek, in Wayne county.

Campbell, a county in East Tennessee, in a triangular form; bounded on the north by Kentucky, on the N. E. by Grainger, south by Anderson and Morgan, and west by Fentress. It contains an area of about 625 square miles. The surface is hilly and in part mountainous. The soil is fertile in the valleys, and along the streams; staples, grain, flour and salted provisions.

This county was erected, Sept. 11, 1806, and contained a population in 1820, of 4244, of which 116 were slaves. Clinch and Powell's rivers water its S. E. border, and the head waters of Cumberland its north.—Seat of justice, Jacksboro.' Population in 1830, 5010.

Campbell's Creek, an east branch of Tennessee, in Stewart county.

Campbell's Station, a post office, in Knox county, 15 miles

---
[59] Discontinued as a post office; mail service through Greeneville.

CAN 125

W. of Knoxville, on the Nashville road.—here is a store, two taverns and a stage office.[70]

Canasauga, a north branch of the Hiwassee river, in the east end of M'Minn county, also the name of a post office in Amoee district.[71]

Cane Creek, an east branch of Tennessee, in Stewart county.[72]

Cane Creek, rises in Hickman county, and running S. W., empties into Buffalo river, in Perry county.

Cane Creek, a post office, in Lincoln county, 65 miles south from Nashville.[73]

Cane Creek, a north branch of Elk river, in Lincoln county. It rises near the Bedford line and falls into the river a short distance below Fayetteville.

Cane Creek, a branch of the Falling water of the Caney Fork of Cumberland, fourteen miles north west from Sparta, in White county. This creek runs with great rapidity, falling in some places 20 or 30 feet, and passes over a fine bed of stone coal.

Caney Spring Creek, a north branch of Duck river, in the N. W. corner of Bedford county.[74]

Caney Creek, a north branch of Holston, in Hawkins county.

Caney Fork, a branch of the Cumberland river, rises in Warren, White and Jackson counties, and flowing N. W., enters Smith, and falls into the Cumberland at Carthage. It is navigable as high up as Shippingsport, at the falls, in Warren county, where the whole stream falls over the rocks one hundred feet.[75]

---

[70] The community of Lovell, near Concord, in Knox County.

[71] The creek is south of Etowah, in McMinn County; the post office (then in the Ocoee District) still exists in Polk County (established in 1839).

[72] Now in Houston County (established in 1871).

[73] Discontinued as a post office.

[74] Now in Marshall County (established in 1836).

[75] Some of the headwaters of the Caney Fork River are in Putnam County (established in 1854) and Cumberland County (established in 1855).

Caney Fork, a branch of Wolf river, in Fentress county.

Canton, a post office, in Warren county, established in 1833.[76]

Caper's Creek, an east branch of Tennessee, in the N. E. end of Perry county.

Carroll, a county in West Tennessee, bounded on the east by Humphreys and Perry, on the west by Gibson, on the north by Henry and Weakley, and on the south by Henderson and Madison. It contains the towns of Huntingdon, (the seat of justice,) Christmasville and McLemoresville, and there is a post office at Wood's store. This county was erected in 1821 and has a population of 9,378. Obion river, Rutherford's fork, North fork of Forked-deer and Sandy river, are its principal waters.

Carrollsville, a post town in Wayne county, ninety-six miles S. W. of Murfreesboro' and 115 from Nashville. This village lies directly on the road between Waynesboro' and Lexington, on the east bank of the Tennessee.[77]

Carrollton, a town established on the land of Robert E. C. Dougherty, in the county of Carroll, 112 miles west from Nashville, at Dougherty's post office—changed to *McLemoresville*.

Carson's Ironworks, a post office in Blount county.[78]

Carter, the extreme eastern county in East Tennessee (erected in April 1796, from Washington county) on the sources of the Watauga branch of Holston; bounded on the E. and S. E. by North Carolina, W. by Washington and part of Sullivan, and north by Sullivan county, and state of Virginia. It is about thirty-five miles long, N. E. and S. W., and about twenty wide, and contains an area of about 700 square miles. The surface is hilly and in part mountainous. The soil with some exceptions, is rather sterile. Iron ore exists in great abundance in this county, and the mines are extensively worked, and the iron and castings here, constitute a

---

[76] Discontinued as a post office.

[77] Carrollsville is the present Clifton, in Wayne County.

[78] Discontinued as a post office.

kind of circulating medium. The agricultural staples are grain, flour, &c. Population in 1820 was 4,835, of which 345 were slaves. Seat of Justice, Elizabethton. Cen. Lat. 36° 20' N., long., 5° 10' W. Population in 1830, 6,418.

Carthage, a flourishing post town, and the seat of justice, for the county of Smith. It is situated on the north-east bank of the Cumberland river, a short distance below the mouth of the Caney Fork. It contains about 700 inhabitants, eight lawyers, three doctors, one divine, thirteen stores, four taverns, one grocery, two tailors, two blacksmiths, one hatter, one cabinet maker, two carpenters, one saddler, one tanyard, one printing office, one house and sign painter, one male and female academy, one church, and an extensive steam mill for sawing and grinding. It is thirty-five miles east from Gallatin, sixty from Nashville, and 654 S. W. from Washington city in lat. 36° 20' N., long. 5° 10' W.

Castalian Springs, these springs are situated at a place heretofore known as Bledsoe's Lick, eight miles from Gallatin in the county of Sumner, on the road leading to Carthage, and thirty three miles from Nashville. The fountains are numerous and the waters are uncommonly cold, clear and palatable: their constituent qualities are somewhat variant, but they all contain portions of sulphur, soda, salts, and magnesia. The virtues of these waters have been fairly tested, and there is no doubt of their medicinal efficacy. The proprietors have erected spacious and comfortable buildings for the accommodation of visitors. The landscape is peculiarly picturesque and beautiful, and it will undoubtedly be a place of fashionable resort during the summer months. See *Bledsoe's Lick*.

Cathey's Creek, empties into Duck river in Maury county, below the mouth of Bigby creek.

Cave Hill, a post office in Greene county.[19]

Cedar Creek, a south branch of Duck River S. E. of Columbia in Maury county.

Cedar Creek, an east branch of Tennessee river, in Perry county, near the Wayne county line.

---
[19] Discontinued as a post office.

Cedar Creek, a south branch of Cumberland river in Wilson county, which falls in above the town of Cairo.

Cedar Creek, a post office in Greene county, established in 1833.[10]

Cedar Grove, a post office in Wilson county, twenty-six miles N. E. from Murfreesboro.' Now *Silver Springs*, on the road leading from Nashville to Lebanon.[51]

Cedar Lick Creek, a south branch of Cumberland, in Wilson county, near the Davidson county line.

Cedar Spring Creek, a north branch of Duck river, which rises in Dickson, and joins the river below Centerville, in Hickman county.

Cedar Spring, a post office in Maury county.[52]

Celina, a post office in Overton county.[53]

Celina, a town established in 1831 on the land of John F. Vass, in Jackson county.

Centerville, the seat of justice of Hickman county, situated on the south bank of Duck river, near the mouth of Defeated creek. It was incorporated in 1824, and contains about 200 inhabitants, two lawyers, two doctors, one preacher, one school, four stores, two taverns, two carpenters, one cabinet maker, one hatter, two saddlers, one tailor, one shoemaker, and one blacksmith. It is 80 miles S. W. from Nashville and 794 from Washington city, in lat. 35° 43' N., long. 10° 30' W.

Celico, a south branch of Little Tennessee, in Monroe county.[54]

Chalk-Level, a post office at J. D. Camp's, in Humphreys county.[55]

---

[50] Mail service through Greeneville.

[51] Discontinued as a post office. It was a well known watering place in the late nineteenth century.

[52] Discontinued as a post office.

[53] Celina is the county seat of Clay County (established in 1870).

[54] Properly, Citico, a south branch of the Little Tennessee River, in Monroe County.

[55] Discontinued as a post office; mail service through Camden, in Benton County.

CHE   129

Chambers' Creek, a branch of Tennessee in the S. W. corner of Hardin county.

Chapel Hill, a post office in Bedford county, on the road from Harpeth to Fayetteville.[86]

Charleston, a town established in 1831, in White county, on the land of Solomon Charles.

Charlestown, a town in the county of Lincoln, at the mouth of Bradshaw's creek, established in 1819, on the lands of David Cowen.[87]

Charley's Creek, a west branch of Collins' river, below McMinnville, in Warren county.

Charlotte, a post town and seat of justice of Dickson county, situated on Jones' creek, a branch of Harpeth, 30 miles west from Nashville, in lat. 36° 6' N., long. 10° 15' W., established in 1804. This village was nearly destroyed by a tornado in 1830. It contains three lawyers, three doctors, one academy, four stores, two taverns and one cabinet maker.

Chattonaga, a south branch of Tennessee, which joins the river within the chartered limits of Hamilton county, S. W. of Brainard Mission station, between Chickamauga and Tunacunhe creeks.

Cheek's X Roads, a post office in Hawkins, 222 miles E. from Nashville.[88]

Cherokee Nation, the Cherokee Indians inhabit an extensive country, within the chartered limits of North Carolina, Georgia and Tennessee, containing 15 or 16,000 square miles. The chief part of their territory lying in this state, is bounded on the N. W. by Tennessee and N. E. by the Hiwassee rivers, and touches Marion, Hamilton, Rhea, McMinn and Monroe counties.

Cherokee Creek, a branch of the Nolachucky, in Washington county.

---

[86] Chapel Hill is in Marshall County (established in 1836).

[87] Neither the White nor Lincoln county towns of Charleston or Charlestown have a corporate entity today; they should not be confused with the incorporated town of Charleston in Bradley County.

[88] Discontinued as a post office.

Cherryville, a town in Haywood county; formerly *Harrisburg*.

Cherry Creek, a branch of Calf-killer in White county.

Cherry Hill, a post office in Hardin county, established in 1833.[89]

Chestnut Grove, a post office in Davidson county (formerly called 'Joslins')—7 miles from Nashville.[90]

Chestua, a north branch of Hiwassee river in McMinn county, between Canasauga and Estanalle creeks.[91]

Chewalee, a post office in Franklin county.[92]

Chickasaw Bluffs.—Three noted bluffs on the Mississippi river. The first below the mouth of Forked Deer, at the town of Fulton, and the second below the mouth of Big Hatchee, at the town of Randolph in Tipton county, and the third and most celebrated one below the mouth of Wolf river, at the town of Memphis in Shelby county.

Chickamauga, a north branch of Tennessee river, in Hamilton county, which passes the former seat of justice, and intersects the river six miles below Sauda creek, and one mile above Falling water creek. Also a south branch of Tennessee which runs by Brainard Mission station.

Chilhowee, a post office in Monroe county.[93]

Chisholm's Creek, a branch of Shoal creek, in Lawrence county, which flows past the town of Lawrenceburg.

Chismsburg, a town established in 1819, on the land of Thomas Burges, on the Caney fork, in Warren county.[94]

Chota, a post office in Blount county, 210 miles east from Nashville.[95]

Christian's Creek, a branch of Sequatchee river, in Bledsoe county. It rises on the top of Walden's ridge, south of the

---

[89-90] Discontinued as a post office.

[91] The mouth of the Chestua and most of its course lie in Polk County (established in 1839).

[92-93] Discontinued as a post office.

[94] Not identified.

[95] Properly, "Chote" or "Chota," the capital of the Overhill Cherokees, on the Little Tennessee River, in Monroe County. Discontinued as a post office; mail service through Maryville.

river, and runs about three miles in a S. W. direction, and falls over a cliff something like three hundred feet. Here is an abundance of large spruce pines through which the sun beams scarcely penetrate. The spray when the sun shines exhibits the colours of the rainbow, and the whole scenery is peculiarly beautiful. From the falls to the mouth of the creek is about four miles.

Christmasville, a post town in Carroll county, on the north bank of the south fork of Obion, 105 miles W. from Nashville, and fifteen miles below Huntingdon."

Chucky Bend, a post office in Jefferson county, 218 miles east from Nashville."

Civil Order, a post office in Bedford county, on the route from Harpeth to Fayetteville, fifty-five miles S. E. from Nashville."

Claiborne, a county in east Tennessee, bounded on the north by Virginia and Kentucky, south west by Campbell county, south east by Grainger, or Clinch river, and east by Hawkins. It was erected Oct. 29, 1801, is fifty miles in length, on the state line, mean width 12, and contains an area of 625 square miles. There are two towns in this county, Tazewell and Speedwell, the first is the seat of justice, and is situated west of Wallen's Ridge on Russel's creek, a south branch of Clinch. The latter is situated on Davis' creek in Powell's Valley, near the Campbell county line, at Speedwell ironworks.

The face of the country is hilly. The principal hills are Cumberland and Log mountains, west of Powell's river, Walden's ridge, Powell's mountain, Newman's ridge, Lone mountain and Raven hill, between Powell's and Clinch rivers. There are two ironworks and furnaces in operation, a number of grist mills, two cotton gins and two wool carding machines within this county. It also contains several mineral springs

---

" Discontinued as a post office; mail service through McKenzie.

" Discontinued. There is, however, a post office, Chuckey, in Greene County.

" Discontinued as a post office.

and lead mines, and copperas mines have also been found near Log mountain.

The first settlement in this county was at the Big spring near Sycamore creek, in 1794 and 5. Population in 1820 was 5,508 of which 377 were slaves. Cent. lat. 36° 25′ N. long. 6° 40′ W. Population in 1830, 8,470.

Clark's Creek, a branch of the south fork of Forked Deer, at the head of navigation.[99]

Clark's Mills, a post office, in Robertson county, on Red River, 11 miles N.W. from Springfield.[100]

Clarksville, a post town and seat of justice of Montgomery county, on the point of land formed by the junction of Cumberland and Red rivers, 45 miles by land below Nashville. It was established by an act of the state of North Carolina, and commissioners for its regulation were appointed by the governor and legislative council in July 1795. In 1819, it was incorporated with a mayor and aldermen. It contains fourteen lawyers, seven doctors, three divines, three churches, one male and one female academy, three common schools, one printing office, twelve stores, three taverns, four blacksmiths, fifteen carpenters, two cabinetmaker's shops, two hatter's shops, two painters, two saddler's shops, two silversmith's shops, one turner's shop, two wagonmaker's shops, one wheelwright, one cotton gin, and one wool carding machine.

Clear Creek, a south branch of Big Hatchee river, in the north west corner of Hardeman county.

Clear Creek, a post office in Hardeman county, 218 miles S. W. from Nashville.[101]

Clear Creek, a north west branch of Tennessee river, in Rhea county, above the town of Washington.

Clear Creek, a north branch of the South Fork of Obion river, which rises in Henry, and joins the river in Carroll county.

Clear Fork, one of the head branches of Cumberland river, which has its source in the Cumberland mountains, and runs

---

[99] In Chester County (established in 1879).
[100-101] Discontinued as a post office.

CLO 133

N. E. with the line between Fentress and Morgan counties. It is the head of the great South Fork of Cumberland, is very rapid and unsuitable for navigation.[102]

Clifty Creek, a north branch of Caney Fork, in White county.

Clifty, a post office, where the Knoxville road crosses Clifty creek, at Eastland's, in White county, 12 miles east from Sparta.[103]

Clinch, a mountain ranging between Clinch and Holston rivers, N. E. and S. W., extending through Grainger and Hawkins counties into Virginia. A vein of grey and variegated *marble* extends along the north side of this mountain for fifty miles; a great portion of it is very fine, and the vein is of a considerable width.

Clinch River, a navigable stream, which has its source in the Clinch mountain, in the state of Virginia, and runs a S. W. direction into this state, touching Hawkins, Claiborne, Campbell and Anderson; and falls into the Tennessee river at South West Point, below Kingston, the seat of Justice of Roane county. This river is said to have been named from the circumstance of an Irishman falling from a raft in 1761, and dolefully exclaiming to his companions, *"clinch me, clinch me."—Haywood's civil History, page 32.*

Clinch Dale, a post office, in Hawkins county, 245 miles E. from Nashville.[104]

Clinton, a post town and seat of justice, of Anderson county, on the west bank of Clinch river. This town was formerly called Burrville, but was changed by an act of the legislature, November 8th, 1809. It is 170 miles E. from Nashville, and 18 north of Knoxville, 559 S. W. by W. from Washington City, in lat. 36° 5′ N., lon. 7° 12′ W.

Cloud's Creek, a north branch of Holston, in Hawkins

---

[102] The mouth of the Clear Fork is in Scott County (established in 1849).

[103] Discontinued as a post office; the community is on the Cumberland County line; mail service through Sparta.

[104] Discontinued as a post office.

county, which has its source near Devil's Nose and Stone Mountains.

Clover Creek, a post office in Madison county, 155 miles S. W. from Nashville.[105]

Clover Creek, a north east branch of Big Hatchee river, in the north end of Hardeman county.

Clover Hill, a post office in Blount county, 162 miles east from Nashville.[106]

Clover Valley, a post office, in Dickson county, established in 1833.[107]

Coal Creek, an east branch of Mississippi, in Tipton county above Fulton.

Coal Creek, a north branch of Clinch river, above the Eagle Bend, in Anderson county.

Cobb's, a post office, in Maury county.[108]

Cocke, a county in East Tennessee; erected October 9th, 1797. It is bounded on the S. E. by Buncome and Haywood counties, N. C., E. by Greene, north and west by Jefferson and Sevier counties, Ten. It contains about 750 square miles. The face of the country adjoining North Carolina is broken and sterile, the balance is generally fertile, even on the hills, and the bottoms on Pigeon, French Broad and Nolachucky, produce from forty to sixty bushels of corn per acre. There is a great variety of timber, pine, poplar, hickory, chestnut, locust, walnut, ash, cherry, beech, &c. Good lime and freestone springs abound throughout the country; and there are two valuable chalybeate springs, one five and the other seven miles from New Port; and a sulphur spring within three miles, which is much resorted to, during the summer months. There are several remarkable caves near New Port; and remains of ancient fortifications, one about two miles below town, containing an area of six acres. There are numerous saw and grist mills in this county, and some cotton gins. The staples

---

[105] Discontinued as a post office.

[106] Discontinued as a post office; mail service through Maryville.

[107-108] Discontinued as a post office.

COL 135

are cotton, corn, wheat, rye and hemp. Corn is the principal, which is fed to stock and driven to market.

It is estimated that five thousand head of hogs are annually driven from this county to the southern market. Cocke contained in 1820, a population of 4,892, of which 468 were slaves. Seat of justice, New Port. Cent. lat. 35° 50′ N., long. 6° 10′ W. Population in 1830, 6,480.

Coffee, a town on the west bank of Tennessee river, in Hardin county, below the mouth of Beoison's· creek, and above Chalk bluff. It contains three or four families.[109]

Cold Spring, a post office in Hardeman county, late *Duncan's.*[110]

Collins' River, a branch of the Caney fork, in the county of Warren. It has its source in the Cumberland mountains, on the line of Marion county, and flows a north west direction through the center of Warren, and falls into the Caney fork on the line of White county, between Rock Island and the Falls.

Columbia, the seat of justice of Maury county, situated on the south bank of Duck river. It was established in 1807, and incorporated in 1817. It is one of the most flourishing towns in Midde Tennessee, and contains about 1,500 inhabitants, a college, an academy, four common schools, one printing office, three churches, three divines, thirteen lawyers, five doctors, twenty stores, three taverns, four groceries, fourteen blacksmiths, three bricklayers, eight carpenters, four cabinetmakers, three gunsmiths, two hatters, two painters, four saddlers, four shoemakers, three silversmiths, four tailors, two tanners, two tinners, two wagonmakers, one cotton gin, two carding machines, and a branch of the Union Bank of the state of Tennessee. It is forty-five miles south from Nashville, twenty-seven from Franklin, and 733 S. W. from Washington City. In lat. 35° 38′ N., long. 10° 3′ W.

[109] Probably the town of Crump; the creek is properly Beason's Creek; there is also a Coffee Landing in Hardin County (mail service through Adamsville).

[110] Discontinued as a post office.

Columbus, a post town in McMinn county, situated on the Hiwassee river, due south from Athens, sixteen miles on the Georgia road. It contains eleven families, one doctor, one merchant, five mechanics, and one tavern.[111]

Commerce, a post town in Wilson, 12 miles above Lebanon, and 34 east from Nashville.[112]

Cool Spring, a post office in Gibson county. Late *Goodman's.*[113]

Copper Ridge, a ridge lying east of Bull run, north west of Knoxville, in the county of Knox.

Cornersville, a post town in the north east corner of Giles county, and near the corners of Maury, Bedford and Lincoln. Incorporated 1831.[114]

Cotton Port, a post office in Williamson county.[115]

Cotton Grove, a post office in Madison county, 163 miles S. of W. from Nashville.[116]

Cottonwood Creek, a south branch of Wolf river, in Shelby county.

Cove Creek, a south branch of Nolachucky, in Greene county, between Camp creek and Baker's fork.

Cove Spring Creek, a south branch of Elk river, in the east end of Lincoln county.

Covington, a post town and the seat of justice of Tipton county. It was laid off in the year 1824, it is situated sixteen miles from the Mississippi river, and six from Big Hatchee, south, in the heart of a rich and fertile country. It was incorporated in 1826, and contains a frame court house, a brick

---

[111] Columbus was the first seat of Polk County (established in 1839). The village is now extinct and the post office of the name is discontinued.

[112] The village of Commerce still exists; the post office has been discontinued; mail service through Watertown.

[113] Discontinued as a post office.

[114] Cornersville is a town and post office, now in Marshall County (established in 1836).

[115] Discontinued as a post office.

[116] Discontinued. Cotton Grove Creek is a north fork of the Forked Deer River in the eastern part of Madison County.

jail, seven stores, two taverns, the surveyor's office for the eleventh District, three or four physicians, about the same number of lawyers, and some thirty or forty families. The buildings are frame and log. This town is watered by an excellent spring of pure and never failing water. It is 200 miles S. of W. from Nashville, and 930 S. W. from Washington City, in lat. 35° 35′ N., long. 12° 45′ W.

Cowan's post office in Henry county, established in 1833.[117]

Cowansville, a post town in Rhea county.[118]

Crab Orchard, a noted gap in the mountains, in Bledsoe county, 136 miles E. from Nashville; at this place there is a toll gate, post and stage office, and a good public house, and it might be rendered one of the most desirable situations in that section of the country.[119]

Cranson's Creek, a branch of Shoal creek, in the north east corner of Lawrence county.

Crawford's Creek, a branch of Caney fork, which rises in the S. W. corner of Warren county.

Criswell's Creek, an east branch of Holston, in Jefferson county. Its mouth is near McBee's ferry, and the corners of Knox, Grainger, Jefferson, Sevier and Blount counties.

Cross Plains, a post office in Robertson county, twelve miles east from Springfield, where the road from Gallatin to Springfield crosses the road from Nashville to Franklin, Kentucky. At this place there is a store, tavern, &c.

Crooked Creek, a branch of Obion, in Henry and Carroll counties.

Crooked Creek, a branch of Loosa Hatchee, in Shelby county.

Crooked Creek, a north branch of the Clear Fork of Cumberland, which rises near Jamestown, in Fentress county.

Crooked Fork, a north branch of Emry, in Morgan county.

---

[117] Discontinued. Not to be confused with the existing town and post office in Franklin County.

[118] Discontinued as a post office.

[119] Crab Orchard is a town and post office in the eastern section of Cumberland County (established in 1855).

Cub Creek, a south branch of Big Hatchee, below Bolivar in Hardeman county.

Cub Creek, a north branch of Cumberland, in Stewart county.

Cullen, a post town in Weakley county, 108 miles W. from Nashville.[120]

Cumberland Gap, a distributing post office, situated in a gap of that name (where the States of Virginia, Kentucky, and Tennessee join, and where the great western road passes) in the corner of Claiborne county.

Cumberland Mountains, one of the ridges of the Appalachian chain, and the continuation in Virginia, Kentucky, and Tennessee of the Laurel mountains of Penn. As a separate ridge, Cumberland mountain distinctly commences S. W. from the great Sandy river, and following a direction of nearly S. W., separates Kentucky from Virginia, and entering Tennessee, traverses this State, and entering Alabama, crosses Tennessee river, and gradually terminates in the north part of Alabama. The ridge is about thirty miles broad, and enlarges in Tennessee to the width of fifty miles. In one place there is a ledge of rocks, near the summit, thirty miles long, with a perpendicular front to the S. E. of about 200 feet. Claiborne, Campbell, Anderson, Morgan, Fentress, Roane, Bledsoe, Overton, White, Rhea, Hamilton, Warren, Franklin, and Marion are the principal mountain counties in this State. The principal mountain, ranges through the State in an oblique direction from N. E. to S. W. between longitudes 7° and 9° W.

Cumberland River, this noble stream rises on the western slopes of Cumberland mountain, and flows westwardly through Harlan, Knox, Whitly, Wayne, Pulaski, Cumberland, and Monroe counties, Kentucky; then turns to the south-west, and enters this State, through which it runs by a general western course, though curving considerably to the south. After having traversed or bounded the counties of Overton,

---

[120] Discontinued as a post office.

Jackson, Smith, Sumner, Wilson, Davidson, Dickson, Robertson, Montgomery, and Stewart, it turns nearly north, and re-enters Kentucky, passing through the counties of Trigg, Christian, Caldwell, and Livingston, and finally enters the Ohio river, eleven miles above the mouth of Tennessee.. The Cumberland, by a comparative course, flows in upper Kentucky 220 miles, in this State 170, and in lower Kentucky fifty. Having an entire comparative course of 440 miles, upwards of 350 of which are navigable at all seasons. The principal towns on this river are Smithland, Eddyville, Dover, Palmyra, Clarksville, Nashville, Haysboro', Cairo, Carthage, Williamsburg, Ten., Burkesville, Williamsburg, Ky., Barboursville, and Mount Pleasant. Steamboats may ascend as high as Burkesville, Ky., in a good stage of water, but they do not often venture higher than Carthage, at the mouth of the Caney Fork.

Cypress Creek, a branch of Big Hatchie, which rises in Haywood county, and flowing west, enters the river, on the east border of Tipton county.

Cypress Creek, a north branch of Tennessee river, which rises in the south part of Wayne County, and joins the river at the town of Florence, in the State of Alabama.[131]

Cypress Creek, an east branch of Tennessee river in Perry county, between Lick and Marsh creeks, opposite to Perryville, and the mouth of Beech river.

Cypress Creek, a west branch of Tennessee, in Humphreys county, which enters the river opposite to Reynoldsburg.[132]

---

[131] There is a town and post office called "Cypress Inn" in the southern part of Wayne County, near Cypress Creek.

[132] This Cypress Creek, tributary of the Tennessee, is in Benton County (established in 1835).

IV.

D

Daddy's Creek, a branch of Emery's river, rising in the north part of Bledsoe county. It joins the river west of Spencer's Hill, in Morgan county, is a beautiful stream, and flows through a romantic country; and its banks are clad with white, and yellow pines.[123]

Daly's, a post office in Montgomery county, 48 miles from Nashville.[124]

Dallas, the seat of justice of Hamilton county, situated on the west bank of Tennessee river. It was established in 1832, and contains about 200 inhabitants, one lawyer, two doctors, four stores, two taverns, a blacksmiths' shop, &c. It is about 150 miles S. E. from Nashville.[125]

Damascus, a small town near the mouth of Goose creek, in Sumner county, adjoining the village of Hartsville.[126]

Dancy's a post office, in Haywood county, established in 1833.[127]

Dandridge, the seat of justice of Jefferson county, situated on the right bank of French Broad river, on the road from Knoxville to Greenville, 45 miles from the former place. It was laid out in the year 1792, on the land of Francis Dean, and established in 1799. It contains about 300 inhabitants, three lawyers, three doctors, two divines, one academy, two schools, four stores, two taverns, four blacksmiths, one bricklayer, two carpenters, three cabinet makers, one painter, one hatter, two tailors, two shoemakers, one saddler, two tanners,

---

[123] Daddy's Creek rises in Bledsoe County; its principal course is through Cumberland County, and it empties into Obed River (in Morgan County), a tributary of the Emery River.

[124] Discontinued as a post office.

[125] In 1838, the seat of Hamilton County was removed from Dallas to the faster-growing town of Chattanooga. Dallas is no longer a post office and has lost its corporate existence.

[126] Damascus has no distinct identity today; it is a suburb of Hartsville, in Trousdale County.

[127] Discontinued. The town, now known as Dancyville, is on the southern border of Haywood County.

one wagonmaker and one wheelwright. It is 245 miles east from Nashville and 497 S. W. from Washington City; lat. 35° 56' N., lon. 6° 20' W.

Danville, a village, in Warren county, near the Rutherford county line, between Readyville and McMinnville.[128]

Davidson, a county in Middle Tennessee, bounded on the north by Robertson, on the north east by Sumner, on the east by Wilson and Rutherford, south by Williamson and west by Dickson; length 26, mean width 24, area about 630 square miles. The surface is rather uneven, but the soil is generally excellent and under a high state of cultivation. This county was erected as early as 1783 by the state of North Carolina, and then included "all that part of this state lying west of Cumberland mountain and south of the Virginia line, beginning on the top of Cumberland mountain, where the Virginia line crosses, extending westward along said line, to the Tennessee river, thence up said river to the mouth of Duck river, thence up Duck river to where the line of marked trees run by the commissioners for laying off land, granted the Continental Line of this state intersects said river, (which said line is supposed to be in 35° 50' north latitude,) thence east along said line to the top of Cumberland Mountain, thence northwardly along said mountain to the beginning."

In 1786 the county of Sumner was erected from it, and sundry alterations of the boundaries were afterwards made. In 1796, John M'Nairy, Andrew Jackson, James Robertson, Thomas Hardeman and Joel Lewis, represented this county in the convention which formed the constitution of the state. In 1820, Davidson contained a population of 20,154, of which 7,899 were slaves and 189 free persons of color. Population in 1830, 15,988 whites, 11,629 slaves, and 472 free blacks—total 28,089.

Cumberland river flows from east to west through this county, past the city of Nashville, the seat of justice for the county, and capital of the state. The other principal streams

---

[128] Danville was originally the name of the present Woodbury, seat of justice of Cannon County (established in 1836).

DEF   143

are White's, Mansker's, Poplar and Sycamore creeks on the north, and Stone's river, Mill creek and Harpeth on the south.

Davidsonville, a post office in Bedford county established in 1833.[129]

Davidson's Bluff, a noted bluff on the north side of Obion river, below the Mouth of North Fork, in Obion county.

Davidson's Creek, a north branch of Obion river, in Obion county, flowing past the town of Troy.

Davis' Mills, a post office in Bedford county, 45 miles S. from Nashville.[130]

Davisville, a small village in Bedford county, on a branch of Duck river, containing three or four families, one store and one physician.

Decatur, a town at the mouth of Tellico, on the little Tennessee river, established in 1820 on the land of John Lowry, below old Fort Loudon.

Defeated Creek, a north branch of Cumberland river, near the line of Smith and Jackson counties, between Carthage and Williamsburg. This creek took its name from a defeat of John Peyton and his party, consisting of his brothers, Ephraim and Thomas Peyton, John Frazer and Squire Grant, in the year 1786. The Indians, about sixty in number, led on by the Fool Warrior, a distinguished Cherokee chief attacked the camp, (situated on a little island just above the mouth of a spring branch, a short distance below where the old Fort Blount road crosses said creek) in the night, during a deep snow, shot a ball through and broke the arm and shoulder of John Peyton. Thomas Peyton was shot through the thigh, Frazier through the leg, and Grant through the knee. Ephraim Peyton escaped without a wound from the Indians, but sprained his ancle in running through the creek. In this naked and mangled condition, these five hardy veterans had to grope their way in crusted snow through a pathless wilderness of cane clad mountains alone, (for no two ever came together) for four days, before they reached the habitation of civilized man—bare-headed, bare-footed, without food, fire,

---
[129-130] Discontinued as a post office.

or any garment except a shirt and pantaloons, marking the desert with their blood. Notwithstanding their situation, they all arrived safely at Bledsoe's Lick, a distance of about 70 miles by the circuitous route they came, recovered of their wounds and fought many Indian battles in defence of the women and children of the frontier. John Peyton, from whom the compiler obtained the above facts, died at his residence on Station Camp, in Sumner county, in 1833, in the 78th year of his age.

Defeated Creek, a north branch of Duck river, in Hickman county, opposite to the town of Centerville.

Deep Spring, a post office in Monroe county, 164 miles S. E. from Nashville.[131]

Delphi, a post town in Marion county, 129 miles S. E. from Nashville, on Farmer's Creek, on the road from Pikeville to Jasper.[132]

Denmark, a post town in Madison county, 163 miles from Nashville, S. W. from Jackson on the road to Estanaula and Sommerville; incorporated in 1831.

Denton, a post office in White county, established in 1833.[133]

Desha's Creek, a west branch of Bledsoe's creek, N. E. of Gallatin, in Sumner county, on which are some excellent mills. The land along this creek is of the first quality, and under a high state of improvement.

Dickson, a county in Middle Tennessee, bounded on the south by Hickman, on the west by Humphreys, on the N. W. by Stewart, on the North by Montgomery, on the northeast by Robertson, and on the east by Davidson and Williamson. Surface, hilly in general, soil but of an inferior quality. This county was erected October 25, 1803, from Robertson and Montgomery; its N. E. corner touches the Cumberland river. The dividing ridge between the Cumberland and Tennessee rivers passes through this county. The principal waters of the

---

[131] Discontinued as a post office.

[132] Delphi, discontinued as a post office, is in Sequatchie County (established in 1857).

[133] Discontinued as a post office.

Cumberland, which rise in this county are Trumbull and Jones' creeks, (branches of Harpeth) Barton's creek, Budd's creek, Yellow and Guise's creeks. And Pine, Cedar, Spring, Eaton's and Blue creeks, which empty into Duck, a branch of Tennessee river.

There is a great deal of Iron ore in this county, and it is extensively worked. In 1820 the population of Dickson was 3,961 whites, 1,305 slaves and 24 free negroes, total 5,190; population in 1830 was 7,260.—Seat of justice, Charlotte; cent. lat. 36° 10′ N., lon. 10° 30′ W.

Dixon's Springs, a noted place in Smith county, on the road from Gallatin to Carthage, at which there is a post office and two or three stores. It is fifty miles N. of E. from Nashville.

Dixon's Creek, a north branch of Cumberland, in Smith county, above Goose, and below Peyton's creek. The land on this creek is first rate and very well improved.[134]

Dodson's Creek, a south east branch of Holston in Hawkins county, nearly opposite to Rogersville.

Doe Creek, a branch of the Tennessee river, in the N. W. corner of Hardeman county, below White Oak creek.[135]

Doe Creek, a branch of Calf-killer, in White county.

Doe or Elk Creek, a south branch of Watauga in Carter county.

Doe River, a post office in Carter county, established in 1833.[136]

Dover, the seat of justice of Stewart county, beautifully situated on the left bank of the Cumberland river. It was established as the seat of justice in 1811. It contains about 225 inhabitants, one academy, one lawyer, two doctors, two blacksmiths, one bricklayer, five or six carpenters, one cabinet maker, one hatter, two saddlers, one shoemaker, two tailors,

---

[134] Dixon's Creek rises in Macon County, flows through Trousdale County; its mouth is in Smith County.

[135] Not identified: all of Hardeman County is drained by the tributaries of the Mississippi River; not the Tennessee. White Oak Creek rises in McNairy County and flows through Hardin County to the Tennessee River.

[136] Possibly Doeville, in Johnson County (P.O., Butler).

one tanner, one carding machine and one steam saw and grist mill. It is thirty-five miles below Clarksville, eighty miles N. W. from Nashville and 787 W. S. W. from Washington city. Lat. 36° 35′ N., long. 10° 45′ W.

Drake's Creek, a north branch of Cumberland, in Sumner county, between Station camp and Mansker's creeks, ten miles west of Gallatin. It rises near the Kentucky line and flows south, past the town of Hendersonville, and through a body of rich land.

Dresden, the seat of Justice of Weakley county, situated near the centre. It contains about 400 inhabitants, one academy, three lawyers, two doctors, two blacksmiths, two bricklayers, four carpenters, one cabinet maker, one gunsmith, two hatters, two saddlers, two shoemakers, one silversmith, two tanners, one tinner, two tailors, one wagonmaker, one Tavern, one school and one church.

It is 144 miles N. of W. from Nashville and 850 W. by S. from Washington city. Lat. 36° 15′ N., long. 11° 45′ W.

Dry Creek, an east branch of Tennessee river, in Hardin county, which has its junction near the Bigbend-shoals.

Dry Creek, a west branch of Cumberland, in Davidson county, which crosses the Gallatin road.

Duck River, an east branch of Tennessee. It rises in the mountains near the line of Marion county, and pursues a comparative course of 150 miles W. N. W. through the counties of Franklin, Bedford, Maury, Hickman, Williamson, Dickson and Humphreys, passing the towns of Shelbyville, Columbia and Centerville. It is navigable for boats following the bends, about 100 miles. It is declared a public high way as high as Shelbyville. Its northern branches are Fox creek, East, Middle and Watrace forks, Jones' and Fall creeks, North fork, Wilson's creek, Cane spring creek, Flat, Burford's, Warrance, Wyman's, Lick, Pine, Cedar-spring, Green's and Blue creeks; and its principal south branches are, Powell's, Sinking, Rock, Cedar, Sandy, L. Bigby, Cathey's, Swan, Indian, and Beaver dam creeks; and Buffalo river.

Duck River Furnace, a post office in Hickman county, established in 1833.[137]

Dugger's Ferry, a post office in Carter county. Late *Julius'.*[138]

Dukedom, a post office in Weakley county, established in 1833.[139]

Dumpling Creek, a north branch of French Broad, in Sevier county, which rises in Jefferson, West of Dandridge.

Duncan's, a post office in Hardeman county, 190 miles S. W. from Nashville.[140]

Durhamsville, the name of a post office at the house of Thomas Durham Esq., on the road from Fulton to Brownsville, at which place there are two stores, blacksmith shop, cotton gin, &c. It is near the western boundary line of Tipton county, in a fine neighborhood.[141]

Dyer, a county in West Tennessee, bounded on the north by Obion, on the east by Gibson, on the south by Tipton and Haywood counties, and on the West by Mississippi river. This county is well watered by the river Obion on the north, and Forked Deer on the south. Seat of Justice Dyersburg. Population in 1830, was 1,904; cent. lat. 36° N., long. 12° 20′ W.

Dyersburg, the seat of justice of Dyer county, situated on the north bank of the north fork of Forked Deer, at its great northern bend nearly in the centre of the county, and due west from Trenton. It contains 100 inhabitants, one lawyer, one doctor, two stores, two taverns, two carpenters, one bricklayer, two tailors, one shoemaker, one blacksmith, &c. Distant from Nashville 168 miles, from Washington city 882.

Dyer's Creek, a north branch of Cumberland in Stewart county, opposite Dover.

---

[137] Duck River, in Hickman County.

[138] Discontinued as a post office.

[139] Dukedom, a post office, lies on the Kentucky line, in Weakley County.

[140] Discontinued as a post office.

[141] In Lauderdale County; mail service through Ripley.

E

Eagle Creek, a south branch of Obey's river, in Overton county.

East Fork, the designation of a branch of Duck river, in the north east corner of Bedford county.

East Fork, one of the main branches of Stone's river, which rises in Warren county, and joins the West Fork at the town of Jefferson, in Rutherford county, N. W. of Murfreesboro.'

East Fork, a large branch of Obid's river, which flows through the north east corner of Fentress county.

East Liberty, a post office in Marion county, 138 miles S. E. from Nashville.[142]

Eaton, a post office in Gibson county, S. of W. from Trenton, on the Middle Fork.[143]

Eaton's Creek, a north branch of Duck river, which rises in Dickson, and joins the river on the line of Hickman and Perry counties.

Eaton's Creek, a north branch of Embree's river, east of Walden's ridge, which rises in Anderson county and has its confluence in Roane county, N. W. of Kingston.

Edward's Fork, a branch of Indian creek, in Washington county.

Effingham, a post office in Bedford county, on the route from Harpeth to Shelbyville, 58 miles S. of E. from Nashville.[144]

Egnew's Creek, a branch of Weakley's creek in Giles county, west of Pulaski.

Elizabethton, a post town, and the seat justice, of Carter county, on the left bank of Watauga river, 130 miles above Knoxville, 275 miles east from Nashville and 449 from Washington city, in lat. 36° 18′ N., lon. 5° 18′ W. It was established in 1799 on the land of Samuel Tipton. In 1833, it

---

[142] Discontinued as a post office.

[143] Eaton, in the west of Gibson County, lies on the Crockett County line.

[144] Discontinued as a post office.

contained 176 inhabitants, one academy, one church, one lawyer, two doctors, two blacksmiths, one cabinet maker, two carpenters, two hatters, three stores, two shoemakers, one saddler, three tailors, one tinner, one grist mill and one set of iron works.

Elk River, a north branch of Tennessee river, which rises on the western slope of the Cumberland mountains, near the corners of Warren, Bledsoe, Franklin and Marion counties; and flowing S. W. by W. through Franklin, Lincoln and Giles, past the towns of Winchester, Fayetteville and Elkton, enters Alabama in Limestone county, over which it meanders and falls into the river at the Muscle Shoals, in the N. E. angle of Lauderdale county. Entire comparative course, about 100 miles; declared navigable as high up as Fayetteville, or mouth of Mulberry creek, Lincoln county.

Elk Fork, a large northern branch of Red river, which rises near Elkton, in Todd county, Ken., enters this state in Robertson, and joins the river three miles from the N. E. corner of Montgomery county. It is one of the best streams for propelling mills in that part of the country.

Elkin's Branch, a small stream, which empties into Big Hatchee, a few miles above Bolivar, in Hardeman county.

Elkton, a post town in Giles county, on the right bank of Elk river, 101 miles from Nashville, 80 from Murfreesboro', 30 north from Huntsville, Ala.

Elkridge, a post office in Giles county, 91 miles south from Nashville.[146]

Elk Creek, a south branch of Cumberland, in Stewart county.

Elk or Doe Creek, a south branch of Watauga, in Carter county, which joins the river below Elizabethton.

Elliott's Branch, a small stream which empties into the Cumberland, three miles south of Gallatin, in Sumner county. Above the mouth of this creek, is Wood's Ferry, Boyer's warehouse and tobacco inspection, being the steamboat landing and port of shipment for the town of Gallatin.

---
[146] Discontinued as a post office.

EVA 151

Ellis' Creek, a north branch of Holston, in Hawkins county.

Embree's or Emery's River, a considerable stream which rises in Morgan county, and running a S. E. course, bends around Spencer's Hill, and falls into Clinch river above the town of Kingston, in Roane county. It receives Obed's, Crab Orchard and Daddy's creeks on the south, and Crooked creek on the north.

Embree's Ironworks, a furnace and forge in Washington county, the property of Elijah Embree, Esq. The furnace is in Bumpass cove, near Nolachucky river, the forge is immediately on the river, three miles below the furnace.

Embree's Ironworks, a post office in Roane county, 141 miles S. of E. from Nashville.[146]

English's Creek, a small branch of Tennessee river, above Savannah, in Hardin county.

Enon's Creek, a branch of Rutherford's creek, in Maury county.

Estanaula, a town, in the south west corner of Haywood county, on the N. E. bank of Big Hatchee river, 181 miles S. W. from Nashville.

Estanallee Creek, a north branch of Hiwassee river in McMinn county. It flows past the town of Athens, and joins the river near the town of Calhoun.

Evans' X Roads, a post office in Williamson county, 32 miles South from Nashville.[147]

[146-147] Discontinued as a post office.

153

F

Factor's Fork, a branch of Chisholm's fork, of Shoals creek, in Lawrence county.

Fall Creek, a north branch of Watauga, in Sullivan county.

Fall Creek, a north east branch of Stone's river, in Wilson and Rutherford counties.

Fall Creek, a north branch of Duck river, in Bedford county, below Shelbyville.

Fall Creek, a south branch of Clinch, in the west end of Grainger county.

Fall Creek, a branch of White's creek, in Rhea county. Four miles and a half east of the Crab Orchard, on the Knoxville road, this creek falls 160 feet; the sheet of water is about six feet wide.[148]

Fallingwater, a north east branch of the Caney Fork of Cumberland, in White county. This stream has its source in the Cumberland mountains, and is about thirty miles long. Seven or eight miles above its junction with the Caney Fork, is the celebrated cascade, which gives name to the creek. "In the course of one mile, the descent is supposed to be three hundred feet. The large fall is a perpendicular descent of water of the depth of two hundred feet, or as some think one hundred and fifty. The country on both sides of the stream, both above and below the fall, is nearly as level as the adjacent country generally; and what is very remarkable, the only difference, in the aspect of the country, as produced by the falls, appears to consist in the depth of the channel, which would seem to have been an excavation out of the solid rock. The perpendicular height of the clifts on each side of the stream, is about three hundred feet. The bottom of the channel below the falls, is almost inaccessible for many miles below the falls, and the descent to it is difficult and even

[148] The spectacular fall of this Fall Creek is at Ozone, in the eastern section of Cumberland County (established in 1855). Fall Creek joins White's Creek at the northern tip of Rhea County. (Not to be confused with Fall Creek and Fall Creek State Park in Van Buren County.)

154 FAL

dangerous. The width of the sheet of water which falls from the rock is about eighty feet, and produces a noise which can be heard for several miles." This is the account given of these falls by Judge Haywood, and it is said to be substantially correct. I have conversed with several gentlemen who have visited them, as well as the falls of Calf-killer and Taylor's creeks, and their descriptions agree with those given by Judge Haywood, in his Natural and Aboriginal History of Tennessee. Mr. Rhea marks this fall at *sixty feet*.[149]

Fallingwater Creek, a north west branch of the Hiwassee river, one mile below Chickamauga, in Hamilton county.

Farmington, a post town, in Bedford county, situated on the main road leading from Nashville to Huntsville. It contains two stores, two taverns, four or five workshops and fifty or sixty inhabitants.[150]

Fayette, a county in West Tennessee, bounded on the east by Hardeman, on the north by Haywood and Tipton, on the west by Shelby county, and on the south by the state of Mississippi. It is about 25 miles square and contains three towns, viz: Sommerville, (the seat of justice) Lagrange and Moscow. Wolf river, Loosa, Hatchee and Big creek, are the principal streams which water this county.

Although this county was only erected in 1823, it has improved very rapidly, and will soon take rank with the best counties in the district. The soil is productive of corn, cotton and the various kinds of grain which usually flourish in this latitude, and the vine flourishes admirably. Population in 1830, 8,654; cent. lat. 35° 10′ N., lon. 12° 20′ W.

Fayetteville, the seat of justice of the county of Lincoln. It was established in 1809, and incorporated in 1819 and 1825; and its population in 1833 was about 800. It contains two academies, two blacksmiths, one bricklayer, three

---

[149] The principal course of the Falling Water River is in Putnam County (established in 1854); the river debouches into Center Hill Lake near the eastern boundary of DeKalb County (created in 1837).

[150] Farmington is a town north of Lewisburg, in Marshall County (established in 1836).

churches, three carpenters, three cabinet makers, two cotton gins, one carding machine, four physicians, two clergymen, three hatters, nine lawyers, one printing office, one painter, one saddler, two shoemakers, three tailors, one tavern, and one wagonmaker. It is thirty miles north from Huntsville, 73 S. from Nashville, and 722 S. W. from Washington City. Lat. 35° 10′ N., lon. 9° 37′ W.

Felicity, a post office in McMinn county, formerly Holt's Store.[161]

Fentress, a mountain county, on the east border of Middle Tennessee. It is bounded on the east and south by Morgan, on the west by Overton, and on the north by the state of Kentucky. It is in a triangular form, and contains about 625 square miles. Nearly two thirds of the county lies on the Cumberland mountains, which range from N. E. to S. W. The soil on the mountains is sandy but clear of rock, and presenting a gentle undulating surface, covered with pine, hickory and chestnut timber. Springs of free-stone water abound, and are mostly of the kind called boiling springs, throw up a clear white sand, and are considered entirely free from any impurities. Below the mountain the face of the country is hilly, but the soil is fertile and covered with every variety of timber common to the western country. Iron ore, coal, and salt petre, can be had in abundance, and lead has been found in several places, but there has been no means used to discover the extent of the mines; alum, copperas and borax are said to abound. A mineral spring, resembling the White Sulphur spring in Virginia, has been discovered in the Poplar cove, five and a half miles from Jamestown. There is an Oil spring on Wolf river, and the oil is said to be very efficacious for burns, &c. A bed of paint, equal, if not superior, to Spanish brown, but of rather a deeper color, has been found near Obed's river. The staples are corn, hogs, cattle and horses, to which may be added, spirits of turpentine, tar, rosin and lampblack, which are manufactured in

---

[161] Discontinued as a post office; the community, a thriving town and post office, now bears the felicitous name of Etowah.

considerable quantities on the mountains. The county and seat of justice (Jamestown) were named in honor of James Fentress, late speaker of the House of Representatives. The first settlement was made at Jamestown in 1827. On the first of June 1830, Fentress contained 2,760 souls.

Firey-Gizzard Creek, a branch of Battle creek, in Marion county.

Five Mile Creek, an east branch of Clinch, above Kingston, in Roane county.

Flat Creek, a N. branch of Holston river, which rises in Grainger county, W. of Rutledge, and east of House mountain, and has its mouth in the east end of Knox county. It crosses the E. and W. road at Mynatt's.

Flat Creek, a north branch of Duck river, on the east side of Maury county, below Cane Spring creek.[152]

Flat Creek, a post office in Bedford county, established in 1833.[153]

Fleming's, a post office, in Weakley county, 130 miles W. from Nashville.[154]

Fletcher's Creek, a tributary of Red river, in Montgomery county.

Flinn's Creek, a south east branch of Cumberland, in Jackson county, below Old Fort Blount.[155]

Forked Deer, a navigable river, in West Tennessee. It has three main forks, designated *North, Middle and South Forks.* The largest is South Fork, which is declared navigable as high up as the mouth of Clark's creek. South Fork takes its rise in McNairy and Henderson counties, and by a south west course, flows through Madison, past the town of Jackson, thence through the N. E. corner of Haywood, into the centre of Dyer, where it joins the united streams of North and

---

[152] Flat Creek rises in Williamson County, and flows through Marshall and Maury counties to the Duck River.

[153] No longer a post office, but a sizeable community in the southeast section of Bedford County.

[154] Discontinued as a post office; mail through Shelbyville.

[155] Nearby is a community now known as Flynn's Lick.

FRA 157

Middle Forks; thence a S. W. direction 'till it joins the Mississippi river above the first Chickasaw Bluff, in lat. 35° 42′ N., lon. 12° 55′ W. Its general breadth is from thirty to forty yards, and depth from three to twelve feet, and is navigable about one hundred miles above Brownsville, in a common stage of water. Its bottoms are fertile, and about one quarter of a mile wide. See *North and Middle Forks.*

Forked Deer, a post office, in Tipton county, established in 1833.[166]

Fort Blount, a post office, in Jackson county, 64 miles N. of E. from Nashville (late Williamsburg.)[167]

Fort Pickering, an old fort at Chickasaw Bluff, one mile below where Memphis now stands.

Fountain Creek, a south branch of Duck river, in Maury county.

Fountain of Health, a post office, in Davidson county, near the Hermitage, on the road from Nashville to Lebanon. Here is a sulpher spring, and a house of entertainment kept by Mr. Saunders.[168]

Fountain Head, a post office, in Sumner county near the Kentucky line, thirty-four miles N. E. from Nashville.[169]

Fourth Creek, a north branch of Holston, in Knox county, between Third and Sinking creeks, west of Knoxville.

Fox Creek, a north branch of Elk river, in the N. W. corner of Franklin county, near the line of Lincoln.

Fox Creek, a south branch of Holston, in the S. W. corner of Hawkins county, between Jones' and Fall creeks.

Franklin, a county in Middle Tennessee, adjoining the mountains. It is bounded south by Alabama, west by Lincoln, N. W. by Bedford, N. E. by Warren, and E. by Marion

---

[166] Discontinued as a post office.

[167] Fort Blount (Williamsburg) was the first seat of justice of Jackson County. The community survives; the post office has been discontinued.

[168] Discontinued as a post office; near the present Donelson.

[169] A community in the northwest portion of Sumner County; discontinued as a post office; mail service through Portland.

county. This county was erected in 1807 off the counties of Warren and Bedford. The surface is hilly, but the soil is fertile and well watered by the numerous branches of Elk river, which traverse a great portion of the county. The towns are, Winchester, (the seat of justice,) Hillsboro', and Salem. Population in 1820, 16,577, of which 4,167 were slaves. Population in 1830, 15,644, being a decrease of 1,133. Cent. lat. 35° 13' N., long. 9° w.

Franklin, the seat of justice of Williamson county, situated on the S. W. bank of Big Harpeth river. It was laid off on the land of Abraham Maury, established in 1799, and incorporated in 1815. In 1833, it contained about 1,500 inhabitants: 5 academies, 3 male and 2 female; 4 churches, 3 clergymen, 8 physicians, 7 lawyers, 4 taverns, 5 blacksmiths, 6 bricklayers, 10 carpenters, 1 cabinet maker, 1 gunsmith, 2 hatters, 3 saddlers, 4 shoemakers, 3 silversmiths, 3 tailors, 2 tanners, 1 tinner, 2 wagonmakers, 13 stores, 1 extensive cotton factory, one carding machine, and one printing office. It is 18 miles from Nashville, S. by the turnpike road, 23 N. E. from Columbia, 23 S. E. from Charlotte, and 732 W. S. W. from Washington city. Lat. 35° 55' N., long. 9° 45' W.

French Broad, one of the sources of Tennessee river. It rises in South Carolina, and crossing the western part of North Carolina, enters Tennessee through a breach in the mountain, on the line of Cocke and Greene counties. After passing through Cocke, *via* Newport, receives Big Pigeon on the south, and Nolachucky on the north; it then turns west, and traverses part of Jefferson, Sevier, and Knox, and joins the Holston 25 miles above Knoxville. It is navigable for boats as high up as the mouth of Nolachucky.

About thirty miles from the mouth of this river, on its margin, 5¼ miles from the Tennessee line, and 32 miles from Ashville, in Buncombe county, N. C. are the celebrated WARM SPRINGS. The waters are of a temperature of 94° to 104°, and are beneficial in cases of palsy, rheumatism, cutaneous affections, &c. The country around is moutainous and healthy, and abounds in romantic scenery, rendering the springs an agreeable resort for the invalid, as well as the gay and the healthful.

French Lick, a noted sulphur spring in the lower suburbs of Nashville. See *Nashville*.

Fulton, a post town in Tipton county. It is beautifully situated at the first Chickasaw bluff on the east bank of the Mississippi river, 18 miles N. W. from Covington. It was laid off and sold in 1827, by a company of speculators who sold the lots at high prices and abandoned the place. That spring and summer the town seemed to flourish, but the fall proving unhealthy many died and others left the place, since which time it has ceased to improve and business is in a great degree stopped. This town, notwithstanding, possesses some advantages, it has a claim to a good share of the Hatchee trade, being only three miles above the upper mouth of Hatchee, which is navigable the principal part of the boating season. And boating can be performed as cheap, and with as much despatch from this place up the Hatchee, as from Randolph, and there is a good road leading out to Brownsville, in Haywood county. Fulton has proved healthy for the last four years, and it contains about half a dozen families. It is 218 miles, W. from Nashville, and 926 from Washington city.[100]

[100] The once flourishing town of Fulton (now in Lauderdale County) consists only of a general store (including a post office, branch of Henning) and a few dwellings.

G

Gainesboro', a post town and seat of justice of Jackson county, on Doe creek, a half mile above the mouth of Roaring river. It was established in 1817, and incorporated in 1820, and named in honor of General E. P. Gaines. It is eighty miles N. from Nashville. It contains a court house and jail, one lawyer and three stores.

Gallatin, a flourishing post town and seat of justice of Sumner county; it is situated on a small branch of Station Camp creek, three miles north of Cumberland river. It was established by an act of the Legislature, Nov. 6, 1801, and incorporated Nov. 7, 1815. It contains a good court house, jail and public offices, a large brick church (free for all denominations of christians, a Cumberland Presbyterian church, a Masonic hall, a printing office, twelve stores, two taverns, eleven lawyers, four physicians, one cabinet-shop, one chair-factory, three tailor's-shops, two shoemaker's-shops, two saddler's-shops, one wagon-maker, one tanyard, one tinner and copper-smith, three blacksmith's-shops, one hatter, one male and two female academies, 666 inhabitants of which 234 were blacks; thirty-five log, thirty-eight frame and twenty-seven brick houses, on the first day of June, 1830. It is 680 miles S. W. from Washington city, twenty-five N. E. from Nashville, twenty-eight E. from Springfield, and thirty-five W. from Carthage, in lat. 36° 16' N., long. 9° 18' from Washington city. The mail stages between Lexington and Nashville pass and repass three times a week, and the eastern stage to Carthage arrives and departs semi-weekly.—The Steam boat landing is at the mouth of Elliott's branch, or Boyer's Warehouse, three miles south from the town.

Garrett's Factory, a post office in Giles county, established in 1833.[161]

Garrison Creek, a western branch of Tennessee river, which empties in at the old Military station, opposite the mouth of Hiwassee river, on the south line of Rhea county.

[161] Discontinued as a post office.

German's Creek, a north branch of Holston river, in Grainger county.

Gibson, a county in West Tennessee, established in 1823. It is bounded on the N. by Weakley and Obion, on the S. by Madison and Haywood, on the E. by Carroll, and on the W. by Dyer. Rutherford's Fork of Obion, and the north and middle forks of Forked Deer, are its principal water courses. It contains an area of about 630 square miles. Seat of justice Trenton. Population in 1830, 5,801.

Gideonsville, a town in Bedford county, on the road from Nashville to Huntsville. It contains one store, two groceries, three taverns, four or five work-shops, and about forty inhabitants.[102]

Giles, a county in Middle Tennessee, established in 1809. It is bounded on the north by Maury, on the east by Lincoln, on the west by Lawrence, and on the south by the state of Alabama. It contains an area of 625 square miles, and four flourishing villages, viz: Pulaski, the seat of justice, Upper Elkton, Lower Elkton, and Cornersville. Its principal water courses are Elk river and Richland a fork of Elk, both of which are navigable during the winter and spring; and the whole county is exceedingly well watered. The face of the country is broken, but the quality of the soil in point of depth and fertility, is not exceeded by any in the state, and is similar to that of Maury, Williamson and Davidson, but more celebrated for the production of *cotton;* corn and tobacco, are also raised in great abundance, and wheat flourishes as well as in any county west of the Cumberland mountains. The inhabitants are wealthy and enterprising, generally. The presbyterian, cumberland presbyterian, baptist and methodist, are the most numerous denominations of christians. Population in 1820, 12,558; in 1830, 18,920. Cent. lat. 35° 12′ N., long. 10. W.

Gillum's, a post office in Sumner county, established in

---

[102] The present-day Chapel Hill, a post office in the northern part of Marshall County.

1833.[143]

Glazebrook's, a post office in Warren county, established in 1833.[144]

Globe Creek, a branch of Fountain creek, in Maury county.

Goodfield, an eastern branch of Tennessee river, in Rhea county, south of Washington;—A *post office* bearing the same name is kept at McDonald's on said creek, 150 miles S. E. from Nashville.[145]

Goose Creek, a large creek in Sumner and Smith counties, which joins the Cumberland on the north; at Hartsville, in the S. E. corner of Sumner. The lands bordering this creek are generally good, and are under a high state of cultivation. In some situations the milk sickness abounds.[146]

Grainger, a county in East Tennessee, between Clinch and Holston rivers, erected in 1796; bounded by Jefferson S. E., Knox and Anderson S. W., Claiborne, N. W., and Hawkins N. E. It is about thirty miles long and fifteen or twenty wide, surface hilly and soil sterile, except along the margin of the streams. Poplation in 1820 was 6,796 whites, 655 slaves, and 199 free blacks, total 7,651. Population in 1830, 10,666. Seat of justice Rutledge. Cen. lat 36° 15′ N., long. 6° 50′ W.

Grantsboro', a town at the junction of Clinch and Powell's rivers, in Campbell county.[147]

Grassy Creek, a south branch of Holston river, in Hawkins county, opposite to Rogersville.

Gravesville, a town established on the land of Daniel Graves, in Knox county, in 1817, north of Knoxville, on the road to Tazewell.[148]

[143-144] Discontinued as a post office.

[145] The community of Goodfield, in Meigs County, has mail service through Decatur.

[146] Goose Creek rises in Macon County, flows through Trousdale County, and debouches into the Cumberland south of Hartsville.

[147] No longer a post office, but a community in southeastern Campbell County; mail service through LaFollette.

[148] Near the border of Knox and Union counties, at or near Graveston and Luttrell.

Grey's Creek, a north eastern branch of Big Hatchee, below Bolivar in Hardeman county.

Greene, a county in East Tennessee, bounded by North Carolina S. E., Cocke county S. W., Jefferson W., Hawkins N., Washington E.; Length thirty-two miles, mean width 22, area about 700 square miles. Surface diversified by mountain, hill and dale. The Nolachucky passes through the center of this county, and affords much good land. This county was erected from Washington in 1783, by the state of North Carolina, and in 1792 the boundaries were circumscribed; and again altered in 1799. French Broad touches the south boundary, and Lick creek the western border of the county. It contains the towns of Greenville the seat of justice, Warrensburg and Rheatown, and there is a post office at Greenville college. Population in 1820, was 11,324, of which 882 were slaves. In 1830, 14,418. Cen. lat. 36° N., Long. 11° 32′ W.

Green River, a south branch of Buffalo river, in Wayne county, flowing past the town of Waynesboro'.

Green Garden, a post office in Sumner county, three miles east from the Castalian Springs, thirty-six miles from Nashville.[169]

Green's Lick Creek, a south branch of Duck river, in Maury county, below Little Bigby.

Green-tree Grove, a post office in Stewart county, ninety-one mile from Nashville.[170]

Green Valley, a post office in Dickson county.[171]

Greenville, capital of Greene county, 75 miles east of Knoxville, 25 miles S. W. of Jonesborough, 25 miles from Newport, 43 miles from Dandridge; 500 inhabitants, 2 taverns, 4 stores, 3 physicians, 4 lawyers, 1 Presbyterian and 1 Methodist church, 1 large brick court house, 1 stone jail, a large spring of good limestone water at the east end of the town, which, about a quarter of a mile from its source, turns an overshot grist mill. Town and surrounding country very healthy.

[169-171] Discontinued as a post office.

Greenville College, a post office in Greene county, at Greenville college.[172]

Greenville College, a Seminary established by the Territorial legislature, Sep. 3, 1794, on the plantation of the Rev. Hezekiah Balch, in Greene county, south of Greenville, and founded chiefly by the exertions of that gentleman. He was President 'till 1810, when he was succeeded by Rev. Charles Coffin, D.D., who presided until 1827, when Henry Hoss, Esq., was elected, who is now in office. Yearly income $5,000. Volumes in the library 3,500. Students, in 1833 twenty-seven.

Greer's Fork, a branch of Indian creek, in Washington county.[173]

Grice's Creek, a south branch of Cumberland, in Stewart county, near Montgomery county line.

Guin's Creek, a branch of Obion, in Henry and Carroll counties.

---

[172] Greeneville College; the post office and college are both known today as Tusculum College.

[173] In Unicoi County (established in 1875).

H

Haggard, a post office in Fentress county, established in 1833.[174]

Hainsville, a town six or seven miles east from Savannah, in Hardin county, on the road leading to Waynesboro'.[175]

Half Pone, a north branch of Cumberland, in Montgomery county.

Hamilton, a county in East Tennessee, bounded north by Rhea, east by the Cherokee nation, south by the state line of Georgia within the Cherokee nation, and west by Marion and Bledsoe. About half the chartered limits lie within the Cherokee nation, and the white and red inhabitants are separated by the Tennessee river. No white settlements under the authority of the U. S. were made in this county until the 1st of January, 1820, and until the session of the legislature in 1819, it was part of Rhea county. Tennessee river enters this county through its N. E. boundary line, and runs in its general course nearly parallel with and about six miles distant from Walden's ridge of Cumberland mountain, 'till within about two miles of its southern boundary, (the Georgia state line) where it buts against the end of Lookout mountain; It then tacts to the north, and running that direction about seven miles, enters Marion county at the lower end of Tumbling shoals. There are numerous large creeks in this county which empty in on the N. W. side of Tennessee. The first of which is Sale, one mile below Rhea county, thence three miles to Rocky, four miles to Oppossum, three to Sauda, six to Little Chickamauga, one to Fallingwater, thence eleven miles to the mouth of Mountain creek, which empties in about four miles above the suck of the Tumbling shoals. At the old court house on the west bank of Tennessee, are some remains of antiquity, an old port enclosing about six acres. The face of the country from Walden's Ridge to the river, is composed of alternate hills and valleys. Cotton is the staple—corn, wheat, rye and oats, are raised in considerable abundance. Population in

[174-175] Discontinued as a post office.

1820, was 821, in 1830, 2,274. Seat of justice Dallas.

Hamlet, a post office in Stewart county, sixty-eight miles S. W. from Nashville.[176]

Hanna's, a post office in Sumner county, established in 1833.[177]

Hardin, a county on Tennessee river, below the Muscle shoals, on the line between Middle and West Tennessee. It is bounded on the north by Perry and Henderson, on the east by Wayne, on the west by McNairy, and south by the state of Alabama. It is twenty-eight miles long from north to south, and twenty-two and a half wide, containing 630 square miles. The first settlement within this county was made in 1816 by Col. James Hardin, and one or two other families near the mouth of Camp or Hardin's creek. The county was organized in 1819, and the first court was held at the house of Col. Hardin, near the mouth of Swift creek, being the temporary seat of justice. In 1822 it was removed and fixed at Hardinsville, where it remained until 1827, when it was permanently established at *Savannah*.

The Tennessee river runs through this county from south to north. It enters about ten miles east of the S. W. corner, and runs in a serpentine direction to the north, until it comes near the boundary; it then turns to the east and leaves the county at the north east corner, near the town of Carrollsville, in Wayne county. The navigation of the river is good from the foot of Big Bend shoals, (eleven miles, above Savannah) for steam boats, except in very low water, and for keel-boats at all seasons, to its mouth. It is narrower in this county than at any other place above, for the distance of 200 miles, being in many places not more than 250 yards wide; but its general width is about 400,--at Savannah it is 275. The face of the country is undulating, and in some places very broken. On the west the land is quite level. Every part of the county is well watered by never-failing springs of lime and free-stone water, and abundantly covered with all the varieties of timber, common in the western

[176-177] Discontinued as a post office.

country. The muscudine and various grapes are common. Limestone is plenty in some places, but not generally so. Millstone grit, iron ore, and dyestones are plenty. Sulphur, saltpetre, chalk and copperas, are found in many places, and a plenty of alum has been found at one place near Savannah. In this county are eleven cotton gins, five saw and nineteen grist mills, and two or three horse mills. Population in 1830, 4,875; in cent. lat. 35° 14' N., long. 11° 10' W.

Hardin's Creek, or Camp creek, rises in Wayne county, and running N. W. discharges its waters in the Tennessee, four miles below the mouth of Indian creek, in Hardin county.

Hardinsville, the former seat of justice of Hardin county.—Vacated.

Hardeman, a county in West Tennessee, erected in 1823. It is bounded on the north by Haywood and Madison, on the south by the state of Mississippi, on the east by McNairy, and on the west by Fayette; it is twenty-seven and a half miles in length N. and S., and twenty-three miles in width E. and W. This county is well watered by Big Hatchee and its tributaries. The Big Hatchee passes nearly through the center of the county from the S. E. to the N. W. corner, passing the town of Bolivar the seat of justice, and receiving on the N. E. side Little Hatchee, Wood's creek, Piney, Gray's, Mill and Clover creeks; on the S. W., Big Muddy, Porters, Cub, Clear, Hickory, Elkin's and Pleasantrun creeks. Loosa Hatchee and Wolf rivers head in the west side of this county. There are post offices at Middleberry, Warnerville and Cross Roads. About one third of the county, viz. the N. E. corner, is poor and hilly, the balance is generally thin timbered level barrens, admirably adapted to the culture of cotton. The first settlements were made in 1822 by William Polk and others. Population in 1830, 11,628.

Hardeman's X Roads, a post office in Williamson county, thirty-four miles from Nashville.[176]

Harpeth, a small river, which has its source in Bedford county, and flows north west through Williamson, past the

---
[176] Discontinued as a post office.

170   HAR

town of Franklin, enters Davidson, and falls into Cumberland river thirty-five miles below Nashville, after a general comparative course of sixty miles, receiving south Harpeth, Trumbull and Jones' creeks on the S. W. and Little Harpeth on the N. E.

Harpeth, a town in Williamson county.

Hartfield, a post office in Tipton county.[179]

Hartsville, a flourishing post town in the south east corner of Sumner county, near the junction of Goose creek with the Cumberland river, on the road from Gallatin to Carthage. It was established in 1817, on the land of James Hart. It contains twenty or thirty families, four stores, two taverns and sundry mechanics. It is eighteen miles east from Gallatin, ten from the Castalian springs, and forty-three from Nashville. Lat. 36° 16′ N., long. 9° 2′ W.[180]

Haskinsville, a town in Gibson county, 151 miles W. from Nashville.

Hatchee, the former seat of Justice of Hardeman county. See *Big Hatchee, Loosa Hatchee, and Little Hatchee* rivers.

Hawkins, a county in East Tennessee, erected in 1786, out of Sullivan, in 1792 the boundaries were circumscribed, and Knox and Jefferson were erected from it in 1796, Grainger was erected from Knox and Hawkins and in 1801, Claiborne was formed out of Hawkins and Grainger, leaving Hawkins 625 square miles. It is bounded by Virginia north, Sullivan county east, Greene and Jefferson south, Grainger west, and Claiborne north west. The surface is considerably broken by mountains and hills. There is a hill two and a half miles east of north from Rogersville, wholly composed of marble; white, grey and sometimes red. Also on the road eight miles west of Rogersville, and at the north of Bean's Station near the top of Clinch mountain. Holston river enters this county at Kingsport, and flows through it in a S. W. direction, and Clinch river waters its N. W. boundary. There are post offices

---

[179] Discontinued as a post office.

[180] Hartsville is now the seat of Trousdale County (established in 1870).

HAY   171

at Black water, New canton, Red bridge, Surgoinsville and Cheek's X Roads. Population in 1820, 10,949; in 1830, 13,683. Seat of Justice Rogersville. Cen. lat. 36° 20′ N., long. 6° W.

Haynes' a post office in Grainger county, 205 miles east from Nashville.[181]

Haysboro' a small town on the north bank of Cumberland river, six miles from Nashville, on the Lexington road, containing about a half dozen families.[182]

Hayes' Creek, a north branch of Harpeth in Williamson county.

Haywood, a county in West Tennessee, erected in 1823. It is bounded on the east by Madison, on the south by Hardeman, as far west as the inset, (5 miles) the balance (17 miles) by Fayette, on the west by Tipton, 17 miles on the north by Dyer, and the remainder by Gibson. It is 30 miles in length from north to south, and 22 miles wide, except the insets of 2½ miles by 5 in the S. E. and N. E. corners, and contains an area of 635 square miles. It contains the towns of Brownsville, (the seat of justice,) Estanaula and Harrisburg. Big Hatchie and the south fork of Forked Deer are its principal streams.

The face of the country is generally level, and "not plentifully supplied with springs, though water is obtained by digging at the depth of from 20 to 60 feet. It is estimated that seven-eights of the county is fit for cultivation, a third of which is first rate land, and heavily timbered. The soil is peculiarly adapted to the culture of cotton; producing from 1,000 to 1,500 pounds per acre. No minerals have been discovered, and but few mineral springs, and those only slightly impregnated with sulphur. Mounds and remains of antiquity are found in this county. About 4 miles west of Harrisburg, there is the remains of an ancient fort, including about ten acres, extending to the bank of Forked Deer, out of which issues a delightful spring. There are four places in the county,

[181] Discontinued as a post office.
[182] Haysboro', in the Madison area, has been encompassed by Metropolitan Nashville, and has no separate identity.

and of the greatest elevation too, that afford a kind of sandstone, which has been most probably removed from the bowels of the earth by some eruption.

About four miles west of Brownsville, Mr. John Rodgers, in digging a well on a ridge, at the distance of 114 feet, came to two logs in a state of petrifaction; at the distance of 20 feet, he came to sand, which continued for 80 feet; he then came to clay again, in which were imbedded the logs, when he ceased digging.

The state of society is highly spoken of for a new county. Population in 1830, 5,356. Cent. lat 35° 35′ N., long. 12° 15′ W.

Henderson, a county in West Tennessee, erected in 1821. It is bounded on the north by Carroll, on the south by McNairy and Hardin, on the east by Perry, and on the west by Madison. It is 27½ miles long N. and S., and 25 wide, containing about 665 square miles. It is watered by Forked Deer, Beech, and Sandy rivers. Beech river runs east through the centre of the county, past Lexington, the seat of justice. There is a post office at Pleasant Exchange. It is a thriving county, and contained a population in 1830 of 8,741. Cent. lat. 35° 38′ N., long. 11° 18′ W.

Hendersonville, a post town in Sumner county, on the west bank of Drake's creek, 10 miles from Gallatin, on the road to Nashville. It contains one store and stage office.

Hend's Creek, a small eastern branch of Clinch river, which empties in at the Eagle bend, in Anderson county.

Hend's Ridge, on the line of Knox and Grainger counties.

Henry, a county in West Tennessee, established in 1821. It is bounded on the north by Kentucky, on the east by Tennessee river, the line of Stewart county, on the south by Humphreys and Carroll, and on the west by Weakley. It is one of the most thriving and populous counties in the Western District. Sandy river and the head of Obion water the interior of the county. Paris is the seat of justice. Population in 1830, 12,230.

Hermitage, the country seat of President Jackson. It is situ-

HIL 173

ated 12 miles N. E. from Nashville, between Stone's and Cumberland rivers, near the east line of Davidson county. It is immediately on the stage route leading from Nashville to Knoxville, *via* Lebanon.

Hesterville, a town in Sevier county, established in 1815, on the land of Ferrill Hester.

Hickman, a county in Middle Tennessee, bounded on the south by Lawrence and Wayne, on the north by Dickson, on the east by Maury, and on the west by Perry and Humphreys. Length 33 miles, width 22, area 726. Surface hilly and soil varied. Its principal water courses are Duck river and branches. Hickman was erected in 1807, and contained a population in 1820 of 6,080, of which 700 were slaves. Duck river runs through the county from S. E. to N. W., passing the town of Centerville, the seat of justice. Population in 1830, 8,132.

Hickman's Creek, a west branch of Caney Fork, in Smith county. Also, a south branch of Cumberland, in Stewart.

Hickory Creek, a post office in Warren county, 70 miles S. E. from Nashville.[183]

Hickory Creek, a branch of Collin's river, in Warren county, which joins the Barren Fork, above McMinnville.

Hickory Creek, a south-west branch of Big Hatchee, in the N. W. corner of Hardeman county.

Hickory Creek, a south branch of Clinch, in the S. W. corner of Knox county.

High Peak, a mountain on the line of North Carolina, W. of Big Pigeon river, and S. E. of New Port, in Cocke county, being a spur of Smoky mountain.

Hightower's Store, a post office in Williamson county. See *Messina.*[184]

Hilham, a post town in Overton county, 84 miles N. of E. from Nashville.

---

[183] The post office is discontinued; the creek is south of McMinnville; mail service through McMinnville.

[184] Discontinued as a post office.

Hillsboro', a post town in Franklin county, 85 miles S. E. from Nashville, and 60 S. S. E. from Murfreesborough.[185]

Hill's Creek, a north-east branch of the Caney Fork of Cumberland, N. W. of Sparta, in White county.

Hiwassee River, a branch of Tennessee, which rises in the N. W. part of Georgia, and flowing N. W., enters this State, and falls into the Tennessee river, at the N. E. corner of Hamilton county, receiving on the north Canasauga, Chestua, Estannallee, Mouse, and Rogers' creeks, and on the south Amoee river. Hiwassee is the north boundary of the Cherokee lands, and the south boundary of McMinn and Rhea counties.[186]

Hilly Creek, a west branch of Shoal creek, in the S. W. corner of Lawrence county.[187]

Holston, a post office in Sullivan county, 300 miles east from Nashville.[188]

Holston, a post office in Knox county, established in 1833.[189]

Holston River, a fine navigable stream, which has its source in the State of Virginia, and enters this State in lat. 33° 30′ N., and long. 5° 40′ W., and flows a south west direction, touching Sullivan on the west, passes through Hawkins, thence through the east corner of Grainger, and bounding the N. W. corner of Jefferson, enters Knox, and after receiving French Broad, passes Knoxville, and enters the Tennessee river at the corners of Blount, Roane, and Monroe counties, in lat. 35° 47′ N., long. 7° 10′ W.

Holston Seminary, a manual labor academy in the town of Newmarket, established by the Methodists.

Holt's Store, a post office in McMinn county, 187 miles S. E. from Nashville.[190]

---

[185] Hillsboro is a town and post office in the southeast portion of Coffee County (established in 1836).

[186] The Hiwassee River forms the boundary between Bradley and McMinn counties.

[187] The mouth of Hilly (now called Holly) Creek is in Lawrence County, but the main course of the stream is in Wayne County.

[188] Discontinued as a post office; mail service through Church Hill.

[189-190] Discontinued as a post office.

Honey Creek, a south-east branch of Holston, between Dodson's and Grassy creeks, in Hawkins county.[191]

Hopewell, a post office in Lincoln county, established in 1833.[192]

Horse Creek, a branch of Lick creek, in the north corner of Greene county.

Horse Creek, a south branch of Watauga, in the west end of Sullivan county. It rises near the Chimney-top mountain, and enters the river opposite to Long Island, above Kingsport.

Horse Creek, a branch of Nolachucky, in Greene county.

Humphreys, a county in Middle Tennessee, on the Tennessee river, erected in 1809. It is bounded on the east by Dickson, on the north by Stewart and Henry, on the west by Carroll, on the south by Perry, and on the south-east by Hickman. Area 625 square miles. Tennessee river passes from south to north, nearly through the centre, and receives numerous rivers and creeks on both sides. Those on the east side are Blue creek, Duck river, Little Dry, Big Dry, Bear, Richland, and Turkey creeks. Those on the west are Eagle, Birdsong, Cypress, Harmon's and Sulphur creeks. Buffalo river, Hamilton creek and Blue creek, branches of Duck river, water the south east corner of the county, and Sandy river and some small tributaries, its N. W. corner, and the head of White oak creek, its N. E. corner. The face of the country on the east side of the river, is generally hilly, except the river bottoms. The uplands are not fit for cultivation, as they consist of rocky hills. Among them are good springs, and the land is well adapted to the depasturing of stock. The west side is generally an uneven low surface, and sandy soil, with no rock except on the highest hills; it is easily cultivated and good for cotton; producing from 1,000 to 1,500 lbs. per acre. On this side of the river, springs are scarce, but water is easily attained by digging from 20 to 40 feet. There is a good sulphur spring in this county, on Sulphur creek four miles from the Tennessee river, which is much resorted to.

[191] Probably Honeycutt Creek, in Hawkins County.

[192] Discontinued as a post office.

Population in 1820, was 4,067; in 1830, was 6,189. Seat of justice, Reynoldsburg.

Humphrey's Mills, a post office in Monroe county, 165 miles from Nashville.[199]

Huntingdon, the seat of justice of Carroll county, situated on Beaver creek, a branch of Forked Deer. It was incorporated in 1824, and in 1833 contained about 600 inhabitants, three lawyers, three doctors, one clergyman, an academy, two schools, seven stores, two taverns, seven carpenters, three cabinet makers, two bricklayers, one hatter, three tailors, two shoemakers, three blacksmiths, one tinner, one tanner, and two painters. It is thirty-eight miles S. E. from Jackson, 109 S. of W. from Nashville, and 823 W. by S. from Washington city. Lat. 36° N., long. 11° 30′ W.

Hunting Creek, a north branch of Clinch river, in the S. E. corner of Claiborne county, between Little mountain and Lost creeks.

Hurricane Creek, a south branch of Stone's river, in Rutherford county.

Hurricane Creek, a north eastern branch of Duck river, which has its source in Dickson county, and is about twenty miles in length. It joins Duck river in the S. E. corner of Humphreys county, above Blue creek. The rich lands along this creek are about two miles wide, and support a dense population of industrious and enterprising citizens. There are three grist mills upon it which run all the year, and one set of iron works which were in successful operation some years since by a Mr. Furguson. Contiguous to the works is the best kind of iron ore. At the mouth of this creek is the beautiful and extensively cultivated farm of the late General Jarmon.

Hurricane Creek, a branch of Wolf river in Shelby county. —also a south branch of Cumberland, in Smith county, above Carthage.

Hurricane Creek, an east branch of Tennessee, in Stewart county.

---

[199] Discontinued as a post office.

Hurricane, a branch of Indian creek, in Tipton county.

Hurricane, a branch of White oak creek, in Hardin county.

Hurricane Creek, a north branch of Stone's river, in Rutherford county.

Hurt's X Roads, a post office in Maury county, thirty-four miles south from Nashville.[194]

---

[194] Discontinued as a post office.

I

Independence, a post office in Hardeman county.[195]

Indian Camp Creek, a south branch of the south fork of Forked deer, in Haywood county. It is formed by the junction of Alpin's and Nixon's Forks, which head near Brownsville, and it joins the river just above Meridian creek.

Indian Creek, a large bold and beautiful creek in Washington county. It rises west of Bald mountain, and flowing north east receives Greer's fork, and East fork, on the east, and Edward's fork on the west, empties into Nolichucky at the Red Bank ferry. The North Carolina road runs along it, and it may at a future day be much used for iron or other factories, as the sites for machinery are numerous and uncommonly fine.

Indian Creek, an east branch of Nolichucky, which rises in Carter and empties in at the bend, below the Baptist meeting house, in Washington county.

Indian Creek, a south branch of the east fork of Obid's river in the west side of Fentress county.

Indian Creek, a north branch of Clinch, in Campbell county.

Indian Creek, or Reinses Creek. It takes its rise in Wayne county, and running west, enters Hardin nineteen miles north of its south east corner, thence flowing a N. N. W. direction, empties into Tennessee river, two miles south of the north boundary of the latter county.

Indian Creek, a south branch of Cumberland, in Stewart county.

Indian Creek, a south branch of Big Hatchee, in Tipton county.

Indian Creek, a south branch of Duck river, in Hickman county, between Swan and Beaver dam creeks. Its mouth is a few miles above Centerville.

Indian Creek, one of the head branches of Shoal creek, in Lawrence county.

---
[195] Discontinued as a post office.

Iron Mountain, a local term for that Ridge of the Appalachian chain, which separates North Carolina from this State. The high peak of which is about 270 miles S. of E. from Nashville. Lat. 35° 50′ N., long. 6° 5′ W.[196]

Iredill, a town established in 1833 at Tollets Mill, in Bledsoe county.

Island Creek, a south branch of Tennessee river, in Monroe county, between Tellico and Bat creeks.[197]

Isom's Store, a post office in Maury county, fifty-three miles S. from Nashville.[198]

---

[196] Iron Mountain, in Carter and Johnson counties, runs from the Virginia line to near Elizabethton.

[197] Island Creek is a tributary of the *Little* Tennessee River, near Fort Loudon.

[198] Discontinued as a post office; mail service through Hampshire.

J

Jacksborough, a post town and the seat of justice of Campbell county, established in the year 1807. In 1833, it contained a population of about 300; two lawyers, one doctor, two stores, two taverns, a female academy, one church, two blacksmiths, two cabinetmakers, one gunsmith, one shoemaker, one saddler and one tanner. It is fifty miles N. N. W. from Knoxville, 215 N. of E. from Nashville, and 543 S. W. by W. from Washington City. Lat. 36° 20′ N., long. 7° 10′ W.[199]

Jack's Creek, a west branch of the Caney Fork of Cumberland.

Jackson, a county in Middle Tennessee, erected in 1801; in 1813, White was erected out of it, and in 1819 it was reduced to its constitutional area of 625 square miles. Cumberland river crosses this county in an oblique direction from N. E. to S. W. The surface is hilly. It contains the towns of Gainsboro', the seat of Justice, Williamsburg, Meigsville, and McLeansville, and there are post offices at White Plains, Beech Hill and Fort Blount. Population in 1820 was 7,593, in 1830, 9,902.

Jackson, the seat of justice for Madison county, situated near the center on the waters of the south fork of Forked Deer river. It was laid out in 1822, in district 10, range 1, sect. 9, and in August the lots were sold to the amount of near $20,000. In 1830 it had a population of 675, and in 1833 near 900. It is rapidly improving and will unquestionably be one of the finest towns in the Western District.

It contains a brick court house 54 by 44 feet, a brick jail, market house, a branch of the Union Bank of Tennessee, a printing office, two academies, one church, ten lawyers, five doctors, two clergymen, eight stores, two taverns, three blacksmiths, six bricklayers, twelve carpenters, three cabinet makers, one hatter, one saddler, three shoemakers, two silversmiths, three tailors, one tinner, three tanners, one painter and one wagonmaker. It is forty miles and a half north of

---
[199] Now known as Jacksboro.

the south boundary of the State, sixty miles in a direct line east of the Mississippi river, fifty-two miles west of Tennessee river, 146 miles by the mail stage route, W. by S. from Nashville, 100 N. E. from Memphis, via Bolivar, and eighty-five via Estanaula and Sommerville, fifty-three E. from Covington, twenty-eight E. from Brownsville, twenty-five north by east from Bolivar, twenty-eight south by east from Trenton, twenty-eight west from Lexington, sixty-three south west from Paris, twenty-eight south of west from Huntingdon, fifty-five south by west from Dresden, forty-five south east from Dyersburg, seventy south east from Troy, ninety south east from Mill's Point, thirty-three north west from Purdy, 110 north east from Florence, Ala., 236 east by north from Little Rock, A. T. and 861 from Washington City. Lat. 35° 40, 30′ long. 12° 7′ W.

Jackson College, a flourishing institution in Maury county, incorporated in 1833. It is ten miles north of Columbia, conducted on the manual labor plan, and has about 150 students.[300]

Jamestown, a post town and the seat of Justice of Fentress county, situated nearly in the center of the county, on the Cumberland mountains. It was established in 1827, and contains thirty houses of different descriptions; eighty inhabitants, two lawyers, two tanners, one hatter, one shoemaker, two blacksmiths, one academy, one clergyman, two stores, and two taverns. The public buildings are a court house and jail. It is 135 miles east from Nashville, seventy-three north west from Knoxville, 150 south from Louisville Ky. and 586 west south west from Washington city. Lat. 36° 18′ N., long. 7° 30′ W.

Jasper, the seat of Justice of Marion county, situated about three miles, on the north side, from Tennessee river. The Sequatchee river is about one mile south east from Jasper, and the Cumberland mountain about one mile, which presents a handsome view from the village. It contains thirty

---

[300] At Spring Hill, chartered in 1829. It later was known as Union Seminary; burned during the Civil War.

dwelling houses, about 180 inhabitants, twenty mechanics, six professional men, five stores, one tavern, and a good court house and jail. Distance 112 miles south east from Nashville, on the main road leading to Athens in Georgia, and where the stage road from Knoxville to Huntsville crosses the Georgia road, and 649 from Washington City, in lat. 35° 10′ N., long. 8° 30′ W. It was incorporated in 1825.

Jefferson, a county in East Tennessee, bounded on the south west by Sevier, north west by Grainger, north east by Hawkins, and east by Greene and Cocke. This county is traversed by Nolichucky and branches, and contains much good soil. It was organized at the formation of the constitution, and contained a population in 1820, of 8,953; in 1830, 11,799. Its towns are Dandridge, the seat of justice, and Russelville, and there are post offices at Chucky Bend and Chunn's store and Moss creek. Cen. lat. 36° 5′, long. 6° 35′ W.

Jefferson, a post town in Rutherford county, in the forks of Stone's river, twenty miles south east from Nashville.[201]

Jenning's Creek, a branch of Cumberland in Jackson county, nearly opposite to Gainesboro'.

Johnsville, a post office in Obion county.[202]

Johnson's Creek, a south branch of Cumberland, in Dickson county.

Jolly's Island, in the Tennessee, at the mouth of Hiwassee, in Rhea county.[203]

Jonesboro', the seat of justice of Washington county, established by the state of North Carolina, in 1779. In 1794 commissioners were appointed by the territorial legislature to erect public buildings; in 1796, commissioners were appointed by the legislature, and the act of '94 repealed, and

---

[201] Jefferson was the original seat of justice of Rutherford County. The community still exists; the post office is discontinued, being served by Smyrna.

[202] Discontinuel as a post office.

[203] Jolly's Island is known as Hiwassee Island, and is a part of Meigs County (established in 1836); an important archaelogical example of the temple mound and Mississippi cultures of prehistoric Indians.

in 1815 it was incorporated. This is the place where the celebrated convention for forming the government of Frankland sat in 1784. In 1833 it contained a population of about 500 inhabitants; eleven lawyers, four physicians, two clergymen, two churches, two academies, four schools, one printing office, four carpenters, three cabinet makers, two bricklayers, one blacksmith, four tanners, two hatters, four tailors, four shoemakers, one silversmith, two tinners, two wagon makers, one mill, a number of stores &c. It is about 100 miles east from Knoxville, 300 from Nashville, forty south west from Abingdon, Va. 160 from Salem, N. C. fifty from the Warm springs, forty-five from Rogersville, twenty from Blountsville, twenty-five from Greenville, sixteen from Elizabethton, 320 from Huntsville, Al. and 449 from Washington City. Lat. 36° 12′ N., long. 5° 18′ W.

Jonesville, a town established on the lands of Joseph Woolfolk, at Spring creek cross roads, in Montgomery county, in 1817.

Jones Creek, a north branch of Duck river, in Bedford county, between Shelbyville and Fall creek.

Jones Creek, a west branch of Harpeth river. It rises in Dickson county, flows a north east course past Charlotte, and Falls into Harpeth near the west line of Davidson, below Turnbull creek.

Jones Creek, a south branch of Holston river, in Hawkins county, south west of Rogersville, between Grassy and Fox creeks.

Joslin's alias *Chestnut Grove*, a post office in Davidson county, seven miles from Nashville.[204]

Joyner's, a post office in Haywood county, 175 miles south of west from Nashville.[205]

---

[204] Joslin's Station was one of the first settlements in the Cumberland area of Davidson County; it has no corporate existence today.

[205] Discontinued as a post office.

185

K

Kendrick's Creek, a south branch of Holston river. It rises in Washington and joins the river above Long Island, in Sullivan county.

Kercheval's, a post office in Montgomery county, sixty-eight miles north west from Nashville.[206]

King Creek, a west branch of Hickory creek, in Warren county.

King's Creek, a west branch of Tennessee, in Roane county.

Kingsport, a post town in Sullivan county, situated on the north side of Holston river, at a place known by the name of the *Boat-yard*, one mile above the junction with the north fork, which is the line between Sullivan and Hawkins. It contains about fifty families, 317 inhabitants; two taverns, two stores, two physicians, one methodist and one presbyterian church, and there is a good bridge across the North Fork.

Athough a number of boats are loaded between this place and the mouth of Wataga, yet it is considered the head of navigation, and it is supposed there are annually shipped from Kingsport about 4,000 barrels of salt, besides considerable quantities of iron, castings, flour, bacon, &c. It is sixteen miles west from Blountsville, forty from Abingdon, Va., twenty-two north west from Jonesboro', thirty-five north from Greenville ninety-three east from Knoxville, sixty east from Rutledge, twenty-seven east from Rogersville, eight south from Scott C. H. Va. and 293 east from Nashville; in lat. 36° 25' N., long. 5° 40' W.

Kingston, the seat of justice of Roane county, near the point between Clinch and Holston rivers, sixty miles by water and forty by land, below Knoxville, at a place known by the name of South West Point. It was established in 1799 on the land of Robert King. In 1801 an act was passed making it the seat of justice, and in 1820 it was incorporated with a mayor and alderman. It is 160 miles south of east from

---
[206] Discontinued as a post office.

Nashville, and 575 south west from Washington City, in lat. 35° 50′ N., long. 7° 30′ W.

Knox, a county in east Tennessee, bounded on the south east by Sevier, on the south by Blount, on the west by Roane, on the north west by Anderson and Grainger, and north east by Jefferson. It is about thirty miles long and twenty wide. It was erected in 1792 by a Territorial Ordinance, and reduced to its constitutional limits in 1801, when Anderson and Roane were erected. Holston and French Broad unite in this county, four miles above Knoxville, and flow a south-west course. Copper, Chestnut and Hend's Ridges, touch the north border of this county, and about fifteen miles north of Knoxville are quantities of Buhr stone. This county contained a population in 1820, of 13,034; in 1830, 14,498. Seat of justice Knoxville and there are post offices at Mecklinburg and Campbell's Station.

Knox's, a post office in Gibson county, ninety-five miles south from Nashville—*now Campbellsville*.[207]

Knoxville, the seat of justice of Knox county. It was laid off about the year 1793 by the late General White, and named in honor of Gen. Knox, the then secretary of war. It is situated on the north side of Holston river, on a considerable elevation. The site is not a good one, and the streets are too narrow. It has been a place of considerable business and was for a long time the seat of government. It was incorporated in 1817, which was the last year the legislature sat there. Knoxville is the largest town in East Tennessee, and the second in the state, though its commercial importance has greatly diminished. Its population at present is about 300 families and 1,500 inhabitants. Its public buildings are a stone court house, stuccoed, a brick jail, bank, the first and second presbyterian churches, methodist church, the Knoxville female academy, and East Tennessee college. The college edifice is one of the best buildings in the western country. As this town will most likely be the seat of learning for East Ten-

---

[207] Discontinued as a post office; the direction in the text should read "west" from Nashville.

nessee, it is proper that some further notice be taken of the flourishing state of her literary institutions. So early as the year 1784 a literary institution styled Blount College, was established in the vicinity of Knoxville by one of the first acts of the territorial government. Under its president, the Rev. Samuel Carrick, who was also pastor of the only church then in the town, it continued in useful operation with some temporary interruptions for several years. In 1807 the college of East Tennessee was established by an act of the state; Blount college was dissolved, and the funds and claims transferred to the new institution, with a proviso that its location should be within two miles of Knoxville. While its first president, the Rev. David Sherman officiated, not a few of the neighboring youths received instruction, and some of them degrees.

The Rev. Dr. Coffin succeeded and presided over the institution till 1833, when the Rev. John H. Piper, was chosen President, and Rev. Stephen Foster, Professor. Number of students in 1833, 28. East Tennessee college may be considered as well endowed; it possesses funds to the amount of about $25,000, and about 15,000 acres of land in the Western District.—The library contains 1,400 volumes; it has a chemical apparatus complete, for illustrating the gases and most of the solid substances; a philosophical apparatus adequate to the greater number of experiments in mechanics, pneumatics, optics and electricity. The college edifice stands on a retired eminence in the western suburbs of the town, commanding a fine view of the river Holston, and the mountains to the north and south.

The Knoxville Female Academy went into operation in December 1828, under very favourable auspices. The building is sufficiently large to accommodate 150 pupils, and is a little removed from the business part of the town. In addition to the literary and scientific branches of education, instruction is afforded in painting, ornamental needle work, music and the French language. Lectures are given on natural philosophy and chemistry, for which purpose an apparatus and other facilities are provided, together with a chosen selection of geological specimens, maps, globes, &c. In August, 1829, the number of students was 80; and it still continues to flourish under the direction of Mr. and Mrs. Estebrook and their assistant teachers. A general superintendence is exercised by a board of nine trustees. Knoxville, likewise, contains twelve stores, two commission houses, one drug store, one book store, three taverns, twenty lawyers, five doctors, four clergymen, 3 printing offices, 2 weekly papers, 1 classical academy, 3 common schools, 3 painters, 2 spinning factories, 2 gins and carding machines, four grist mills, three saw mills, one brass foundery, six blacksmiths' shops, six carpenters, two bricklayers, two cabinet makers, three hatters' shops, six saddlers, eight shoemakers, one tinner and coppersmith, five tanyards, two coachmakers and two waggon-makers. It is 200 miles east from Nashville, and 538 S. W. by W. from Washington City, in lat. 35° 58' N., lon. 7° 50' W.

L

La Grange, a thriving post town in the south east corner of Fayette county, on Wolf river. In 1828 it contained sixty houses, 240 inhabitants, four stores, two taverns, and a dozen mechanics. In 1831 it was incorporated, and it bids fair to be one of the most interesting villages in that section of the state. Distant from Nashville 168 miles. Lat. 35° 5′ N., long. 12° 10′ W.

Lake Oliver, a post office in Dyer county, established in 1833.[308]

Lancaster, a post town in Smith county, established in 1817 on the land of Richard Lancaster, on the Caney Fork, twelve miles south east of Carthage and fifty-three east from Nashville. In 1833 it contained about 100 inhabitants; two stores, two doctors, a tavern, grocery, shoe shop, blacksmith and wagon maker.

Laurel Furnace, a post office in Dickson county, forty-four miles west from Nashville.[309]

Laurel Gap, a post office in Greene county, established in 1833.[310]

Laurel Mountains, a range of mountains west of the main Alleghany range. They extend from Pennsylvania across Virginia to Kentucky, then under the name of Cumberland mountains, divide Virginia and Kentucky, and cross Tennessee, terminating near its south border; Laurel mountain proper, lies in Kentucky, in lat. 37° N., long. 6° about the source of the Cumberland river.

Lawrence, a county in Middle Tennessee, erected in 1817. It is about twenty-eight miles long and twenty-three wide; area, 644 square miles. It is bounded on the east by Giles and Maury, on the west by Wayne, on the north by Hickman, and on the south by the state of Alabama, immediately opposite the Muscle Shoals. It is well watered by Shoal creek and other branches of Tennessee on the south, and Buffalo river on the north. It contained a population in 1820, of

[308-310] Discontinued as a post office.

3,271; in 1830, 5,412. Seat of justice *Lawrenceburg*. Cen. lat. 35° 15′ N., long. 10° 50′. W. There are two iron works on the waters of Buffalo river, and one on Shoal creek.

Lawrenceburg, a town, established in 1815, on the land of David Campbell, in the county of Knox.[111]

Lawrenceburg, the seat of justice of Lawrence county, on Chisholm's fork of Shoal creek; established in 1819, and named in honor of Capt. James Lawrence, late of U. S. Navy. It is eighty-eight miles west of south from Nashville, and 780 west south west from Washington City; in lat. 35° 15′ long. 10° 36′ W.

Leatherwood Creek, an eastern branch of Tennessee river, in Stewart county, and has its intersection at Leatherwood Island.[113]

Lebanon, a flourishing village, and seat of justice of Wilson county; established in 1801, and incorporated in 1807. It was laid out in a beautiful cedar grove, at the head of one of the branches of Barton's creek, 8 miles south of Cumberland river. The spring rises within a few rods of the court house, and forms a creek 15 or 20 feet wide. The environs and unimproved lots are thickly clad with cedar like those in the city of Nashville, which adds greatly to the beauty of the town. It contains upwards of 100 houses, a good court house and jail, one Methodist and one Presbyterian meeting house, three taverns, ten stores, one hatter, two tailors, three shoemakers, one tinner and coppersmith, one tanyard, three cabinet makers, one painter, three blacksmiths, one rope and bagging factory, ten lawyers, four physicians, one male and female academy. It is 23 miles E. from Nashville, 16 S. from Gallatin and 686 W. S. W. from Washington City, in lat. 36° 15′ N., lon. 9° 14′ W. Population in 1830, 700.

Leesburg, a post town, in Washington county, 5 miles from Jonesboro'. It contains 30 houses, 200 inhabitants, one store and a Presbyterian church. It is 80 miles from Knoxville,

---

[111] Discontinued as a post office.

[113] There is also a Leatherwood Creek in Dickson County, tributary to Yellow Creek.

on the stage road leading E. from Greenville, and was established in 1799, on the land of Michael Fraker and Abraham and John Campbell.

Lee Valley, a post office, in Hawkins county, 250 miles E. from Nashville.[213]

Lewis', a post office, in Hickman county, established in 1833.[214]

Lexington, the seat of justice of Henderson county, situated on Beech river, a branch of Tennessee. It is 114 miles S. W. from Nashville, 28 miles E. from Jackson, and 823 S. W. by W. from Washington City, in lat. 35° 38′ N., lon. 11° 18′ W.

Liberty, a post town, in Smith county, established in 1817, on the land of Adam Dale, on Smith's Fork, on the stage road from Nashville to Sparta *via* Hermitage and Lebanon. It was incorporated in 1831, and contained in 1834 about 200 inhabitants, three stores two taverns, two carriage maker's shops, two tailor's shops, one tanyard, one shoe shop, one saddler shop, one carpenter, two churches and two doctors. It is 22 miles S. from Carthage and 50 E. from Nashville.[215]

Lick Creek, a large creek which rises in McNairy county, and runs into Tennessee river below the Big Bend Shoals, and above Snake creek, in Hardin county—also a branch of Cumberland, in Stewart.

Lick Creek, a large northern branch of Nolichucky, which has its source in the north corner of Greene county, and flowing west parallel with, and east of Bay's mountain, enters the river in the S. W. corner of said county, above the Chucky Bend. It is navigable for small boats.

Lick Creek, an east branch of Tennessee river, in Perry county, north of Perryville.—*Lick creek, a west* branch in said county below Cub creek.[216]

---

[213] Discontinued; the community is served by Sneedville.

[214] Discontinued as a post office.

[215] Liberty is a town in the western section of DeKalb County (established in 1837).

[216] Lick Creek, a west tributary of the Tennessee River, is in Decatur County.

Lick Creek, a north branch of Duck river, in the N. E. corner of Hickman county.

Little Bigby Creek, a south branch of Duck river, below Columbia, in Maury county.

Liddonsville, a post town, in Wayne county.[217]

Lieper's Fork, a west branch of Harpeth, in Williamson county.

Limestone Creek, a north branch of Nolichucky. It rises near Jonesboro', in Washington, and joins the river above Sinking creek, near the east line of Greene county.

Lincoln, a county in Middle Tennessee, erected in 1809. It is bounded on the east by Franklin, on the west by Giles and part of Maury, on the north by Bedford, (the line running on the ridge dividing the waters of Duck and Elk,) and the south by the state of Alabama. It lies nearly in a square form, and contains about 625 square miles. This county is divided into nearly two equal parts by Elk river, which flows from east to west. The surface is diversified, and the soil very productive; cotton is the staple. Population in 1820, 14,761, in 1830, 22086, making an increase in ten years of 7,325. Seat of justice, Fayettville, and there are post offices at Lynchburg, Mulberry and New Hope. Cen. lat. 35° 15′ N., lon. 9° 28′.

Linseyville, a post town, in Obion county.[218]

Lionel, a town in Hardeman county, in the S. E. corner, between Big Hatchee river and Potter's creek, S. E. of Bolivar.

Little Barren Creek, a north branch of Clinch river, between Big Barren and Hunting creeks, in Claiborne county.

Little Doe River, a branch of Wataga, which rises in the north east corner of Carter county; the extreme east end of the state.

Little Hatchee, a north east branch of Big Hatchee river, which rises in McNairy county, and falls into the river below Warnersville, on the east side of Hardeman county.

Little Pigeon, a post office, in Sevier county, established in 1833.[219]

[217-219] Discontinued as a post office.

LOO

Little Pigeon river, a branch of French Broad, which rises in Cocke, and flowing a south west direction, through Sevier, receives the West Fork at Sevierville, and joins the river above Dumpling creek ferry.

Little River, a north east branch of Holston. It rises on the line of North Carolina, in the east end of Blount, and running through the north east side, falls into the river below the mouth of Knob creek, S. W. of Knoxville.

Little Rock Creek, an east branch of Rock creek, one of the south branches of Duck river, on the line of Bedford and Maury counties.[220]

Little Sycamore Creek, a north branch of Big Sycamore, which rises between Powell's mountain and the Spur of Wallen's ridge, and joins the main creek between Raven hill and Lone mountain, a few miles above its junction with Clinch river, in Claiborne county.

Log Mountain, a small mountain, lying west of Cumberland mountain, and east of the Clear Fork, S.W. of Cumberland Gap, in the N. W. corner of Claiborne county.

Lone Mountain, in Anderson county.

Lone Mountain, a solitary hill, north of Clinch river, between Sycamore and Straight creeks, S. W. of Wallen's ridge, in Claiborne county.

Long Creek, a south branch of Cumberland river, above Dover, in Stewart county.—*Long Creek,* a branch of Barren river, in Sumner and Smith counties.

Long Island, an island in Holston river, above Kingston, in Sullivan county. It is about three miles in length, and lies just above the point where the north fork joins the river. This place is rendered memorable by the battle of 'Long Island Flats,' fought in June 1776.[221]

Look Out Mountain, a range of mountains, extending about thirty miles across the boundary between Georgia and Tennessee, and terminating abruptly six miles east of the Suck,

---

[220] Now in Marshall County (established in 1836).
[221] The entry should have read "Kingsport."

in Tennessee River, eight miles west of Brainerd Mission. It is about 200 feet high.

Looneyville, a town, in Lincoln county, established in 1819, on the land of Peter Looney.

Loosa Hatchee, a river, which rises in Hardeman county, and flows west through Fayette, past Sommerville, and falls into the Mississippi nine miles above Memphis, in Shelby county."[222]

Lost Creek, a north branch of Clinch river, which rises in the south corner of Claiborne, and joins the river a short distance above the road from Clinton to Tazewell, in Campbell county, above the mouth of Powell's river.

Lost Creek, a west branch of Caney Fork, in White county. Upon this creek are extensive falls, some of them thirty feet in perpendicular height. It affords sufficient water to propel machinery about half of the year, and is about ten miles in length. "And nature, after exhibiting much variety in the romantic appearance of its falls, and the impetuosity of its current, has, as if weary of its passage, directed its course to the foot of a stupendous mountain, where the stream is ingulphed and lost in the silent grandeur of the surrounding objects."—*Haywood.*[223]

Lost Creek, an east branch of Tennessee, in Stewart county.

Louisville, a post town, in Blount county, on the south side of Holston river, about one quarter of a mile from the bank. It contains four dwelling houses, one store, one blacksmith, one cotton gin, two grist mills and three sawmills; and there is one set of iron works a quarter of a mile from the town. It is 175 miles S. of E. from Nashville.

Loveville, a town, established in 1815, on the land of Robert Love, in Knox county, between Campbell's Station and Knoxville.[224]

---

[222] Properly one word, Loosahatchie.

[223] The text should read "north" branch of the Caney Fork; the stream is southeast of Sparta.

[224] The community is east of Campbell's Station, near Concord, in Knox County.

Lowe's, a post office, in Robertson county, 20 miles N. W. from Nashville.[225]

Loy's X Roads, a post office in Anderson county, established in 1833.[226]

Lynchburg, a post town, in Lincoln county, 70 miles S. from Nashville, on Mulberry creek, in the north east corner of the county.[227]

Lynn Creek, a post office, in Giles county, 124 miles W. of S. from Nashville.[228]

Lyon's Creek, a south branch of Holston, in the east end of Knox county, below Carswell's creek.

[225-226] Discontinued as a post office.

[227] Lynchburg is the county seat of Moore County (established in 1871).

[228] Correctly, Lynnville, a town and post office in northern Giles County.

197

M

McAdoe's Creek, a north branch of Cumberland, in Montgomery county.

MacAllis' X Roads, a post office, in Montgomery county, 61 miles N. W. from Nashville.[229]

McCrory's Creek, a south branch of Harpeth, in Williamson county.

McKoysville, a post office, in Cocke county, established in 1833.[230]

MacLean's Mills, a post office, in Rutherford county.[231]

McLeansville, a post town, in Jackson county, 77 miles E. from Nashville.

McLemoresville, a post office, in Carroll county, late *Dougherty's.*

McMinn, a county in E. Tennessee, erected in 1819. It is bounded on the N. E. by Monroe, on the S. by Hiwassee river, on the N. W. by Rhea, on the E. by the Cherokee lands. Its chartered limits extend S. to the Southboundary of the state, and bounding W. on Hamilton county, including lands yet owned by the Indians. It is well watered by Canasauga, Chestau, Estannalle Mouse and Rogers creeks, branches of Hiwassee, on the north side, and Amoee and other branches on the south. It contains the towns of Athens, the seat of justice, Calhoun and Columbus. And there are post offices at Holt's store and Cobb's. The population in 1820 was 1623, in 1830 it was 14,497, making an increase in ten years of 12,874. Cent. lat. 35° 20′ N., lon. 7° 35′.

McMinnville, the seat of justice of Warren county, established in 1809, on Collin's river, a branch of the Caney Fork of Cumberland. It was incorporated in 1813, and in 1833, it contained about 700 inhabitants, five lawyers, five doctors, two academies, one school, three blacksmiths, two bricklayers, five carpenters, five cabinet makers, two painters, one printing

---

[229] McAllister's Cross Roads; mail service through Cunningham.
[230-231] Discontinued as a post office.

office, six saddlers, five shoemakers, one silversmith, eight tailors, five tanners, two taverns and several stores.

It is 73 miles S. E. from Nashville, 40 E. from Murfreesboro', 26 S. of W. from Sparta, and 644 W. S. W. from Washington City. Lat. 35° 50′ N., lon. 8° 42′ W.

McNairy, a county in West Tennessee, erected in 1823. It is bounded on the east by Hardin, on the west by Hardeman, on the north by Henderson and Madison, and on the south by the state of Mississippi. It is about 28 miles long and 22 wide. It is watered by the head branches of Big Hatchee and some small branches of Tennessee river on the south, and on the north by the head waters of the south fork of Forked Deer. Population in 1830, 5,697; seat of justice, Purdy.

McMillan's, a post office, in Knox county, established in 1833.[132]

McReary's, a post office, in Robertson county, 43 miles from Nashville, on the Lexington road.[133]

Madison, a county, in West Tennessee, erected in 1821. It is bounded on the north by Gibson, on the south by McNairy and Hardeman, on the east by Henderson, and on the west by Haywood. It is 25 miles square. The south and middle fork of Forked Deer waters this country. It contains the towns of Jackson, (the seat of justice,) and Denmark; and there are post offices at Clover Creek, Mount Pinson, Point Center, Spring Creek, Whiting and Cotton Grove. Population in 1830, 11,750. Cent. lat. 35° 37′ N., lon. 11° 50′.

Madisonville, the seat of justice of Monroe county, on the waters of Bat creek, a south branch of Little Tennessee. It contains about four hundred inhabitants, four lawyers, five doctors, four clergymen, three churches, one academy, two schools, five stores, three taverns, six carpenters, two cabinet-makers, three bricklayers, four blacksmiths, two hatters, three tailors, two shoemakers, two saddlers, one printing office, two tanners and two painters. It is 168 miles S. E. from Nashville, and 593 S. W. from Washington City, in lat. 35° N., lon. 7° 20′ W.

---

[132]-[133] Discontinued as a post office.

MAR 199

Mansker's Creek, a north branch of Cumberland river, and the dividing line between Sumner and Davidson county. This creek took its name from Casper Mansker, who discovered Mansker's Lick about the year 1772. The Gallatin road crosses it at the Dismuke's Ferry, 12 miles from Nashville.

Marion, a county, in East Tennessee, erected in 1817. It is bounded on the east by Hamilton and in part by Tennessee river, on the north west by Franklin, on the north by Bledsoe, and on the south by the state of Alabama. Length 32 miles, mean width 18 miles; area 756 square miles. The surface is hilly and in part mountainous. This county is drained by Sequatchee river. Marion occupies the vally between two ridges of the Cumberland Mountains. The land in the valley is generally good, is mixed with sand, and covered with oak, hickory, sweetgum and walnut timber. The products are corn, cotton, wheat, hemp and tobacco—cotton is the staple. Mills are not plenty in this county. Population in 1820, 3,388; in 1830, 5,516. *Jasper* is the seat of justice, on Sequatchee river, cen. lat. 35° 15′ N., lon. 6° 34′ W.

Marrowbone, a north branch of Cumberland, in Davidson county.[234]

Marsh Creek, an east branch of Tennessee river, between Cedar and Cypress Creeks, in Perry county.

Marshall's Ferry, a post office in Grainger county 250 miles east from Nashville.[235]

Marshall's Creek, a north branch of Holston above Rogersville, in Hawkins county.

Martin's Creek, a branch of Cumberland river, in Jackson county. It is considered navigable from Robert's mill to its junction with the river, which is in the west side of the county, below Beech hill.

Maryville, the seat of justice of Blount county, established in 1796 on the land of John Craig. It is situated on the great stage road leading from Knoxville to Huntsville, about 15

---
[234] Marrowbone Creek rises in Davidson County; its mouth is in Cheatham County.
[235] Discontinued as a post office.

miles from the former place, and contained in 1833 about 600 inhabitants, four lawyers, four clergymen, three physicians, three churches, five stores, two taverns, six bricklayers, three blacksmiths, one gunsmith, three hatters, one painter, four shoemakers, three saddlers, two silversmiths, three tanners, three tailors, one turner, three waggonmakers, four cabinet-makers, one cotton gin, one carding machine, three gristmills, one printing office, &c.

The South Western Theological Seminary of the Presbyterian church is located at this place. It was established in 1821, and in 1832, it had 22 students, three professors, and 5,500 volumes in the library. It is 190 miles S. of E. from Nashville, 556 S. W. by W. from Washington City. Lat. 35° 46′ N., lon. 7° 4′ W.

Maury, a county, in Middle Tennessee, erected in 1807. It is bounded on the south by Giles, on the west by Hickman and Lawrence, on the north by Williamson, and on the east by Bedford, and part of Lincoln. This county is exceedingly well watered by Duck river and its numerous branches, it is also watered on the south by north branches of Elk river. The lands in Maury, in point of fertility, are equal to any in the state, including a great portion of what is denominated the Duck river country. It is about 25 miles wide and 30 long. Population in 1820, 22,140, and in 1830 it was 28,153; Columbia is the seat of justice, and there are post offices at Moorsville, Williamsport, Mount Pleasant, Cedar spring, Hurt's X Roads, Isom's store, Pleasant Grove and Spring Hill. Cen. lat. 35° 30′ N., lon. 10° 5′ W.

Meadow Creek, a south west branch of Caney Fork, above Caney Bend, in Warren county.

Mecklenburg, a post town in Knox county, situated at the confluence of French Broad and Holston rivers, four and a half miles from Knoxville, on the main road leading to the Warm springs, N. C., *via* Greenville and Jonesboro'. The situation of this village combines all that is wild and romantic with the sublime and beautiful, and in the neighborhood are lofty cliffs and extensive subterraneous caverns. It is 205 miles

MID 201

east from Nashville.[236]

Meigsville, a post town in Jackson county, 84 miles N. of E. from Nashville.[237]

Memphis, a post town in Shelby county, situated on the east bank of Mississippi river, one mile above the site of old Fort Pickering, at one of the Chickasaw Bluffs, below the mouth of Wolf river. This town stands on one of the most noble bluffs on the river, commanding a fine view of the surrounding country, and from its relative position to the Western District, and the late Chickasaw Purchase, it must undoubtedly become the emporium of one of the finest agricultural districts in the western country. Already it is a place of considerable business, and is improving faster than any town in the state.

Meridian Creek, a south branch of south Forked Deer. It rises west of Brownsville, in Haywood county, and flows north ten or fifteen miles nearly with the Meredian line of the district, when it intersects the river between Indian Camp and Turkey creeks.

Middleburg, a post town in Hardeman county, on Pleasant Run, S. W. of Bolivar. It contains one store, tavern, &c. It is 206 miles S. W. from Nashville.[238]

Middle Fork, a tributary of *Duck River*, in the N. W. corner of Bedford county.

Middle Fork, a branch of Forked Deer, in West Tennessee. It waters part of Henderson, Madison, Carroll and Gibson counties, and joins the North Fork in the east side of Dyer county, in lat. 36° N., lon. 12° 13' W.

Middle Fork, a branch of Obion river, in West Tennessee. It rises near the centre of Henry county, and flows west

---

[236] No longer a post office; sometimes identified as "Fork of the River," or "Ramsey's." Mecklenburg was also the name of the home of J. G. M. Ramsey, author of *The Annals of Tennessee*; the house stood at the confluence of the two rivers, which from that point is known as the Tennessee.

[237] Discontinued as a post office.

[238] Discontinued as a post office; Middleburg is between Bolivar and Hickory Valley in Hardeman County.

MID

through the south part of Weakley, and joins the main river in the S. E. corner of Obion county.

Midway, a post office in Monroe county, established in 1833.[239]

Mifflin, a post office in Henderson county, 110 miles S. W. from Nashville, on the road leading from Lexington to Mount Pinson.[240]

Mill Creek, a south branch of Cumberland river, in Davidson county, above Nashville.

Mill Creek, a north east branch of Big Hatchee, between Gray's and Clover creeks, below Bolivar. It is declared navigable as high up as Goodlet's mill.

Mill Fork, a branch of Limestone creek, in Washington county.

Milledgeville, a post office in White county, 10 miles W. from Sparta.[241]

Miller's Cove, a post office in Monroe county, established in 1833.[242]

Miller's Island, between Fulton and Randolph, in the Mississippi, Tipton county.

Milton, a post town in Rutherford county, on Bradley's creek, 37 miles S. E. from Nashville, established in 1820, on the land of Gideon Thompson.

Mississippi River. This noble river rises in about lat. 47° 47' N., lon. 15°, amidst lakes and swamps, in the north western territory, and after a south east course of about 800 miles, reaches the falls of St. Anthony, in lat. 44° N. where it descends perpendicularly 16 or 17 feet. Some places above the falls, it is narrow and rapid, in other places it is near six hundred yards wide, and has a smooth and even current. Im-

---

[239] The present post office of Midway is in Greene County, and has no relationship to the earlier one in Monroe County.

[240] The community of Mifflin is in Chester County (established in 1879).

[241] Discontinued; the present-day post office of Milledgeville is on the line between Chester, Hardin, and McNairy counties.

[242] Discontinued as a post office; in Blount County; postal service through Walland.

mediately above the falls, it contracts to a width of two hundred yards. Ninety miles below the falls, and between 44° and 45°, it receives Rapid and St. Croix rivers; the former from the west and the latter from the east. Near 44° comes in Cannon river from the west. Between lake Pepin and the parallel of 43° come in three or four inconsiderable rivers, of which Buffalo, Bluff and Black rivers from the east, are the principal. Between 43° and 42° are Root, Upper Ioway, and Yellow rivers from the west, and LaCroix and Bad Axe rivers from the east. Ouisconsin comes in from the east in about lat. 42°, near Prairie du Chein. A little below this comes in Turkey river from the west, and La Mine from the east. On the opposite side comes in Tete de Morte river. A little below, lat. 42°, comes in from the west, the Wapisipinacon river, and a little lower, down on the same side, comes in the Little Laoutoux; and still lower from the east, Rock river. Near the mouth of Rock river, on the west side of the Mississippi, is Fort Armstrong. Below Fort Armstrong comes in Lower Ioway river. Below 41°, comes in from the eastern side, two or three inconsiderable streams. Near lat. 40°, on the west side, in the state of Missouri, comes in the Des Moines, the largest tributary from the west above the Missouri, being 150 yards wide at its mouth. Between Des Moines and the Illinois, come in from the W. the Waconda, Fabrian Jaustioni, Oahaha, or Salt river, Bœuf or Cuivre, and Dardenne rivers. These rivers are from 50 to a 100 yards wide at their mouths. In lat. 39°, comes in the Illinois from the east, near 400 yards wide at its mouth, and about 400 miles long. A little below 39° from the west, comes in the Missouri river, which is longer and affords more water than the Mississippi. The next principal stream below Missouri on the west side, is the Maramee, 20 miles below St. Louis, a little above lat. 38°. It is nearly 200 yards wide at its mouth. Nearly in 38° comes in from the E. Kaskaskia, river 30 yards wide at its mouth, and 200 miles long. On the opposite side enter two or three small streams below St. Genevieve. Forty miles below Kaskaskia from the east comes in Big Muddy. A little below 37°, on the east side, comes in the Ohio river, by far the largest tributary on the east. At its junction, and for an hundred miles above, it is as wide as the parent stream, though not so rapid in its course. In lat. 36° 30′ above New Madrid, the Mississippi touches the N. W. corner of the state of Tennessee. The next stream on the east side, is Reel Foot, in Obion county. A little below 36° comes in Obion river, in Dyer county. The next is Forked Deer, in Tipton county, at the First Chickasaw Bluff; the next is Big Hatchee, in the same county, at the 2nd. Chickasaw Bluff, the next is Loosa Hatchee, in Shelby county, and 9 miles below comes in Wolf river, just above the town of Memphis or 4th Chickasaw Bluff. This river is 50 yards wide at its mouth, and is navigable as high up as LaGrange, for small boats. The next and last stream in Tennessee, is Nanconnah creek, which joins the river opposite to President's Island. A few miles below is the south west corner of this state, and north west corner of the state of Mississippi in lat. 35° N., lon. 13° 10′ W. From the mouth of Ohio to the south west angle of Tennessee, the Mississippi flows a general S. W. course, bounding part of Kentucky and the whole west end of Tennessee; a distance of 150 miles by its meanders. On the west side, between 35° and 34° enters the St. Francis, which is 200 yards wide at its mouth, and has a comparative course of 400 miles; 300 of which are considered boatable. A little above 34° enters White river. It has a comparative course of 1200 miles, and is 300 yards wide at its mouth. Thirty miles below and between 34° and 33°, comes in the Arkansas, the next largest tributary to Missouri on the west. Its course, including its meanders, is computed at 2500 miles. Between 33° and 32°, a little above the Walnut Hills, in the state of Mississippi, enters from the east the Yazoo river, 300 yards wide at its mouth. Below the Yazoo, on the same side, Bayou Pierré, Big Black, Cole's creek and Homochitto enter the river. Eighty miles below Natchez, and a little above 31°, on the west side, enters Red river ,a stream nearly as large as Arkansas. Immediately below this river, the Mississippi carries its greatest volume of water. A league and a half below this river, is seen the first bayou of note, which leaves the channel for the Gulf. It is the Atchafalaya and is supposed to be the ancient bed, by which Red river made its way to the Gulf, without joining the Mississippi. Twenty leagues below, on the east side, comes in bayou Sarah, the only stream of importance that enters below the outlet of Atchafalaya. The next bayou is Manchac or Ibberville, an outlet from the east bank, a little below Baton Rouge, through which in high waters, passes off a considerable mass through lakes Maurepas, Ponchartrain and Borgne, to the Gulf of Mexico. At no great distance below on the west side, is another considerable efflux, bayou Plaquemine; and at some distance below bayou LaFouche.—Thence to New Orleans the banks are but slightly broken. Below the city there is no outlet of any importance until you reach the four mouths by which the Mississippi enters the Gulf of Mexico.

From the falls of St. Anthony, to the mouth of Missouri, is 843 miles, and from thence to its mouth, in the gulf of Mexico, is 1396, making the whole length of the Mississippi, more than 3000 miles. It is estimated that there are 130 steamboats now running on this river; about 100 of which are of a large size.

Monroe, a county in East Tennessee, erected in 1819. It is bounded on the N. E. by Tennessee river, the line between it and Blount, on the N. W. by Roane, on the S. W. by Mc-Minn, and on the S. E. by North Carolina. It is drained by Tellico river, and other south branches of Tennessee river. Population in 1820, 2,529; in 1830, 13,709, making an increase in ten years of 11,180. It contains the towns of Madisonville, the seat of justice, Philadelphia, Rockville, Tellico, &c. And there are post offices at Humphrey's mills, mouth of Tellico and Tellico Plains. In this county the milk sickness prevails at times, amongst the knobs. Cent. lat. 35° 30′ N., lon. 7° 20′ W.

Monroe, the former seat of justice of Overton county, on a small branch of Obid's river, 96 miles N. E. by E. from Nashville, and 616 from Washington City, in lat. 36° 25′ N., lon.

8° 11' W. It contained in 1829, four stores, three taverns and the usual public buildings.—The seat of justice has been removed to Livingston.

Montgomery, a county in Middle Tennessee, erected in 1796, at the same time Robertson was formed, out of the district then called Tennessee county. It is bounded on the north by the state of Kentucky, on the east by Robertson, on the south by Dickson, and on the south west by Stewart. It is about 40 miles in length, with a mean breadth of about 18. Cumberland river traverses the southern part of this county, and at Clarksville, receives from the N. W. Red river. The soil is not generally productive, but in some parts it is highly so. The surface is rather uneven than hilly, and about one third of the county is brushy barrens.—Seat of justice, Clarksville; and there are post offices at Brookhill, Fredonia, Dayly's, Kercheval's, McAllis's X Roads, Mount Henry, Palmyra, Port Royal, Red River Forge, Searcy's, Williams' and Yellow creek. —In 1820, this county contained a population of 12,219. and in 1830 it was 14,365. Cent. lat. 36° 25' N., lon. 10° 15' W.

Montgomery, a post town and seat of justice of Morgan county, established on the land of Samuel Scott, on the turnpike road, in 1825. It is situated on the border of Emery's river, and contains five or 6 families, two stores and two taverns. It is 153 miles E. by N, from Nashville.[243]

Montgomery's, a post office in Sumner county, on Drake's creek, on the upper Nashville road, nine miles W. from Gallatin, and 18 miles north east from Nashville.[244]

Moody's Fork, a branch of Sugar creek, in the south east corner of Lawrence county.

Moorsville or Moorsburg, a town in Hawkins county, between Bean's Station and Rogersville, not far north of Holston river, and two miles east of Grainger county. It contains eight or ten families, one tavern and one store. It is 247

---

[243] Discontinued as a post office and county seat; the latter is now at Wartburg.

[244] Discontinued as a post office.

MOS   207

miles east by north from Nashville.[245]

Mooresville, a post town in Maury county, 61 miles south from Nashville, and 15 miles S. E. from Columbia. It contains two stores, one grocery, one doctor, two tailors, one cabinet maker, one saddler, one blacksmith, and half a dozen families.[246]

Morgan, a county in East Tennessee; bounded on the north by Kentucky, on the east by Campbell, on the south east by Anderson, and on the west and N. W. by Fentress. It is watered by the great South Fork of Cumberland river and branches on the west, and Emery's river on the south. On the east side of this county, there is some excellent land, but the surface in general is hilly and the soil sterile. Population in 1820, 1,676; in 1830, 2,582. Seat of justice, Montgomery.

Morganton, a post town established in 1813, at the mouth of Baker's creek, on the east bank of Little Tennessee river, in Blount county, eleven miles above its junction with the Holston. It was originally called Portsville. It contains eighteen dwelling houses, one hatter's shop, one cabinet shop, one smith's shop, one silversmith, one gunsmith, a merchant gristmill, sawmill, hemp-factory for making rope and bagging, one physician and seventy inhabitants. It is 200 miles E. by S. from Nashville.[247]

Morrison's X Roads, a post office in Warren county, S. E. by E. from Nashville, 70 miles.[248]

Morristown, a post office in Jefferson county, established in 1833.[249]

Moscow, a post town in Fayette county, on the north bank

---

[245] Now known as Mooresburg.

[246] Discontinued as a post office; the town is in Marshall County (established in 1836); postal service through Lewisburg.

[247] Morgantown, no longer a post office, is a community in the southeast corner of Loudon County (established in 1870); postal service through Greenback.

[248] Now listed as Morrison, in Warren County, near the Coffee County line.

[249] Morristown is the county seat and principal city of Hamblen County (established in 1870).

of Wolf river. It contains about a dozen houses, five mechanics and one inn. It is 146 miles S. W. by W. from Nashville.

Moss Creek, a post office in Jefferson county, 225 miles E. from Nashville.[160]

Mossy Creek, a bold stream in the county of Jefferson, on which are established six mills in a distance of four miles.

Mossy Run, a north branch of Cumberland, in Stewart county.

Mountain Creek, a west branch of Collin's river, in Warren county.

Mountain Creek, a north branch of Tennessee river, in Hamilton county, eleven miles below Falling Water creek.

Mount Airy, a post town in Bledsoe county, 115 miles S. E. from Nashville.[161]

Mount Carmel, a post office in Jackson county, established in 1833.[162]

Mount Comfort, a post office in Hardeman county, 153 miles S. W. by W. from Nashville.[163]

Mount Henry, a post office in Montgomery county, 85 miles N. W. from Nashville.[164]

Mount Pinson, a post office in Madison county, 166 miles W. by S. from Nashville, and 12 from Jackson. Here is a mound 60 or 70 feet high, and an ancient fortification.[165]

Mount Pleasant, a post town in Maury county, 52 miles S. from Nashville, and 11 miles S. from Columbia. It is a beautiful village and the largest town in the county, except Columbia. It was incorporated in 1832, and is a point in the Columbia rail road, 46 miles from Tennessee river.

Mount Pisgah, a post office in Blount county, 200 miles E. by S. from Nashville.[166]

---

[160] Discontinued as a post office.

[161] Discontinued; the community is in Sequatchie County; postal service through Dunlap.

[162-164] Discontinued as a post office.

[165] The town and post office is now "Pinson." Pinson Mounds, nearby, is now a registered national historic landmark.

[166] Discontinued as a post office.

MUR 209

Mount Richardson, a post office in Jackson county.[257]

Mount Sterling, a town in Hawkins county, established in 1817, on the road from Dotson's Ford to Cheek's X Roads, 245 miles east from Nashville.[258]

Mount View, a post office in Davidson county, 13 miles from Nashville, on the road leading to Murfreesboro'.[259]

Mouth of Paintrock, a post office in Roane county, at the junction of Paintrock creek with Tennessee, above Kingston, 165 miles E. by S. from Nashville.[260]

Mouth of Tellico, a post office in Monroe country, 180 miles E. by S. from Nashville.[261]

Mud Creek, a south fork of South Forked Deer, on the east side of Haywood county, which joins the river about a mile below Harrisburg.

Muddy Creek, a south branch of French Broad, in Jefferson county, south of Dandridge, near Sevier county line.

Mulberry, a post office in Lincoln county, 84 miles E. of S. from Nashville, on a creek by that name (a north branch of Elk river,) above Fayetteville.

Mulberry Creek, an eastern branch of Powell's river, N. E. of Wallen's ridge, near the Virginia line, in the N. E. angle of Claiborne county.

Mulloy's, a post office in Robertson county, 33 miles N. W. from Nashville.[262]

Mulherring's Creek, a branch of Smith's Fork, in Smith county, below Hickman's creek.[263]

Murfreesboro', the seat of justice for Rutherford county. It was established in 1811, and incorporated in 1817, and was the seat of government from that time until 1826. In 1830 it

---

[257-258] Discontinued as a post office.

[259] No longer a post office; a community called Mountain View is in Davidson County between Una and LaVergne.

[260] Discontinued as a post office.

[261] Discontinued; the site was near Fort Loudon and Vonore, Monroe County.

[262] Discontinued as a post office.

[263] Mulherring's Creek is a tributary of the Caney Fork, not of Smith's Fork.

contained a population of 786, and in 1833, about 1000. It is well laid out and handsomely situated near the west branch of Stone's river, surrounded by a body of rich farming land, under a high state cultivation. It has an academy and two schools, three churches, four clergymen, ten lawyers, four physicians, a printing office, two cotton factories, two cotton gins, one carding machine, one grist mill, four blacksmiths, four bricklayers, six carpenters, five cabinet makers, one gun smith, three hatters, one painter, three saddlers, five shoemakers, one silversmith, four tailors, two tanners, one tinner, two taverns and ten or twelve stores. It is 32 miles S. E. from Nashville, and 686 W. S. W. from Washington City. Lat. 35° 52′ N., lon. 9° 15′ W.

211

N

Nanconnah Creek, an east branch of the Mississippi river, in the south west angle of the state, opposite to President's Island, in Shelby county.

Naples, a town established on the lands of Micajah Thomas, in Henry county, in 1831.[264]

Narrimore, a post office in Bledsoe county, established in 1833.[265]

Nash's Bluff, a post office in Dyer county, 190 miles west from Nashville.[266]

Nashoba, a village established by Frances Wright, on Wolf river, in Shelby county.

Nashville, the metropolis of the State of Tennessee, and the seat of justice of the county of Davidson, is elegantly situated on the south bank of Cumberland river, in lat. 36° 9′ 43″ N., long. 9° 47′ 15″ west from Washington City, or 86° 47′ 15″ west from London. The site is undulating and rocky, with unequal elevations from fifty to one hundred and seventy-five feet above low water mark. The ground plat is interspersed with beautiful cedar groves, and the environs present the richest variety of landscape scenery; the river seems to meander where it should, and the evergreen hills have the proper elevation and position to give boldness and symmetry to the picture; in short it is altogether one of the most romantic, healthy and flourishing little cities in the Valley of the Mississippi.

The first settlement was made in the year 1779 by the late General James Robertson and company but it had for some time previous been the occasional rendezvous of the French traders, and was then called the French Lick. In 1783 the legislature of North Carolina established the county of Davidson, and the first county court was held here on the 6th day of October, by the commissioned justices of the peace. They appointed Andrew Ewing clerk, and Daniel Williams

[264-266] Discontinued as a post office.

Sheriff, and made an order for the erection of a temporary court house and jail by the first day of January ensuing, at Nashboro' as they then called the seat of justice. In 1784 a town was established by law, by the name of Nashville, in honor of the brave and patriotic General Nash, who fell at the battle of Germantown, October 4, 1777. The commissioners, Thomas Mulloy, Samuel Barton, Daniel Smith, James Shaw and Isaac Lindsey, were authorized and required to cause to be laid off two hundred acres of land at the Bluff, near to, but not so as to include the French Lick, in lots of one acre each, with convenient streets, lanes and alleys, reserving four acres for the purpose of erecting public buildings. And provision was made to allot to citizen subscribers, such number as they should draw, for which they were to receive a deed, upon condition that within three years they would make certain specified improvements thereon. This year there were two licensed taverns in Nashville, and a few shops. In 1787 there were about a half a dozen frame and log houses and twenty or thirty cabins. In November 1788, the Hon. John McNairy held the first superior court of law and equity for the county of Davidson and Sumner. John Macay was appointed clerk and Andrew Jackson, state's attorney pro tem.

In 1796 the legislature of Tennessee appointed additional trustees, and made some slight alterations in the registered boundaries of the town. In 1801 it was placed under the government of an Intendent and six commissioners. In 1804 it had a population of about 400 and in 1806 it was incorporated with a mayor and six aldermen, and Joseph Coleman was elected the first mayor. In 1810 the population was about 1100 and in 1812 the legislature sat here for the first time. In the spring of 1818 the citizens of Nashville hailed the arrival of the first Steam Boat she carried 110 tons: was called the General Jackson, and built in 1817 at *Pittsburg for Governor Carroll*, who sold her to Messrs. Fletcher, Young and Marr, for $33,000 cash. Freight was then five cents from New Orleans to this place.

In 1822 a fine bridge was built across the Cumberland opposite the public square, which cost about $85,000. In 1823 the population was 3,463, and in June 1830 there were 5566 of which 1108 were slaves, and 204 were free persons of color. At present (1834) the population is about 7000, and there are about three hundred brick and two hundred frame and log dwelling houses; eighty brick and fifteen frame stores, twenty brick warehouses, fifty brick and twenty-five frame offices, and one hundred work shops. The public buildings are a court house, jail, penitentiary, lunatic asylum, university, female academy, theatre, episcopal, presbyterian, cumberland presbyterian, methodist, baptist, and catholic churches, several banks a masonic hall, two market houses, water works, &c. And there are also two steam saw mills, one steam rolling mill, two brass and iron foundries, three hardware stores, three iron stores, four auction stores, eighteen wholesale stores, fifty-five retail stores, four groceries, six taverns, and a number of refectories, confectionaries, coffee houses, fancy stores, &c. Here are likewise six merchant tailors, ten saddlers, twelve shoemakers, four boot and shoemakers, four shoestores, two tanyards, about a dozen blacksmiths, one gunsmith, six silversmiths and jewellers, three extensive apothecary and drug stores, one hatter, three cabinet makers, a number of carpenters, three carriage makers, three wagon makers, three tallow chandlers, four tobacconists, two coppersmiths, five tinners, one engraver, four portrait painters, four house and sign painters, six bricklayers, four stone cutters, one marble worker, and several plasterers, glaziers, &c. There are four extensive printing offices, four large bookstores, three book binderies, two classical schools, two female academies, ten common schools, an infant school, and a number of sunday schools. There are about a dozen clergymen including the collegiate and the academical instructors, upwards of forty practising lawyers, and about twenty-five physicians.

The *Court House*, which stands on the public square, is a spacious and commodious edifice. It presents a handsome front of 105 feet and is sixty-three feet deep. The basement story contains a number of rooms, designed for public offices, and on the second and third floors there are two rooms forty by sixty feet each, two others thirty-six by forty, and two others twenty-three by forty. The basement story is eleven feet high, and the two principal ones are eighteen feet each, and the height of the whole building to the top of the dome is ninety feet. The foundation and part of the lower story is of fine hewn stone, and the remainder of brick, and the two fronts are ornamented with four white pilasters each. The dome contains a good town clock, and is supported by eight columns of Ionic order.

The Sheriff's office is on the first floor, the marshal's on the second, and the Secretary of State's on the third. All the state courts are held in the north room of the second story, and the Federal court occupies the south room in the same. The two large rooms in the third story are handsomely fitted up for the use of the legislature until a state house shall be built.

The *Market House* on the square, is one of the finest buildings of the kind, to be found in the west. At each end there are spacious rooms, one of which is occupied as a City Hall and recorder's office.

The *Nashville University*. This institution is located on a handsome elevation, at the upper end of College street. Its buildings are brick, and consist of a college edifice, three stories high, 200 feet long and 50 broad, containing a chapel, recitation rooms, and forty four rooms for students; a building of one story 100 feet by 40, containing a laboratory, apparatus, &c.; a house for the stewart, refectory, &c., and a house for the President, which is in a beautiful grove east of Market street, a short distance from the college. The mineralogical cabinet contains upward of 10,000 specimens; the philosophical apparatus cost $6000; there is a good chemical apparatus, and also a museum of natural history.—The library contains 2000 volumes, and there are libraries belonging to the students containing 1200 volumes.

The institution originated in the Davidson county academy, established by the state of North Carolina, Dec. 29, 1785.

The academy was converted into Cumberland College by the legislature of Tennessee, Sept. 11th 1806. In 1826, the name was changed to the 'Nashville University.' The value of its property in and near Nashville, exclusive of the college buildings, &c., is estimated at about $50,000; and it owns 25,000 acres of land in the Western District.

FACULTY IN 1834.

REV. PHILIP LINDSLEY, D. D., President and Professor, Mor. Phil., Pol. Econ., &c.

Gerard Troost, M. D., Prof. of Chemistry, Mineralogy and Geology.

James Hamilton, A. M., Prof. Mathematics and Natural Philosophy.

N. S. Parmantier, Prof. French Language and Literature.

George Ely and *Abednego Stephens,* Tutors in the Greek and Latin.

Number of students in the four classes, from 70 to 100; whole number of alumni, 118, in 1833. *Commencement* is on the first Wednesday in October.—*Vacations,* 1st from commencement, five and a half weeks; second, from 1st Wednesday in April, five and a half weeks.

Annual Expenses:—Tuition, room rent, servants hire, &c., $50; for board, $1.75 per week; for the year $70.00—total $120. Candidates for the ministry of all denominations are admitted at half price.

The *Episcopal Church* is a fine stone building handsomely stuccoed, and in the Gothic style of architecture. It is fifty three feet deep in front, on Spring street, from the extremities of the buttresses, and extends back along high street nearly, eighty feet. It contains a basement story nine feet high, embracing a room forty by forty five feet, for lectures and sunday schools, together with rooms for the vestry and clergymen, communicating with the body of the church by private stairs behind the pulpit. The body of the church is forty five feet wide, sixty nine long and twenty four high; containing sixty two spacious pews, with extensive galleries on three sides. The pulpit and desk are in good taste, and the front gallery is ornamented with a fine toned organ. The windows are five feet wide and twenty one high, having buttresses or projections of two feet square between them, terminating in points.. The whole is surmounted with a Gothic cupola, in which is a bell, weighing 544 lbs. The corner stone was laid with appropriate ceremonies on the 5th of July 1830, and it was consecrated by the name of Christ Church, in July, 1831. The whole cost was about $16,000. Rev. George Weller, Rector, and the number of communicants, thirty four.

The *Baptist Church,* also on Spring street is a neat brick building two stories high, forty five by sixty feet, with a tall steeple, and an excellent bell. The whole cost about $6000.

The Baptist association was formed in 1820, and in 1825, there was a division, and the Reformers as they are denominated, seceded from the regular Baptists, retained the church, and declined any further connexion with the Association, deeming it unwarranted by word of God. They reject all confessions of faith, and profess to be guided by the scriptures alone. They receive all persons professing faith in Jesus Christ by Immersion, for the remission of sins, and they meet every Lord's day, in order to engage in worship, by reading the scriptures, exhortation, prayer, praise, breaking of bread and contribution for the poor. The number of members in April, 1834, was 456, of which 280 were colored. The regular Baptists have about 100 members, and hold their meetings in the Masonic Hall.

The *New Methodist Church,* is situated on Spring between High and Summer streets, nearly opposite to Christ church; is a spacious and elegant building. Its form is that of a parallelogram, being sixty feet in front and extending ninety feet back. It has a basement story containing two rooms, thirty by sixty feet each, intended for sunday schools and class meetings. The front approached by stone steps, is composed of three parts—an inverted portico, supported by two massive stone columns of the Doric order, and enclosed between rusticated stone piers flanked by antis, containing each a flight of stairs to the galleries, and lighted by well proportioned windows. The extent of the first story is marked by a handsome stone cornice extending the whole length of the front, and surmounted by a blocking course on which rest four pilasters that embellish the second story, the most striking feature of which is a large Grecian window in the centre, surmounted by a noble arch, and two others with square heads, immediately above and corresponding with those in the lower story. The second story is surmounted by a well proportioned ballustrade, that conceals the roof, and lends to the whole composition a light and pleasing effect. The main body of the building is lighted by two ranges of windows in good proportion. The interior of the building is finished in corresponding style. The pulpit is richly draperied, and fronted by a spacious altar. The pews are free, and well arranged, and will accommodate about 1500 persons.

It is contemplated during the present season, to surmount the whole structure with a turret, in uniformity of proportion with the other parts of the building, in which will be placed a bell weighing 1100 lbs., which has been presented to the church by a gentleman of New Orleans. The cost of the building when completed will be upwards of $12,000. It was solemnly dedicated to the worship of God on the last Sunday in October, 1833, by the venerable Bishop McKendree, assisted by the Rev. Messrs Douglass, McMahon and Maddin.

The Methodists have three other places of preaching the old church on Spring street, Gwinn's Chapel, on College side, and the African church. As early as 1796, they had a small society here, and had erected a meeting house on the public square. About the year 1809, they held their meetings in the jail, and in 1815, a small brick church was erected in South Field, and they had 20 or 30 members. In 1822, the society contained 90 members, and there has been a gradual increase ever since. The number in April 1834, was 780 whites, and 819 blacks in the city and vicinity.

The *Presbyterian Church,* also on Spring street, between the new Methodist church and the river. It is built on the site of the old church, which was burnt in 1832, and is ninety-one feet long and sixty-nine wide, and when completed will be one of the handsomest buildings in the city. It has a basement story eleven feet high and sixty four feet square in the clear, which is comfortably fitted up for a lecture room and sunday school. The main room is sixty-five feet square, contains 124 pews, and will accommodate eight hundred persons. The gallery is very spacious and will hold about 500. The vestibule is approached by a flight of stone steps, extending the whole width of the building and is supported by six massive brick columns cased and fluted. The whole building when completed will have cost about $16,000.

The presbyterian church here had no regular pastor until the installation of the Rev. Aaron Campbell, in 1821; previous to that time it was occasionally supplied, and doctors Craighead and Blackburn, may be considered the fathers of this branch of the church. Dr. Blackburne organized a church in 1813, and when Dr. Campbell was called to the charge, there were about one hunded members. Dr. Campbell resigned in 1826, and there was a vacancy for about a year, when the Rev. Dr. Obadiah Jennings took charge; he died in January 1831, and there was a vacancy again until the call of the Rev. John T. Edgar, the present pastor. He was installed on the 25th December, 1833. Number of members in May 1834, two hundred.

The *Cumberland Presbyterian Church,* is situated on Summer street. It is a plain but neat brick building fifty seven by seventy feet. It is two stories high exclusive of the basement story which is partly below the surface.. The front presents a parapet wall variegated with recessed arches, resting on pillars which forms an open vestibule; from whence on either side winding flights of stairs ascend to the galleries. Three doors open to the main room, which is a spacious sanctuary sixty by fifty-five feet. The pews below will accommodate about 600, and the galleries about 400 persons. The whole interior is light and comfortable, and fitted up in good taste. The cost, exclusive of the steeple which has not yet been erected, is seven thousand dollars. It was dedicated to the worship of God in May 1832. The clergymen of this denomination began to labor statedly in Nashville, in 1829, and the succeeding year a society was organized with about a dozen members. This year the Rev. A. M. Dowell, had the pastoral charge, and they held their meetings in the city hall and catholic church. In May 1831, the Rev. Messrs. Donnell, Smith and others, held a five day's meeting in the new market house; the novelty drew thousands to the scene, and about thirty were added to the church. Arrangements were soon made for the erection of a church, which was ready for the reception of the General Assembly in May 1832, shortly afterwards Messrs. Lowry and Smith, editors of the Revivalist, located in the place and jointly exercised the pastoral charge for one year.—At present there is no regular pastor, but the church have the alternate labors of several gentlemen. Number of members, seventy-two.

The *Catholic Church*, stands upon the northern declivity of Campbell's hill, which gives it a handsome appearance. It is, however, in a state of dilapidation, and there is no organized body of members, or officiating priest.

The *Nashville Female Academy*, a flourishing institution, is situated in the western suburbs of the city, near Spring street, in a handsome bowling-green. It was instituted in 1816, and incorporated in 1817. Dr. Berry was the principal for a time, but he resigned and was succeeded by the Rev. Mr. Hume, who presided 'till his death in 1833, when the present incumbent, the Rev. Robt. A. Lapsley was appointed. The school rooms will accommodate upwards of 200 pupils, and 70 or 80 may obtain boarding at the public boarding house. The greatest number of scholars at any one time was 239, but the number at present does not exceed 130.

The *Bank of the State*, is situated upon College street, immediately opposite Yeatman and Woods'.—It was chartered in 1820 for twenty-three years, with a branch at Knoxville and agencies in every county in the state. The whole capital, which belonged to the state, has been appropriated for the promotion of internal improvement and common schools; and William M. Berryhill, Esq. has been appointed agent to close the concerns of the mother bank.

The bank of *Yeatman Woods' & Co.*, a private institution, presents a stucco front, with arches, a recess and iron doors and windows. It is on the west side of College street, between the square and Union street. It is a very solvent institution. John P. Erwin, Esq. Cashier.

The *Branch Bank of the United States*, is a handsome brick building with plain columns, and is situated on the north corner of the public square. This branch which was established in 1827, has done an extensive business. The amount of specie reported in Jan. 1832, was $167,866.36. Thos. H. Fletcher, Esq. is president and John Sommerville, Esq. cashier.

The *Union Bank of Tennessee*, was chartered in 1832, with a capital not to exceed $3,000,000. It went into operation in 1833 under very favourable auspices. The state owns half a million of stock, and individuals two millions. It is a bank of public deposite, both for the state and the United States, and the president is a pension agent. It has branches at Knoxville, Columbia and Jackson, and agencies at Baltimore, Philadelphia and New Orleans. The present banking house, is at the corner of College and Union streets, but a splendid house on the style of the United States Bank at Philadelphia, has been commenced at the corner of Union and Cherry streets, and will be finished by January 1835. George W. Gibbs, Esq., president, A. Vanwyck, Esq., Cashier.

The *Planters' Bank of Tennessee* was chartered in 1833, and organized in 1834. Capital $2,000,000.—The temporary banking house, is on the north side of the public square, one door west of the Nashville Inn. Edward B. Littlefield, Esq., President, and Nicholas Hobson, Esq., Cashier.

The *Penitentiary*, is a beautiful and substantial Prison, located in the western suburbs of the city, on the right of the road leading from spring or church street, about one mile from the court house. The building was commenced in 1830, and finished so far as to receive convicts by the first of January

1831. It presents a front of three hundred and ten feet, and is three hundred and fifty in depth. The two wings of the front building contain two hundred cells, and half of the center building is occupied by the Keeper, and the other half is used for a hospital, guard rooms, &c. The yard walls are four and a half feet thick at the bottom, and three at the top, and have an average height of twenty feet. The whole cost of the edifice up to the reception by the State was less than $50,000. It was built by David Morrison, an experienced architect under the direction of the Governor and Commissioners. By the report made to the legislature in September 1833, the income for the preceding year was $23,223, and after deducting $16,771 for expenses &c., left a balance in favor of the institution of $6,552. Inspectors, William Carroll, Samuel G. Smith, Robert C. Foster, Moses Ridley and Eastin Morris. Keeper, John McIntosh. In April 1834, there were eighty convicts engaged in shoemaking, hatting, tailoring, coopering, blacksmithing, wagonmaking, carding, &c.

The *Lunatic Hospital,* is pleasantly situated on an elevated spot south of Vauxhall Garden. The act for its establishment was passed October 19th, 1832, and ten thousand dollars appropriated to purchase the site and commence the building. In 1833 one half of the State tax of the years 1834 and 1835 for the county of Davidson, was appropriated in addition. With the exception of the penitentiary, it is the largest building in the State, and when completed will be an ornament to the city, as well as a monument of the humanity and charity of the State. It is three stories high including the basement story, with an additional tier of rooms in the centre building. The base and front walls are of stone, and the remainder of brick. When the whole is finished, upwards of one hundred unfortunate persons may be comfortably provided for, and secured in separate rooms.

Commissioners, Joseph Woods, H. R. W. Hill, Felix Robertson, John Shelby and Boyd McNairy.

The *Water Works,* for supplying the city with water, are located on the bank of the river above the city.

They were constructed by Albert Stein, an experienced engineer, at the expense of the corporation, and completed in November, 1833. The water is raised from the river by a high pressure steam engine. The engine house is built of stone and brick, thirty six by thirty feet, and fifty feet above low water mark. The reservoir stands on an elevation of one hundred and sixty-six feet above low water mark, and 45 above the level of the public square, near a fine cedar grove, which partially obstructs the view of the city, but it adds much to the comfort and beauty of the spot as a summer evening's retreat. It is distant from the public square, by the line of the main pipe, 5879 feet, and from the lower pump, by the ascending main, 472 feet, seventy feet six inches long, eighty feet six inches wide, and ten feet six inches deep. Both of them when filled to the depth of ten feet, will contain 695,520 gallons. The quantity of water which may be raised in twenty four hours, at twenty strokes per minute, is 950,000 gallons, and at sixteen strokes per minute, 750,000. The main pipe leading from the reservoir, is of six inch bore, and extends as follows: 1838 feet to the circular pipe in Market street, with a fall of fifty and a half feet, from thence to the branch pipe with stop cock on Market street, 1628 feet, with a descent of sixty one and a half feet, making a fall of 112 feet from the top of the reservoir; from thence to the square, 2413 feet with an ascent of sixty-seven feet. The whole cost of the works up to Nov. 1833, was $49,264.56, including $8,727.77, paid for the ground and for superintendency. Since which time, the city authorities have been actively engaged in extending the pipes, and will, in a short time, have an ample supply of good water in every part of the city. Strangers in the city during the summer months, will find it an agreeable excursion to visit the Water Works, Vauxhall Garden and the Sulphur spring.

Vauxhall Garden, is a place of fashionable resort, and is situated in the southern border of the city, near the Franklin turnpike. Here is an ingenious circular rail-way, two hundred and sixty two yards in circumference. The cars are so constructed that persons are enabled to propel themselves at a most rapid rate, simply by turning of a crank with the hands. There is also a large assembly room, handsomely decorated; and the promenade, walks and other places of amusement and recreation, are laid off and arranged in good taste. It is owned and kept by Mr. John Decker, a gentleman who spares no pains to render his parterre acceptable to visiters.

The *Sulphur Spring*, is situated in the lower suburbs, on French Lick creek, between Cherry and Summer streets. The water is a strong salt sulphur, but clear, cold and palatable, and is said to contain about the same properties of the celebrated Harrowgate waters.—Here are also cold and warm baths; and the curious observer can spend a leisure hour very satisfactorily, in examining the fragments of Indian pottery ware, ancient furnaces for making salt, and various aboriginal remains which exist here in great abundance.

The *Post Office* is situated on Cherry and Deaderick streets. It is a distributing office, and receives about fifty mails per week. The net revenue for the first quarter of 1834 was $1,431.50.

The Louisville and Northern stages arrive and depart daily, the Lexington via. Gallatin, Glasgow, &c. every other day,—Russellville, Hopkinsville, Shawneetown, &c: tri-weekly,—Clarksville, Dover, Paris &c: tri-weekly,—Columbia, daily, —Memphis, Bolivar, &c: daily, three times a week via Jackson, and three times via Florence,—Florence, Natchez, New Orleans, &c: tri-weekly,—Huntsville, daily, three times a week via Columbia, and three times via Murfreesboro',—Murfreesboro', Shelbyville, Fayetteville, &c: tri-weekly,—and the Lebanon, Knoxville, &c: tri-weekly—and there is a weekly mail to Shelbyville carried on horse back.

Nashville is 329 miles from Abingdon, Va., 200 from Knoxville, eighty-six from Sparta, twenty-eight from Lebanon, twenty-five from Gallatin, 200 from Lexington, Ky., 259 from Maysville, Ky., 175 from Louisville, Ky., 285 from Cincinnati, Ohio, 240 from Memphis, 147 from Jackson, thirty-eight from Charlotte, 115 from Florence, Ala., forty-two from Columbia, eighteen from Franklin, 119 from Decatur, Ala., seventy-five from Pulaski, 110 from Huntsville, Ala., seventy-nine from Fayetteville, seventy from Hopkinsville Ky., and forty-six from Clarksville.

For a more complete list of roads and distances, see Appendix.

Nelson's Creek, a north branch of Tennessee river, in Blount county—also a branch of Harpeth in Williamson county.

Nevin's X Roads, a post office in the Cherokee nation.[467]

New Canton, a post town in Hawkins county, 244 miles N. of E. from Nashville.[468]

New Hope, a post office in Lincoln county, 81 miles E. of S. from Nashville.[469]

Newman's Ridge, one of the spurs of Cumberland mountain, in East Tennessee, lying in the N. E. angle of Claiborne county, west of Clinch river, and east of Powell's mountain. It took its name from a Mr. Newman who discovered it in 1761.[470]

Newmarket, a post town in Jefferson county, 15 miles from Dandridge, and 24 east from Knoxville. This village has sprung up within the last eight years. It is situated in a beautiful valley, about four miles west of Mossy creek, on which there are a number of mills.—The town is watered by Lost creek, and contains almost 250 inhabitants, and a number of stores, taverns, workshops, &c. The inhabitants are moral and industrious, and the Methodist Episcopal church have here a manual labor school, styled the Holston Seminary, which is a promising institution. A newspaper called the Newmarket Telegraph is published at this place.[471]

New Port, the seat of justice of Cocke county. It was established in 1799 on the land of John Gilleland, on the bank of the French Broad river above the mouth of Big Pigeon. In

---
[467] Discontinued as a post office.
[468] Discontinued; mail service through Church Hill.
[469] Discontinued; mail service through Fayetteville.
[470] Newman's Ridge is in Hancock County (established in 1844).
[471] Properly, "New Market."

1833 it contained 150 inhabitants; two lawyers, two doctors, two clergymen, two churches, one school, two taverns, two stores, three blacksmiths, two carpenters, one cabinetmaker, two hatters, two tailors, two shoemakers, two saddlers, one tanner, and one wagonmaker. It is twenty-five miles S. W. from Greenville, fifty from Jonesboro', 250 E. from Nashville, and 491 S. W. from Washington City. Lat. 35° 55' N., lon. 6° 10' W.[272]

New River, an east branch of the south fork of Cumberland in Morgan county, and has its mouth east of Jamestown, and north of the new turnpike road leading to Jacksboro.[273]

New York, a town at the mouth of Blooming Grove, in Montgomery county.

Nettle Carrier, a branch of Obid's river, in Overton county.

Nimble Creek, a north branch of Tennessee, in Blount county, 200 miles south of east from Nashville.

Nixon's Fork, a branch of Indian creek, in Haywood county. It joins Alpin's Fork, north of Brownsville.

Noah's Fork, a post office in Bedford county, 51 miles E. of S. from Nashville.[274]

Nolensville, a post town in Williamson county, 32 miles S. from Nashville, on the Huntsville road.

Nolachuckey, a post office in Green county, 255 miles E. from Nashville.[275]

Nolachucky, a river which rises in the northern part of Buncombe county, N. C. and flowing north west, enters Washington, in this state, and crossing Washington and Greene, joins French Broad 40 miles above its junction with the Holston.

North Cross Creek, a north branch of Cumberland, in Smith county.

---

[272] Properly, "Newport."

[273] The greater part of the New River's course is in Scott County (established in 1849).

[274] A community northwest of Manchester in Coffee County (established in 1836); postal service is through Beechgrove.

[275] Discontinued as a post office.

North Chickamauga, a post office in Hamilton county, established in 1833.[376]

North Fork, a branch of *Duck river,* in Bedford county, in the N. W. corner, above Wilson's creek.

North Fork, a large branch of *Obion river,* which rises in Henry county, N. W. of Paris, and flowing through Weakley, joins the river in the south east corner of Obion, above Davidson's bluff.

North Fork, a branch of *Forked Deer,* rising in Carroll, and flowing through Gibson, joins the river in the east end of Dyer county. It is navigable from its mouth to Page's mill in Gibson county.

---

[376] Discontinued; absorbed into Chattanooga.

227

O

Oak Grove, a post office in Jefferson county, 230 miles east from Nashville.[277]

Obids River, a south eastern branch of Cumberland river. It takes its rise in the Cumberland mountains, in Overton and Fentress counties. It has a remarkably smooth and regular current, and excepting some small obstructions, which might easily be removed, it is safe and convenient for the descent of boats fifty or sixty feet long, and from ten to twelve wide, from as high up as the Poplar and Buffalo Coves, on the east fork, in Fentress county. And from the junction of the east and west forks, down, it is considered but little inferior to Cumberland, for small boats. Its general course is west; and after watering the north of Overton, falls into the Cumberland, near its north west corner. It is generally called *Obies* river. It has been declared navigable as high up as Donaldson's Cove.[278]

Obed's river, a branch of Emery's river, in Morgan county.

Obion, a county in West Tennessee, in the north west angle of the State. It was erected in 1823, and is bounded on the north by Kentucky, on the east by Weakley, on the south by Gibson and Dyer counties, and on the west by the river Mississippi. It is about twenty-three miles wide, and thirty-five long. Its principal streams are Obion and Reel Foot rivers. Seat of justice, Troy. Population in 1830, 2,099.[279]

Obionsville, a post office in Obion county, established in 1833.[280]

Obion River, an east branch of the Mississippi, in West Tennessee, watering the counties of Carroll, Weakley, Obion and Dyer. After the junction of the principal forks in the

---

[277] Discontinued as a post office; mail service through Dandridge. There are 14 communities in Tennessee called Oak Grove.

[278] Properly, "Obey's River," not to be confused with "Obed River" which is in Cumberland and Morgan counties.

[279] Union City is now the county seat of Obion County.

[280] Officially, the simpler "Obion."

south east corner of Obion, it flows a general south west course, and falls into the Mississippi at the western bend, below the grand cut off, in Dyer county, in lat. 35° 56′ N., long. 12° 40′ W. It is navigable as high up as the mouth of Beaver creek, in Carroll county.

Old Town, a post office in Claiborne county.[281]

Old Town Creek, a west branch of Powell's river, in Claiborne county. It heads near the Cumberland Gap.

Oliver's, a post office in Anderson county, 190 miles east from Nashville.[282]

Oporto, a post office in Fentress county.[283]

Oppossum Creek, a north branch of Tennessee, in Hamilton county, four miles below Rocky creek.

Oppossum Creek, a south branch of the Caney Fork, in Warren county.

Overall's Creek, a west branch of the west fork of Stone's river, in Rutherford county, above the town of Jefferson.

Overton, a county in Middle Tennessee, erected in 1806. It is bounded on the north by the state of Kentucky, and east by Fentress, on the south and south west by the Walton Road, which is the line between it and White, and on the west by Jackson county. It is twenty-eight or twenty-nine miles long from north to south, and twenty-two wide from east to west, and contains an area of 625 square miles. The principal water courses in this county, are, Wolf, Obid's and Roaring rivers; all rising about the base of the range of mountains, which run through the south eastern part of the county, and taking their courses northwestwardly to the Cumberland river. Obid's river runs through the most populous and wealthy part. In addition to these, there are a great many creeks suitable for mills and other machinery. There is a spring about two and a half miles from Monroe, that rises near the summit of a high hill, and in running 300 yards falls 250 feet, in a column of water a foot in diameter. It has been used to propel a

---

[281] Discontinued as a post office.
[282] Officially, "Oliver Springs."
[283] Discontinued as a post office.

OWL 229

grist mill for many years, but is at present unoccupied. There are numerous grist and saw mills in the county, and one spinning establishment about four miles from Monroe, with sixty spindles and a wool carding machine, grist mill, and cotton gin at the same place. The only towns in the county are Livingston, Monroe and Hilham. About one fourth of the land is good, and the balance is poor and hilly, but affording a tolerable range for stock. About 2000 head of hogs and 2 or 300 head of cattle are annually raised for market. Grain is the staple. Iron ore and stone coal may be had in great abundance. Oak, ash, hickory, beech, and on the spurs of the mountains, pine, constitute the growth of timber. Population in 1820, 7,128; in 1830, 8,246. Monroe was the former seat of justice, but it has lately been removed to Livingston.

Owl Creek, an east branch of Tennessee river, between Tom's and Caper's creeks, below Perrysville in Perry county.

231

P

Pactolus, a post town in Sullivan county, six miles above Kingsport, on the south side of Holston. There was established in this place, a very extensive Nail Factory, which supplied nearly the whole country east of Huntsville, Al. with first rate nails. The factory is owned by Elijah Embree, Esq. It is twelve miles from Blountsville, and 268 from Nashville.[284]

Page's Mills, a post office in Gibson county, 150 miles west from Nashville.[285]

Paint Rock, a very noted rock on the French Broad river, six miles below the warm springs, near the line between this State and N. C. It is about 200 feet at its base, 150 perpendicular; the paintings are scattered over the surface of the rock, commencing twenty or thirty feet from the ground, and extending to the top, and are supposed by some to be artificial, but they are probably occasioned by the oozing of mineral waters.

Paint Rock Creek, a south branch of Tennessee river, between Bud and Stamp creeks, in Roane county.

Paint Rock Creek, a north branch of New river, in Campbell county.[286]

Palmyra, a post town in Montgomery county, established in 1796, on the south bank of Cumberland river, forty-eight miles below Nashville, and ten below Clarksville. It was laid out on the land of Dr. Morgan Brown, at the mouth of Deason's creek.

Panther Creek, an east branch of Tennessee, in Stewart county.

Paperville, a post town twelve miles east of Blountsville, in Sullivan county, on Sinking creek, a north branch of Holston

---

[284] Pactolus is a community southeast of Kingsport; no longer a post office; postal service through Kingsport.

[285] Discontinued as a post office.

[286] The stream is in Scott County (established in 1849).

river. It contains about 100 inhabitants, a paper manufactory, one wagon maker, one blacksmith, two saddlers, one tavern, one physician and one presbyterian church. It is 300 miles north of east from Nashville.[287]

Paris, the seat of Justice of Henry county. It was laid off in a thick forest in the year 1823, on the dividing ground between the waters of Obion and Sandy rivers, near the Baily Fork of the latter. In 1833 it contained about 800 inhabitants, twelve lawyers, twelve doctors, two clergymen, one church, one printing office, one academy, three schools, ten stores, two taverns, five carpenters, four bricklayers, two cabinet makers, two hatters, eight tailors, two shoemakers, five blacksmiths, one silversmith, four tanners, two tiners, seven saddlers, one cotton gin and two factories. It is twenty-three miles east from Dresden, thirty north east from Reynoldsburg, twenty-five north from Huntingdon, thirty south west from Dover, thirty-five south from Wadesboro', Ky. 110 north of west from Nashville, and 812 west by south from Washington city. Lat. 36° 19′ N., long. 11° 19′ W.

Paschal, a post office in Weakley county, established in 1833.[288]

Pea Ridge, a post office in Shelby county, established in 1833.[289]

Perry, a county in Middle Tennessee, erected in 1820. It is bounded on the north by Humphreys, on the south by Wayne and Hardin, on the east by Hickman, and on the west by Henderson and Carroll. It is thirty miles long N. and S. and twenty-six wide, and contains an area of about 825 square miles. Tennessee river flows from south to north a little west of the centre of this county, and receives on the west Beech river, Lick creek, &c.; on the east side, Cedar, Marsh, Cypress, Lick, Spring, Toms, Owl and Caper's creeks. Buffalo river flows through the east side of the county, and joins Duck river, in the S. E. corner of Humphreys. That part of Perry

---

[287] A community on the southeast outskirts of Bristol; discontinued as a post office.

[288-289] Discontinued as a post office.

lying west of the river is in West Tennessee. It contained a population of 2384, in 1820; and in 1830, 7038. Seat of justice Perryville; and there is a post office at Locust Grove.[290]

Perry's, a post office in Giles county, eighty miles south from Nashville.[291]

Perryville, a post town and the seat of justice of Perry county, situated on the east bank of Tennessee river, about the mouth of Spring creek, In lat. 35° 40′ N., lon. 10° 38′ W. 112 miles W. S. W. from Nashville, and 812 W. by S. from Washington City. It contained in 1833 about seventy-five inhabitants, three lawyers, two doctors, three stores, two taverns, a blacksmith, saddler, tanner and shoemaker.[292]

Person's Creek, an east branch of Red river, in Montgomery county.

Petersburg, a town estabilshed in 1809, on the north bluff of the Caney Fork of Cumberland, on the land of Joseph Franks, in White county.[293]

Petersville, at the mouth of Big Sandy, in Henry county.

Peyton's Creek, a north branch of Cumberland river, in Smith county.

Philadelphia, a post town in Monroe county, near the Roane county line, established in 1823, on the land of William Knox and Jacob Pearson, on Sweet-Water creek, a south branch of Tennessee. It is thirty miles S. W. from Knoxville, and 180 E. by S. from Nashville.[294]

Pigeon Roost, a post office in Henry county, 109 miles west by north from Nashville.[295]

---

[290] The portion of Perry County lying west of the Tennessee River is now Decatur County (established 1845). The county seat of present-day Perry County is Linden.

[291] Discontinued as a post office.

[292] Perryville, on the west bank of the Tennessee River, is a town and post office in Decatur County, the county seat of which is now Decaturville.

[293] Discontinued; the present town and post office of Petersburg, in Lincoln County, has no relation to the White County community.

[294] Now in Loudon County (established in 1870).

[295] Discontinued as a post office.

Pigeon Creek, an eastern branch of Richland creek, north of Pulaski, in Giles county.

Pigeon River, or *Big Pigeon*, a south branch of French Broad river. It rises in the state of North Carolina, and running a south west course, enters this state in Cocke county, and falls into the river a little below New Port, south of the Chucky Bend. It is navigable for small boats—see *Little Pigeon*.

Pikeville, the seat of justice of Bledsoe county, established in 1813, when the seat of justice was removed from the town of Madison. It is situated on the left bank of Sequatchee river, twenty miles from its source. In 1833 it contained 150 inhabitants, an academy, one lawyer, two doctors, five stores, two taverns, two blacksmiths, one carpenter, one cabinet maker, four shoemakers, one saddler, three tailors, one wagonmaker and two cotton gins. It is 109 miles E. S. E. from Nashville, and 608 W. S. W. from Washington City. Lat. 35° 37′ N., lon. 8° 11′ W.

Piney River, a north branch of Duck river, in Hickman county, passing the town of Vernon. It heads in Dickson.

Piney River, a post office in Dickson county, fifty miles W. by S. from Nashville.[***]

Piney Creek, a branch of White's creek, in Roane county.

Piney Creek, a north eastern branch of the Big Hatchee. It joins the river east of Bolivar, in Hardeman county.

Piney Creek, a north western branch of Tennessee river, in Rhea county; between White's and Spring creeks, above Washington.

Pinhook, a *quasi* village in Wayne county, on the waters of Rutherford's Fork, of Indian creek.

Pistol Creek, a south branch of Little river, at Maryville, in Blount county.

Playball Creek, a south east branch of Tellico river, in Monroe county.

Pleasant Exchange, a post office in Henderson county, 108

[***] Discontinued as a post office. Subsequently Pinewood, then Graham; postal service through Nunnelly.

miles S. W. by W. from Nashville.²⁹⁷

Pleasant Grove, a post office in Maury county, sixty-eight miles S. from Nashville.²⁹⁸

Pleasant Hill, a post office in Hickman county, late *Lewis'.*²⁹⁹

Pleasant Run, a south west branch of Big Hatchee river, below the town of Bolivar, in Hardeman county.

Pleasant Shade, a post office in Smith county, established in 1833.³⁰⁰

Pleasant Town, a post office established in 1832, at Love's store, in Henry county.³⁰¹

Pleasant View, a post office in Henry county; late *Gate's.*³⁰²

Plum Creek, a branch of Calf-killer, in White county.

Plum Point, on the Mississippi, in Tipton county, above Fulton.³⁰³

Pocahontas, a village in Hardeman county, at the intersection of Muddy creek with the Big Hatchee.³⁰⁴

Point Centre, a post office in Madison county, 150 miles S. S. W. from Nashville.³⁰⁵

Polkpatch Creek, a west branch of Caney Fork, in White county.

Pond Creek, a post office in Roane county, 175 miles S. of E. from Nashville.³⁰⁶

Pond Creek, a south branch of Cumberland in Davidson county.³⁰⁷

---

[297] No longer a post office; it was once a noted racetrack and gambling resort; virtually abandoned after the Civil War.

[298] Discontinued as a post office; now a railroad station.

[299] Discontinued.

[300] Settled before 1800 on the Revolutionary War land grant of William Young.

[301-302] Discontinued as a post office.

[303] Plum Point is not in Tipton County, but in Lauderdale.

[304] Pocahontas is a post office and town in the southeastern corner of Hardeman County.

[305-306] Discontinued as a post office.

[307] The course of Pond Creek now lies largely in eastern Cheatham County (established in 1856).

Poorvalley Creek, a north branch of Holston, in Hawkins county.

Poplar Creek, a north branch of Clinch, in Anderson and Roane counties, between Clinton and Kingston, on which are ironworks.

Poplar Creek, a south branch of Duck river, in Maury county.

Poplar Creek, a north east branch of Cumberland, above Sycamore creek, in Davidson county.

Poplar Grove, a post office in Gibson county.[308]

Porter's Creek, a south branch of Big Hatchee. It rises in the state of Mississippi, and joins the river below Warnerville, in Hardeman county.

Portersville, a post town in Tipton county, established in 1832, on James Hodges' land.[309]

Port Royal, a post town in Montgomery county, established in 1797, on the lands of Samuel Wilcox, on the south bank of Red river, at the junction of the Sulphur Fork, thirty-four miles N. N. W. from Nashville. A number of flat boats are annually built here for the shipment of tobacco.[310]

Powell's Mountain, one of the Appalachian ridges, lying east of a spur of Wallen's ridge, in the north east corner of Claiborne county, and extending into Virginia, between Clinch and Powell's rivers. It was named in 1761 by Wallen, Scaggs, & Co. from seeing the name of Ambrose Powell inscribed on a tree, near the mouth of Wallen's creek, on Powell's river.

Powell's River, a north west branch of Clinch. It rises in Scott and Lee counties, Va., flows south west, and enters Claiborne county, Tennessee, and joins the river at Grantsboro', in the southern part of Campbell county, thirty-eight

---

[308-309] Discontinued as a post office.

[310] No longer a post office, but a community of some importance in Montgomery County, well-known for including one of the few surviving covered bridges in Tennessee; postal service through Adams.

PUR 237

miles north west from Knoxville. It is navigable for boats nearly 100 miles.

Powell's Valley, a valley between Powell's and Cumberland mountains, eighty or ninety miles long, and from ten to eighteen wide, nearly equally divided between Virginia and Tennessee.

President's Island, an Island in the Mississippi river, near the Ten. shore, below Memphis, and opposite to Nanconnah creek, in Shelby county.

Prestonville, a post office in Rhea county, at Mr. Gillenwaters', 153 miles E. S. E. from Nashville.[311]

Princeton, a post town in Jackson county, eighty miles N. of E. from Nashville.[312]

Proctor's Creek, a west branch of Cumberland, in Jackson county.[313]

Pulaski, the seat of justice of Giles county, established in 1809, and incorporated in 1819. In 1830 it contained a population of 905, and in 1833 about 1200. It is situated on Richland creek, a north branch of Elk river and is quite a flourishing and interesting village. It has a good court house and jail, public offices, a branch of the Planter's Bank, three churches, two academies, masonic hall, eleven lawyers, six doctors, one clergyman, one common school, fifteen stores, three taverns, ten carpenters, six cabinet makers, eight bricklayers, one stone cutter, two hatters' shops, two shoemakers' shops, four blacksmiths shops, three tanyards, three saw and gristmills, three silversmiths, a printing office, &c. It is seventy-five miles south from Nashville, forty-four N. W. from Huntsville, fifty from Florence Al. a little E. of N., and 770 W. S. W. from Washington City. In lat 35° 10′ N., lon. 10° 5′ W.

Purdy, a post town and the seat of justice of McNairy county, situated on the waters of Snake creek, near the centre of the county, fifteen miles west of Tennessee river, and ten east of Big Hatchee, 160 miles S. W. by W. from Nashville,

---

[311-312] Discontinued as a post office.
[313] Proctor's Creek is in Clay County (established in 1870).

thirty three miles S. E. from Jackson, and 860 W. S. W. from Washington City. In lat. 35° 10′ N., lon. 11° 30′ W.[314]

---

[314] Purdy has been superceded by Selmer as the county seat of McNairy County. The village, northeast of Selmer, survives, though not as a post office; postal service through Selmer.

Q

Quincy, a post office in Gibson county, late *Harmony.*[315]

---
[315] Discontinued as a post office.

R

Raccoon Creek, a west branch of Holston, in Roane county.

Raccoon Creek, a branch of Shoal creek, in Lawrence county.

Raleigh, a post town and seat of justice of Shelby county, established in 1826. It is on the north bank of Wolf river, and incorporated in 1832. Memphis is the commercial capital.[316]

Randolph, a post town in Tipton county, established in 1827. It is situated on the east bank of Mississippi river, at the second Chickasaw Bluff, immediately below the lower mouth of Big Hatchee, 18 miles N. W. from Covington. It contained in 1829, three commission warehouses, six dry goods stores, ten physicians, one tavern and twenty or thirty families. Here is an excellent harbor for steam and flat boats at all stages of the water, and the port is a convenient one for the shipment of the produce of the adjoining counties of Fayette, Haywood, Madison and Hardeman.—It is 237 miles W. by S. from Nashville, in lat. 35° 32′ N., lon. 12° 55′ W.; incorporated in 1831.[317]

Raspberry, a north branch of Holston, south of Hend's Ridge, in Knox county.

Rat Creek, an eastern branch of Tennessee, in Stewart county.

Readyville, a post town in Rutherford county, on the east fork of Stone's river, 15 miles a little N. of E. from Murfreesboro', and 42 miles south west from Nashville.

Red Bridge, a post office in Hawkins county, 254 miles N. of E. from Nashville.[318]

Red Hill, a post office in Grainger county, established in

---

[316] Raleigh now has no corporate existence outside of Memphis, which supplanted it as the county seat of Shelby County.

[317] Randolph has, like Raleigh, been superceded by Memphis as a river port town. It exists today as a community; no post office; service through Atoka.

[318] Discontinued as a post office.

1833.[319]

Red River, a north branch of Cumberland. It rises in Kentucky and waters the counties of Robertson and Montgomery, in this state. It flows a general S. W. course and falls into Cumberland River at Clarksville, in Montgomery county, after a comparative course of seventy miles. Its principal branches are Sulphur and Elk Forks. It is navigable for flat boats as high up as the mouth of Elk Fork.—West and Barren Forks united have their junction a short distance above Clarksville.

Reed's Creek, a south branch of Obion river, in Dyer county.

Reedy Creek, a south branch of Forked Deer, in Carroll county.

Reedy Creek, a post office in Sullivan county.

Reel Foot River, a north branch of Obion river in Obion and Dyer counties.

Reinse's Creek, an east branch of Tennessee, in Wayne county; see Indian creek.

Renfro's Creek, a north branch of Holston, in Hawkins county.

Reynoldsburg, a post town and the seat of justice of Humphreys county, situated immediately on the east bank of the Tennessee river, on a beautiful level, rising from the margin of the river of about fifteen feet elevation, and entirely above high water mark. It was located in the year 1812, and is about 12 miles below the mouth of Duck river. Its population in 1829, was 108; and it contained 28 dwelling houses, two taverns, three stores, one blacksmith, one saddler, one cabinet maker, one shoemaker and one tanner. The houses are all built of wooden materials, except the court house and jail. It is 73 miles S. of W. from Nashville and 782 W. by S. from Washington City, in lat. 35° 38′ N., lon. 11° W.[320]

[319] Now known as Dotson's Camp Ground with mail service through Washburn.

[320] Reynoldsburg has been superceded by Waverly as the seat of justice of Humphreys County. Near the town of New Johnsonville, Reynoldsburg is largely under the waters of Kentucky Lake.

Rhea, a county in East Tennessee, erected in 1807. It is bounded on the south east by McMinn, on the west by Bledsoe, on the north east by Roane, on the south by Hamilton and the Cherokee lands, and on the N. W. by Morgan; and contains about 625 square miles. Population in 1820, 4215; in 1830, 8182. Tennessee river flows through this county from N. E. to S. W. and receives the Hiwassee river from the east, on the south line. Cumberland mountain ranges the western border, and is the dividing line between it and Bledsoe. Washington is the seat of justice; and there are post offices at Prestonville, Goodfield and Ten-mile stand. Cent. lat. 35° 40′ N., lon. 7° 48′ W.

Rheatown, a post village in Greene county, established in 1823, on the road leading from Greenville to Jonesboro', 285 miles E. from Nashville.[321]

Rice's, a post office in Campbell county.[322]

Richland Creek, a west branch of Tennessee in Rhea county.

Richland Creek, a large northern branch of Elk river, about thirty miles in length, rising in Maury county and flowing southardly thro' Giles, past the town of Pulaski, falls into the river near the Alabama line, below lower Elkton.

Richland Creek, a post office in Giles county, 70 miles S. from Nashville.[323]

Richland Creek, a north branch of Holston, flowing past the town of Rutledge, in Grainger county.

Richland Creek, a south branch of Cumberland, in Davidson county, west of Nashville.

Richland Creek, an eastern branch of Tennessee, in Humphreys county. It empties into the river about five miles below Bear creek. Its length is about 20 miles, and on it are one saw and four grist mills.

Richland Grove, a post office in Tipton county, 233 miles W. by S. from Nashville.[324]

---

[321] Discontinued as a post office. The community is just north of Chuckey.
[322-324] Discontinued as a post office.

Richmond, a post town in Bedford county, established in 1831.[335]

Riley's Creek, a south branch of Tennessee, in Roane county, opposite to Kingston.

Roane, a county in East Tennessee, bounded on the east by Knox and Blount, on the south east by Monroe and McMinn, on the south west by Rhea, on the north west by Morgan and on the north east by Anderson.—It contains an area of about 625 square miles. This county is well watered by Tennessee, Holston, Clinch, and Embree's rivers. It was erected in 1801, and contained a population of 7,885 in 1820, and in 1830, 11,340. The land is generally poor and uneven.—Kingston is the seat of justice, and there are post offices at Embree's Iron works, Blair's Ferry and Wood's Hill.

South east from Kingston, in this county, are several remarkable sinkholes, one of which could not be fathomed by a rope 380 feet in length. Cent. lat. 35° 55′ N., lon. 7° 30′ W.

Roane's Creek, a north east branch of the Watauga, in Carter county, which unites with Little Doe, East of Elizabethton.

Roane's Creek, an east branch of Tennessee, in Perry county.

Roaring Creek, a south branch of Elk river, in Franklin county.

Roaring River, an east branch of Cumberland, rising about the base of the Cumberland mountains, and flowing a north west direction through the S. E. corner of Overton, joins the river not far from the centre of Jackson county, above Williamsburg.

Robertson, a county in Middle Tennessee, erected in 1796. It is bounded on the north by the state of Kentucky, on the east by Sumner county, on the south by Davidson, and on the west by Montgomery. It is about 40 miles long from N.E. to S.W., with a mean width of 16. It is watered by Red river on the north west, and by the Cumberland on the south, and Sulphur Fork in the middle, which flows past

---

[335] Discontinued as a post office; the community is in the southwestern part of Bedford County; mail service through Petersburg.

ROC 245

Springfield, the seat of justice.

In 1820, Robertson contained a population of 9,938, and in 1830, 13,302. There are post offices at Turnersville, McReary's, Mulloy's, Lowe's and Cross Plains. Cen. lat. 36° 28′ N., lon. 9° 40′ W.

Robertson, a post office in Giles county.[326]

Robertson's Fork, a post office in Giles county, 75 miles south from Nashville.[327]

Robertson's Creek, a south branch of Holston, in Hawkins county.

Robertson's Springs, very noted sulphur springs in Robertson county, on the head waters of Sulphur Fork, 14 miles from Springfield, 16 from Gallatin and 24 from Nashville, near the road leading to Franklin, Ken. See *Tyree's Springs*.

Robinson's Creek, a south branch of Holston, in Knox county.

Rockcastle Cove, near Jamestown, in Fentress county.

Rocky Springs, a post office in Grainger county, 200 miles E. from Nashville.[328]

Rock Creek, a south branch of Duck river, in Bedford county. It rises near Cornersville—a post office in said county.[329]

Rocky Creek, a north branch of Tennessee river, in Hamilton county, three miles below Sale creek.

Rocky Creek, a branch of Cumberland, in Sumner county.

Rock Island, a post office in White county, at Parris, 13 miles south from Sparta.[330]

Rockville, a post town in Monroe county, and former seat of justice.[331]

---

[326] Discontinued as a post office.

[327] Now Lynnville, in the northern part of Giles County; Robertson's Fork, now in Marshall County, has postal service through Lynnville.

[328] Discontinued as a post office.

[329] Now in Marshall County (created in 1836).

[330] Rock Island, near the junction of Warren, White, and Van Buren counties, is in Warren County.

[331] The county seat of Monroe County is now Madisonville.

Rogers' Creek, a south branch of Cumberland, in Jackson county.

Rogers' Creek, a north branch of Hiwassee river, on the line of Rhea and McMinn counties.

Rogers' Creek, a post office in McMinn.[332]

Rogersville, the seat of justice of Hawkins county, situated about two miles north of Holston river. On the 5th day of November, 1791, a printing press was established at this place by a Mr. Roulstone, and a paper issued entitled the 'Knoxville Gazette,' being the first paper ever printed in the Territory. In 1833, it contained about three hundred inhabitants, four lawyers, two doctors, two divines, one academy, seven stores, three taverns, six blacksmiths, three bricklayers, four carpenters, four cabinet makers, two painters, two hatters, four tailors, four shoemakers, two saddlers, one silversmith, three tanners, one tinner and four wagonmakers. It is 66 miles S. of W. from Abingdon, Va., 268 N. of E. from Nashville, and 451 S. W. by W. from Washington City. Lat. 36° 20′ N., lon. 6° 3′ W.

Rome, a town in the county of Smith, situated at the mouth of Round Lick creek, on the left bank of the Cumberland, eight miles west from Carthage. It contains about 200 inhabitants, five stores, two taverns, one grocery, two tailors' shops, two carpenters, one blacksmith's shop, one saddler's shop, one stone mason, one cabinet shop, one shoemaker's shop, two ware houses and one doctor.

Roseton, a post office in Warren county, established in 1833.[333]

Rosetta, a post office in Hickman county established in 1833.[334]

Ross', a post office in Anderson county.[335]

Rotton's Fork, a branch of Wolf river, in Fentress county.

Round Lick Creek, a south branch of Cumberland river in

---

[332] In McMinn County, near the Meigs County line; the post office is discontinued.

[333-335] Discontinued as a post office.

Wilson county, and flowing north east, joins the river at Rome in Smith county.

Round Lick, a post office in Smith county, 31 miles E. from Nashville.[336]

Rural Hill, a post office in Wilson county, established in 1833.[337]

Russell's Creek, a branch of Powell's river, in Claiborne county. It flows N. E. past the town of Tazewell, N. W. of Wallen's ridge.

Russellville, a town in the north east corner of Jefferson county, established in 1826. It contains about twenty houses, eighty inhabitants, one physician, and a dozen mechanics.—250 miles E. from Nashville.

Rutherford, a county in Middle Tennessee, erected in 1803. It is bounded on the east by Warren, on the west by Davidson and Williamson, on the north by Wilson, and on the south by Bedford. It has an area of 625 square miles. It is drained by Stone's river, which flows from the S. E. to the N. W. corner. The land in this county is generally of an excellent quality, and well adapted to the growth of cotton. It contains the towns of Murfreesboro', the seat of justice; Jefferson, Readyville, Milton and Fosterville. Population in 1820, 19,552; in 1830, 26,133 of which 8654 were slaves. Cen. lat. 35° 50′ N., lon. 9° 15′ W.

Rutherford, a post office in Dyer county, established in 1833.[338]

Rutherford's Creek, a north branch of Duck river, in Maury county.

Rutherford's Fork, a large south branch of the Obion river. It rises in Henderson, and flows a north east course, through Carroll and Gibson, and has its junction in the S. E. corner of Obion county.

Rutledge, the seat of justice of Grainger county, established in 1797, and named in honor of George Rutledge, Esq.. It

---

[336-337] Discontinued as a post office.

[338] The post office (and town) of Rutherford is in northern Gibson County, not Dyer.

is situated on Richland Creek, a small branch of Holston river. In 1833 it contained about 150 inhabitants, two lawyers, one doctor, one school, one church, three stores, two taverns, two blacksmiths, two hatters, one tailor, one shoemaker, one saddler and two tanners. It is 33 miles E. from Knoxville, 235 from Nashville, and 483 S. W. by W. from Washington City. Lat. 36° 10′ N., lon. 6° 27′ W.

S

Sale Creek, a north west branch of Tennessee river, in Hamilton county, one mile below the Rhea county line.

Salem, a post town in Franklin county, ninety-four miles S. E. from Nashville, at the crossings of Beans' creek, on the Huntsville road, S. W. of Winchester.[339]

Salt Lick Creek, a post office in Smith county, established in 1833.[340]

Sam's Creek, a south branch of Cumberland, in Davidson county, on which is a fine sulphur spring.

Sandy Creek, a south branch of Duck river, in Maury county, above Columbia.

Sandy Hill, a post office in Henry county.[341]

Sandy River, a considerable stream, arising in Henderson, and flowing a north course through the east side of Carroll, and the N. W. corner of Humphreys, enters the Tennessee river, on the west side, in the north east corner of Henry county. It has been declared navigable as high up as Filpots, in Henderson county. The lands along the margin of this stream are not of the first quality, but the adjoining hills are rich, of a dark sandy mould, and well adapted to the growth of cotton.

Sauda Creek, a north branch of Tennessee, in Hamilton county, three miles below Oppossum creek.

Savannah, a post town and the seat of justice of Hardin county, situated on the east bank of the Tennessee river, fifteen miles north of the south boundary of the county, and within four miles of its center. The first improvements made at this place, were in March 1827. It is considered one of the healthiest situations on the river, below the Muscle Shoals.

---

[339] Salem is in southwestern Franklin County; the post office has been superceded by that of Huntland; the community is called "Old Salem."

[340] Discontinued as a post office; the community, now called "Salt Lick," is in Macon County (established in 1842) and has mail service through Red Boiling Springs.

[341] Big Sandy, in Benton County, is the successor to Sandy Hill.

On the first of January 1829, this village contained 150 inhabitants; two lawyers, two merchants, three hatters, two tailors, two tanners, one stone mason, two brick masons, two saddlers, two shoe and boot makers, one tavern, two groceries, one school-master, three house carpenters, and one minister of the Gospel. It is forty-nine miles S. W. from Florence Al., twenty-eight from Waterloo, seventeen E. from Purdy, McNairy county, forty-six S. E. from Jackson, twenty-eight E. of S. from Lexington, thirty-two W. of S. from Perryville, twenty-three from Carrollsville, thirty-one W. from Waynesborough, 152 S. W. from Nashville, and 850 W. S. W. from Washington City. In lat. 35° 15′ N., long. 11° 11′ W.

Searcy's a post office in Montgomery county, N. W. by W. from Nashville.[149]

Sequatchee River, a north branch of Tennessee river, in Bledsoe and Marion counties. It has its source near the Crab Orchard, and after winding its way through the hills for six or eight miles into the Grassy Cove, it enters a large cavern, and is lost for eight of ten miles under a mountain, at the foot of which, on the south, it bursts out in a clear cold fountain. This is the head of what is called *Sequatchee Valley.* The river then flows nearly a S. W. direction through Marion, and falls into the Tennessee, five miles above the N. W. angle of Georgia. Entire comparative course about sixty miles: and it is sixty or seventy yards wide at its mouth. The land in the Sequatchee valley is rich and well timbered and for eight miles from the head of the valley it is three miles wide encompassed on each side by the mountains and hills, and presenting a rich view of stupendous cliffs, clad with evergreen. Products of the valley, corn, cotton, hemp, wheat and tobacco. Population about 2500.

Sevier, a county in East Tennessee, erected in 1795. It is bounded on the south west by Blount, on the north west by Knox, on the north east by Jefferson and Cocke, and on the south east by the Iron mountains, or line of North Carolina. Length thirty-three miles, mean width twenty, area 660 square

---

[149] Discontinued as a post office.

SHE 251

miles. The surface is generally hilly and soil sterile. Little Pigeon and French Broad rivers are its principal streams. Population in 1820, 4772; in 1830, 5717. Seat of justice Sevierville. Cen. lat. 35° 50′ N., lon. 6° 34′ W.

Sevierville, the seat of justice of Sevier county, established in 1795. It is situated on the south bank of Little Pigeon river, below the junction of the south Fork. In 1833 it contained a population of about 150, and four lawyers, two doctors, one church, one clergyman, one academy, one school, three stores, two taverns, two carpenters, one cabinet maker, two bricklayers, one hatter, two tailors, one shoemaker, one tanner, one saddler and two mills. It is twenty-five miles S. E. from Knoxville, 225 S. of E. from Nashville, and 515 S. W. by W. from Washington City. Lat. 35° 50′ N., lon. 6° 34′ W.

Shannonsville, a town established on the land of Robert Shannon, on the west bank of Tennessee river, in Perry county, in the year 1824.[345]

Shelby, a county in West Tennessee, erected in 1819, in the S. W. angle of the state, containing 625 square miles, having Tipton county on the north, Fayette on the east, Miss. State on the south and Miss. river on the west. Wolf river and Loosa Hatchee are the principal branches of the Mississippi in this county. Memphis is the commercial capital, but the seat of justice is at Raleigh on Wolf river. Population in 1820, 354; in 1830, 5,625.

Shelbyville, the seat of justice of Bedford county, established in 1809, and incorporated in 1819. It is situated on the northeast bank of Duck river, considerably elevated, but on rather an uneven and rocky surface, surrounded by cedar groves. In 1830 this town was almost entirely demolished by a storm, four persons were killed and above forty wounded. Most of the buildings have been rebuilt which gives the village a very thriving and handsome appearance. In the summer of 1833 the cholera raged with great malignancy, and about one tenth of the population fell victims to the scourge. It is how-

---

[345] The site of this town is now in Decatur County (established in 1845).

ever, considered a healthy place, and contains at present about 600 inhabitants, and three lawyers, eight doctors, two clergymen, two churches, two academies, one common school, one printing office, thirteen stores, two taverns, two carpenters, two cabinet makers, three bricklayers, two stone-masons, one hatter, four tailors, four shoemakers, four blacksmiths, one silversmith, one tinner, one tanner, and a number of grist mills, saw mills, cotton gins, &c. in the town and vicinity. A good McAdamized turnpike road from this place to Nashville, *via* Murfreesboro', is now under contract and will be completed during this year. It is twenty-six miles S. from Murfreesboro', fifty-five from Nashville *via* turnpike, and 700 W. S. W. from Washington City. Lat. 35° 25' N., lon. 9° 27' W.

Shepherdsville, a town on Martin's creek, in Smith county.[344]

Shippingsburg, a town at Rudd's Bluff, on the Tennessee river, in Hardin county.[345]

Shippingport, a post town in the county of Warren, on the Caney Fork of Cumberland. It was one of the places proposed, to locate the Penitentiary, being at the head of navigation of that branch of the river.[346]

Shoal Creek, a north branch of Tennessee river, which rises in Lawrence county, and flowing S. W. touches the corner of Wayne, and joins the river opposite the Muscle Shoals, in Alabama.

Short Creek, an eastern branch of Tennessee, in Stewart county.

Short Creek, a south branch of Tennessee, in the north east corner of Hardin county.

Siloa, a post office in Green county.[347]

Silver Springs, a post office in Wilson county, fifteen miles below Lebanon.[348]

Simpson's, a post office in Sumner county, in the N. E. corner, forty-five miles N. E. from Nashville.[349]

Sinking Cane, a post office in Overton county, 120 miles E. of N. from Nashville.[350]

[344-350] Discontinued as a post office.

SMI 253

Sinking Creek, a south branch of Duck river, in Bedford county, below Powell's creek.

Sinking Creek, a north branch of Holston, in Knox county, nine miles west of Knoxville.

Sinking Creek, a north branch of Holston, in Sullivan county, on which there is a paper mill, and a village called Paperville.[351]

Sinking Creek, in the N. E. corner of Washington county.

Sinking Creek, a north branch of Nolichucky, in Greene county, just below the mouth of Limestone creek.

Smith, a county in Middle Tennessee, erected in 1799. It is bounded on the north by Kentucky, on the east by Jackson county, on the south east by White and Warren, on the south west by Wilson, and on the west by Sumner. It is about forty-five miles long, north and south, and twenty wide. This county is well watered by the Cumberland river and branches: the principal of which are, Defeated creek, Peyton's creek, Dixon's creek and Goose creek on the north, and Caney Fork on the south, which joins the river at Carthage. The principal branches of the Caney Fork, are, Smith's Fork, Hickman and Mulherrin. The towns in Smith, are Carthage, the seat of justice, Alexandria, Lancaster, Liberty and Rome, and there are post offices at Dixon's Springs, Round Lick and Bratton's. Population in 1820, 17,580; in 1830, 21,492. Cen. lat. 36° 23' N., lon. 8° 50' W.

Smithville, a post office in Dickson county.[352]

Smithfield, a post office in Hamilton county, S. E. from Nashville.[353]

Smith's, a post office in McMinn county, established in 1833.[354]

Smith's Fork, a branch of the Caney Fork of Cumberland, which has its source in Wilson near Statesville. It runs a

---

[351] Sinking Creek and Paperville are in the eastern outskirts of Bristol in Sullivan County.

[352] The post office of Smithville in Dickson County is discontinued; Smithville, in DeKalb County, is the post office and seat of justice of that county.

[353-354] Discontinued as post offices, or towns by the name.

north east course into Smith county, passes the town of Liberty and falls into the river below the town of Lancaster. It has been declared navigable from its mouth to Stump's mill.

Snake Creek a north branch of Tennessee river, and has its junction at the Head of Diamond Island, in Hardin county. Its source is in McNairy county, near Purdy.

Sommerville, a post town and the seat of justice of Fayette county, established in 1824, and named in honor of Robert M. Sommerville, who fell at the battle of the Horseshoe. It is situated on the Loosa Hatchee river, and contained in 1828, 100 houses, 400 inhabitants, twenty mechanics, seven professional men, eight stores, two groceries, three taverns, a court house and jail. It was incorporated in 1826. It is 175 miles S. W. by W. from Nashville, and 900 from Washington City, in lat. 36° 15′ N., lon. 12° 25′ W.[355]

South Branch of Holston, a river which rises in the state of Virginia, and enters this state in Sullivan county, through which it flows by a general west course, until it joins the main river, at the town of Kingsport, or Boat Yard. It receives from the S. E. the Watauga, a branch draining Carter county, on which are several iron works.[356]

South Cross Creek, a south branch of Tennessee, in the Cherokee nation, on which is situated Brainerd Mission.[357]

South Fork, a south branch of *Little Pigeon*, in Sevier county.

South West Point, the name given to the point at the confluence of Clinch and Tennessee rivers, in Roane county, where Kingston now stands. Here was established a military garrison during the Indian wars.

Sparta, a post town and the seat of justice of White county, established in 1809, and incorporated in 1813. It is situated at the foot of the Cumberland mountain, near the Calf-killer, a

---

[355] Properly, Somerville.

[356] The North and South Branches of Holston meet at Kingsport (the Boatyard) in Sullivan County.

[357] In Hamilton County, east of Chattanooga.

branch of the Caney Fork of Cumberland. It contained in 1833, about 200 inhabitants, four stores, three taverns, three doctors, one divine, six lawyers, one printing office, six cabinet makers, two hatters, two shoemakers, four tailors, three brick layers, three blacksmiths, five carpenters, two saddlers, two tanners, one tinner, three wagonmakers, an academy, one church, &c. It is 86 miles east from Nashville via Lebanon, and 99 via Murfreesboro', and 628 miles from Washington City, in lat. 35° 53' N., lon. 8° 22' W.

Speedwell, a post town in Claiborne county, situated on Davis' creek, a west branch of Powell's river, near the line of Campbell county, in Powell's Valley, 186 miles N. of E. from Nashville.

Spencer's Creek, a south branch of Cumberland, in Wilson county.

Spencer's Creek, a branch of Harpeth, in Williamson county.

Spencer's Hill, a spur of the Cumberland mountains in Morgan County, in lat. 36° N., lon. 7° 50' W. Named for Thomas Sharp Spencer, who was killed here by the Indians.

Spring Creek, a south branch of Big Hatchee, near the town of Bolivar, in Hardeman county.

Spring Creek, a north branch of Shoal creek, east of Lawrenceburg, in Lawrence county.

Spring Creek, an east branch of Tennessee, below Perryville, in Perry county.

Spring Creek, a west branch of Tennessee, which has its junction at Washington, in Rhea county. It is now called *Clear Creek.*

Spring Creek, a south branch of Cumberland, east of Lebanon, in Wilson county.

Spring Creek, a branch of Sulphur Fork of Red river, in Robertson county.

Spring Creek, a post office in Madison county, 150 miles W. S. W. from Nashville, in the N. E. corner of the county.

Springhill, a post office in Maury county, 35 miles S. from Nashville, on the road from Franklin to Columbia.

Springmount, a post office in Dyer county, 178 miles W. from Nashville.[358]

Springfield, a post town and the seat of justice of Robertson county, established in 1796; and incorporated in 1819. It is pleasantly situated on a commanding elevation, about one mile south of the Sulphur Fork of Red river, 25 miles N. by W. from Nashville. It contains 300 inhabitants, a good court house and jail, four stores, two taverns, three blacksmiths, two tailors, one shoemaker and two saddlers. It is 25 miles S. from Russellville, 29 miles E. from Clarksville, 720 miles W. S. W. from Washington City in lat. 36° 26' N., lon. 9° 40' W. A four horse stage from Nashville to Louisville passes and repasses three times a week.

Standing Stone Creek, an east branch of Tennessee, in Stewart county.

Standing Rock, a post office in Stewart county.[359]

Statesville, a post town in Wilson county, formerly called Maryville, established in 1819 on Smith's Fork, 17 miles S. of E. from Lebanon, and 43 E. from Nashville. In 1833, it contained about 200 inhabitants, one church, one male and one female school, five retail stores, one large cotton factory, one wool carding machine, two cotton gins, one tread saw mill, one horse and one water grist and saw mill, two tan yards, five saddlers, six tailors, six blacksmiths, three cabinet makers, three carpenters, two brick and stone masons, four shoe makers and one potter's shop.[360]

State Line, a post office in Fayette county, established in 1833.[361]

Station Camp Creek, a north branch of Cumberland, in Sumner county; the east branch of which is two and the main branch is five miles west of Gallatin, on the road leading to Nashville. The lands on these creeks are first rate generally, and afford as many good farms as any part of the county.

[358-359] Discontinued as a post office.

[360] Not a post office, but a community in the southeastern part of Wilson County.

[361] Discontinued as a post office.

STO 257

Station Camp Creek, a western branch of the South Fork of Cumberland, in the north corner of Fentress county, between Big Branch and Pecan creeks.

Stewart, a county in Middle Tennessee, erected in 1803. It is bounded on the north by Kentucky, on the east by Montgomery and part of Dickson, on the south by Humphreys, and on the west by the Tennessee river, the dividing line between Stewart and Henry, and part of Kentucky. Cumberland river enters this county near the corners of Dickson and Montgomery, and flows a western direction as far as Dover, when it turns a north west course, and enters Todd county, Kentucky. Seat of justice, Dover; and there are post offices at Bowlingreen, Hamlet, Center Grove and Trousdale. Cen. lat. 36° 20′ N., lon. 10° 40′ W. Population in 1830, 6988.

Stewart's Creek, a south branch of Stone's river, in Rutherford county, west of Murfreesboro'.

Stewart's Ferry, a post office in Davidson county, established in 1833.[362]

Stiffeetown, a town established on the land of John Stiffee, in Grainger county.

Stock Creek, an east branch of Tennessee, on the line between Knox and Blount counties.

Stone Fort, a post town in Franklin county, in the two most northern of the three forks of Duck river, 62 miles S. E. from Nashville, on the Georgia road.—Here is an ancient fortification of stone work, from which it takes its name. "At its northern extremity, on the front of the wall, are two mounds of stone, about six feet in height, and circular. Directly in the rear is the north wall, which extends from the river, and is situated exactly at the foot of the falls about fifteen feet. This wall has one gate-way, and is about ten feet in height, on the inner side. In the rear of the gate is a stone building of about sixteen feet square, with a smaller one by its side. Running south with the wall, it still maintains the same height, until you arrive again at the foot of the falls about

[362] Discontinued; the site is under Percy Priest Lake; a county road still bears the name.

twenty feet, where this part of the wall terminates, and is discontinued for some distance in consequence of a bold rising bluff of solid limestone rock, at about mid way of which there has been excavated a foot path to the river. The like occurs at the foot of the falls on the opposite side of the Fort. On passing this bluff the stone is again continued to its most southern angles; on the south side the wall is again continued, with the same interposition of falls, bluff and foot path, as on the east, until it joins the western extremity of the north wall—on the south wall there appears to have been an excavation of the earth from 80 to 100 feet in breadth, and about 40 feet in depth, at the bottom of which, and next to the stone wall, is a ditch of about twenty feet in width.— Both the excavation and the ditch extends from river to river. The form of the fort is nearly triangular, the north wall being but a few yards in length. The whole ground contained within the wall of the fort is from 30 to 32 acres.

"These walls are about 16 or 20 feet in thickness at the base, and on top from four to five. The present appearance of the walls are, as might be expected, quite rough. The whole area as well as the excavation was covered with heavy forest trees as large as any in the neighboring counties."— *Haywood.* Lat. 35° 30′ N., lon. 9° W.[363]

Stoner's Creek, a branch of Stone's river, in Davidson county, near the Hermitage.

Stone's River, a south eastern branch of Cumberland river, rising in Warren, and flowing S. W. through Rutherford, joins the Cumberland a short distance below the Hermitage, in Davidson county. It is declared navigable as high up as Bowman's mill on the west fork, above Jefferson, in Rutherford county. This river was named after *Uriah Stone,* who composed one of an exploring party with *Col. James Smith,* late of Bourbon county, Kentucky, in the year 1766.[364]

---

[363] The site, near Manchester, Coffee County (established in 1836), is under development as a state park.

[364] The source of Stone's River is in Cannon County (established in 1836).

SUL 259

Stone Mountain, in Campbell county.

Stony Creek, a north branch of the Watauga, in Carter county, N. E. of Elizabethton.

Straight Creek, a north branch of Clinch river, between Lone mountain and Big Barren creek, in Claiborne county.

Sugar Creek, a post office in Giles county, established in 1833.[365]

Sugar Creek, a north branch of Big Hatchee, in Haywood county, rising near Brownsville.

Sugar Creek, a north branch of Duck river in Hickman county.

Sugar Creek, an east branch of Cumberland in Jackson county.

Sugar Loaf, see Bald mountain.

Sugg's Creek, a north branch of Stone's river, in Davidson county.

Sullivan, a county in East Tennessee, erected in 1779, by the state of North Carolina. It is bounded on the north by Virginia, on the south east by Carter, on the south by Washington, and on the west by Hawkins. It is about 45 miles long and 15 wide. This county is somewhat broken, but it contains no mountains. There is a chain of hills about two miles wide, running north eastwardly from Blountsville to the Virginia line, and some knobs between Reedy creek and Holston river. This river runs from E. to W. through the county, making a southern curve to the line of Washington, at the mouth of Watauga. There is some good land in places along the river, but a great deal of it is broken; on the smaller streams the land is pretty good and produces excellent timothy grass. Clover grows well, particularly where gypsum is used, which can be procured in great abundance in Washington county.—The principal growth of timber is hickory, walnut, buckeye, sugar-tree, poplar, oaks of various kinds, chestnut, &c. Productions, wheat, corn, hay and oats. There is one iron and one nail factory in extensive operation in this county. It contains the towns of Blountsville, the seat of justice, Kings-

[365] Discontinued as a post office.

port, Pactolus, and Paperville. In 1820, the population was 7015, in 1830, 10,073. Cen. lat. 36° 23′ N., lon. 5° 24′ W.

Sulphur Creek, a west branch of Tennessee, in Humphreys county, below Hurricane creek. On this creek about four miles from the river is a sulphur spring, which is much resorted to during the summer months. Mammoth bones were found here in 1820, and among them a tusk, which was eight feet six inches in length, and was said to weigh above 100 weight.[444]

Sulphur Fork, one of the east branches of Red river, in Robertson county. It rises near the road leading from Nashville to Franklin, Kentucky. It takes its name from the Sulphur springs owned by Mr. Cheatham, called '*Robertson's Springs*,' which are situated near its source, two miles from Tyree's springs. This creek runs a N. W. direction, 15 or 16 miles, until it passes the town of Springfield, it then turns, and flowing a S.W. course falls into Red river at Port Royal, in Montgomery, after a comparative course of forty miles. A great portion of the country through which it flows is hilly, and of that class of land denominated brushy barrens.

Sulphur Fork, a branch of Obid's river, in Morgan county.

Sulphur Lick Creek, an eastern branch of Tennessee, above Savannah, rising near the Florence road, in Hardin county.

Sumner, a county in Middle Tennessee, erected in 1786, and reduced to its constitutional limits, 625 square miles, in 1799. It is bounded on the north by Kentucky, on the east by Smith county, on the south by Wilson, the south bank of Cumberland river, and on the west by Robertson and Davidson. About one half of Sumner county is equal in point of fertility to any part of Middle Tennessee. There is a rich body of land extending from Mansker's to Goose creek, the extreme west and east lines, about 34 miles long and eight wide, between the ridge and the river, which is settled by wealthy and enterprising farmers. Cotton and corn are the staples south of the ridge, and tobacco on the north. Sumner is celebrated for the raising of fine horses. Goose, Bledsoe's, Station

[444] Now in Benton County (established in 1835).

SYC   261

Camp, Drake's and Mansker's creeks are the principal streams. It contains the towns of Gallatin, Hartsville, Cairo and Hendersonville, and two celebrated watering places, *Castalian and Tyree's Springs*. Population in 1820, 19,211; in 1830, 20,606. Seat of justice, Gallatin; cent. lat. 36° 22' N., lon. 9° 15' West from Washington City.

Surgoin's Creek, a north branch of Holston, above Marshall's creek, in Hawkins county.

Surgoinsville, a post town at the mouth of Surgoin's creek, on Holston river, 12 miles east from Rogersville, containing about 30 families. The surrounding country is poor. It is 275 miles north of east from Nashville.

Swan Creek, a north branch of Elk, in the east end of Giles county.

Swan Creek, a south branch of Duck river, in Hickman county.

Sweet-water Creek, a south branch of Tennessee, in Monroe and Roane, passing Philadelphia.[367]

Swift Creek, a south east branch of Tennessee river, in Hardin county, and joins the river below Lee's Bluff.

Sycamore Creek, a north branch of Cumberland river, on the line of Davidson and Robertson counties.[368]

---
[367] Its course is now in Loudon County (established in 1870).
[368] Its course is now in Cheatham County (established in 1856).

263

T

Tacket's Creek, a south branch of the Clear Fork of Cumberland, in the N. W. corner of Claiborne county.

Tallassee, a north branch of Elk river, in Franklin county, below Bean creek.

Taylor's Creek, one of the tributaries of the Caney Fork, three miles S. of Falling water, in White county. On this creek is a beautiful cascade, about 80 yards wide; above the principal fall, the stream is about 60 feet wide, and falls over a rock ten feet; and about 40 further, the water falls 25 feet, and in 40 yards more the whole stream pitches over a rock 100 feet; twenty yards below this, on the south side, is a cascade still more beautiful; a creek six or eight feet wide falls from the summit of an overhanging rock, a distance of at least three hundred feet. The chasm below these falls is something like 100 yards wide and 3 or 400 hundred deep.

Tazewell, a post town and the seat of justice of Claiborne county, situated on Russel's creek, a branch of Powell's river. In 1803, the first house was built, and in 1833, it contained about 400 inhabitants, three lawyers, two doctors, one clergyman, one Presbyterian and one Methodist church, one male and one female school, seven stores, four taverns, two bricklayers, four blacksmiths, two carpenters, two cabinet makers, one hatter, three tailors, two shoemakers, three saddlers, one silversmith, two tanners and one gristmill. It is 240 miles N. of E. from Nashville, 45 N. from Knoxville and 490 S. W. by W. from Washington City. Lat. 36° 25' N., lon. 6° 28' W.

Tellico, the former seat of justice of Monroe—see Madisonville.

Tellico River, a south branch of Tennessee, in Monroe county, rising in the Smoky mountains, and running a south west direction, falls into the river south west of Maryville, at old Fort Loudon.

Tellico Plains, a post office in Monroe county, 190 miles E. by S. from Nashville.

Tennessee River, this river, properly speaking, rises in

Virginia, and is described in the article 'Holston.' The Tennessee, or Little Tennessee, above the junction of the Holston, is, comparatively speaking, a small river, boatable only thirty or forty miles above its confluence. After the union of the two streams, now bearing the name of Tennessee, it receives from the north, Clinch river at Kingston, and then flows S. W. through Rhea county, and at the south line of Rhea, adjoining the Cherokee lands, it receives from the east, the Hiwasee river. It then makes a curve, westwardly bounding Hamilton county on the south and the Cherokee lands on the north; or rather enters the chartered limits of Hamilton through its north and east boundary lines, and runs in its general course, nearly parallel with, and about six miles distant from Wallen's ridge of Cumberland mountain, 'til within about two miles of the line of the state of Georgia, where it butts against the end of Lookout mountain; it then tacks to the north and running that direction about seven miles, enters Marion county, at the Suck, which commences immediately at the lower end of the Tumbling shoals. These shoals in a low stage of water are great obstructions to the navigation. A few miles further south, the river crosses the line of Tennessee and enters the state of Alabama in the north east corner, and receives the Sequatchee from the north. It then makes a great southern bend in that state, passing Crow Town, Coosauda Village, Fort Deposit, Triana, Cotton Port, Decatur, Marthon, Fort Hampton, Bainbridge, Florence, Tuscumbia, Havana, &c., and re-enters Tennessee state, at the S. W. corner of Alabama and N. E. of Mississippi. Its general course from thence is north, through Hardin, Perry, Humphreys, Stewart and Henry, bounding Stewart on the west and Henry on the east. At the N. W. corner of Stewart, it leaves the state of Tennessee, and flowing N. W. enters the Ohio river, 13 miles below the mouth of Cumberland, and 57 above that of Ohio. It is by far the largest tributary of the Ohio, and contributes nearly as much water as the main river. It is susceptible of boat navigation for at least 1000 miles, 130 of which lie in the state of Alabama. All that part of Tennessee and Kentucky which lies west of Tennessee river and east of Mississippi river, was purchased of the Indians in 1818, and is denominated the Western District. From the mouth of Tennessee to the Muscle Shoals in Alabama, is 260 miles. This part of the river is navigable at all seasons. From the shoals to the Suck in Marion county, Tennessee, is 250 miles.

Tennessee Ironworks, a post office in Dickson county, 55 miles west from Nashville.[369]

Ten-mile Stand, a post office in Rhea county, 150 miles E. by S. from Nashville.[370]

Three Forks, a post office at N. Smith's, in Wilson county, at the forks of Round Lick.[371]

Third Creek, a north branch of Holston in Knox county, between Second and Fourth creeks.

Thompson's Creek, a post office in Bedford county.[372]

Tipton, a county in West Tennessee, erected in 1823. It is bounded on the north by Dyer, on the east by Haywood, on the south by Fayette and Shelby, and on the west by the Mississippi river. It is well watered by the Forked Deer and Big Hatchee rivers. It contains the towns of Covington, the seat of justice, Fulton and Randolph; and there are post offices at Durhamsville and Richland Grove. Population in 1830, 6317; cent. lat. 35° 35′ N., lon. 12° 45′ W.[373]

Todd's, a post office in Lincoln county, established in 1833.

Totten's Wells, a post office in Overton county, 160 miles W. of N. from Nashville.[374]

Tisdale's Creek, a south west branch of Forked Deer, in the N. W. corner of Haywood county.

Tom's Creek, an eastern branch of Tennessee, in Perry county, between Spring and Owl creeks, below Perryville.

Toulon, a post office in Haywood county, late *Belmontaine.*[375]

[369] Discontinued; near Tennessee City, Dickson County.
[370] The present "Ten-Mile," in the northern tip of Meigs County.
[371-374] Discontinued as a post office.
[375] Discontinued as a post office; postal service through Ripley.

Trace Creek, a post office in Jackson county, established in 1833.[376]

Trace Creek, an east branch of Tennessee, in Humphreys county. It is about twenty miles long, and has its source in the edge of Dickson county. The stage road from Nashville to Jackson runs along the margin of this creek.

Trenton, a post town and seat of justice of Gibson county, incorporated in 1826. It is 150 miles west from Nashville, and 875 W. by S. from Washington City, in lat. 36° N., lon. 12° W., on the north fork of Forked Deer, 50 miles east of Mississippi river.

Trousdale, a post office in Stewart county, 89 miles N. W. from Nashville.[377]

Troy, a post town and seat of justice of Obion county, 175 miles N. of W. from Nashville, and 900 from Washington City, in lat. 36° 20′ N., lon. 12° 30′ W. It is situated on Davidson's creek, a north branch of Obion river, about 25 miles W. from Dresden and 20 S. from Mills Point, Ken., Incorporated in 1831.[378]

Tuckaluchee Cove, a post office in Blount county.[379]

Tuckahoe Creek, a north branch of French Broad, west of Bay mountain, in Sevier and Knox counties.

Tumbling Shoals. Noted shoals in the Tennessee river above the *Suck,* opposite to Lookout mountain in Hamilton county, 250 miles above the Muscle Shoals. Here the river breaks through the Cumberland mountains and is compressed to a width of about 70 yards from a width of near half a mile. Just as it enters the mountain, a large rock projects from the northern shore, which causes a sudden bend of the river; the water is then thrown with great rapidity against the southern shore, whence it rebounds around the point of the

---

[376] Discontinued as a post office.

[377] Discontinued. Trousdale is the name of a county in Tennessee, established in 1870; north of Wilson, west of Smith, east of Sumner, and South of Macon.

[378] Troy is a town and post office of Obion County; the county seat is now Union City.

[379] Discontinued as a post office.

rock, and produces a tremendous whirl or suck. If boats enter the chute a little veering to the left, they are precipitated with great violence against the rocks of the southern shore.

Tunnacunhe Creek, a south branch of Tennessee, rising in Georgia and has its junction at Ross's, in the Cherokee nation, above the Tumbling Shoals.

Tunnell's, a post office in Monroe county.[380]

Turkey Creek, a south west branch of the S. fork of Forked Deer, between Meridian creek and Wheaton's creek, in the north west corner of Haywood county.

Turnbow's Creek, a north west branch of Tennessee, on the line between Perry and Hardin counties, above Eagle-nest Island.[381]

Turnbull's Creek, a south west branch of Big Harpeth, above Jone's creek, in Dickson and Davidson counties.[382]

Turnersville, a post town in Robertson county, ten miles west from Springfield, where the road from Nashville to Hopkinsville crosses the road leading from Springfield to Clarksville. It contains a store, tavern, physician, shoemaker and blacksmith. It is thirty-three miles north west from Nashville.[383]

Tusculum, a post office in Williamson county.[384]

Two mile Creek, a west branch of Caney Fork, in White county, above the mouth of Calf-killer.

Tyree's Springs, the most celebrated watering place in the state. The house of entertainment is situated on the right side of the road leading from Nashville to Franklin, Kentucky, twenty miles from the former place. The establishment for-

---

[380] Discontinued as a post office.

[381] Turnbow's Creek is in Decatur County (established in 1845); near the village of Bath Springs.

[382] Most of the course of Turnbull's Creek is in Cheatham County (established in 1856).

[383] No longer a post office; a community in the western section of Robertson County; postal service through Cedar Hill.

[384] Discontinued; there is a post office, Tusculum College, in Greene County.

merly belonged to Richmond C. Tyree, now deceased, and was for some years kept by Mr. Hagan. It is now kept by Mr. Cheatham, and extensive improvements both ornamental and convenient have been made. This delightful situation presents many allurements, the situation is high, dry, and commanding, where the purest air never fails to circulate. There is a spring of pure cold water issuing from the hill; and the shades and pleasure grounds are tastefully exhibited. The Robertson's springs, distant about one mile and a half, a pleasant ride for excursion and exercise, have been attached to the establishment, which adds much to its value. Tyree's Springs are in Sumner and Robertson's Springs in Robertson county. A post office is kept here, and the mail stages pass and repass every day and it is alternately a regular breakfasting and dining place. The waters contain sulphur, and small portions of neutral salts, which are known to be serviceable in obstructions of the liver, and other abdominal viscera. These springs are fourteen miles west from Gallatin, and fourteen east from Springfield.

U

Unica Mountains, these mountains lie south of Little Tennessee, and north of Hiwassee, on the line between North Carolina and this state about 225 miles east by south from Nashville. In lat. 35° 15′ N., lon. 7° W. Unica in the cherokee language signifies *white.*

Unitia, a post town in Blount county, near the Holston river, containing about a dozen families, seventy inhabitants, one store, one blacksmith, one hatter, one doctor, a tanyard and a wool carding and cotton picking machine. It is 158 miles east from Nashville.[385]

Union, a post office in Humphreys county, seventy-five miles west from Nashville.[386]

Upper Elkton, a town in Giles county, on Elk river, incorporated in 1831.[387]

---

[385] Discontinued as a post office; the community of Unitia (postal service through Greenback) is now in Loudon County (established in 1870).

[386] Discontinued as a post office.

[387] Now known as Elkton, a town and post office in southeastern Giles County.

V

Valley Town, a post office in the Cherokee nation, 160 miles south east from Nashville.[388]

Van Buren, a town established in 1831, in Hardeman county, at Robson's cross roads.

Vaughn's Creek, a branch of the West Fork of Stone's river, in Rutherford county.

Vernon, a post town and former seat of justice of Hickman county, situated on Piney river, a north branch of Duck river, forty-five miles south west from Nashville. It was disfranchised in 1823.

---

[388] Discontinued as a post office.

273

W

Wallen's ridge, lying north west of Powell's mountain and east of Powell's river, in Claiborne county. It was named in 1761, after a Mr. Wallen who composed one of an exploring party. There are other spurs south west which bear the same name, or Walden.[389]

Walnut Grove, a post office in Fayette county, established in 1833.[390]

Warnersville, a post town in Hardeman county, on the W. bank of Big Hatchee river, a short distance above the mouth of Little Hatchee, some ten or twelve miles above Bolivar. It contains a store and tavern—164 miles south west by west from Nashville.[391]

Warren, a county in Middle Tennessee, adjoining the mountains, erected in 1807. It is bounded on the south by Franklin, on the north east by White, on the east by Bledsoe, on the west by Rutherford, and on the north west by Wilson. Length forty miles, mean width twenty. The Caney Fork is the line between Warren and White. It flows a north west direction and joins the Cumberland at Carthage, in Smith county. The other principal water courses are south west branches of the Caney Fork. McMinnville is the seat of justice, and there are post offices at Danville, Cave mills and Pleasant Spring. Population in 1820, 10,343, in 1830, 15,351. Cent. lat. 35° 45′ N., lon. 8° 40′ W.

Warrensburg, a post town on the Little Chucky, in the western angle of Greene county, seventy miles a little north of east from Knoxville, and 245 miles east from Nashville.[392]

War Trace Creek, a north branch of Cumberland, in Jackson county.

---

[389] Correctly, "Walden's Ridge." It extends southward to Marion County.

[390-391] Discontinued as a post office.

[392] The post office is discontinued; the community exists, in the western section of Greene County, postal service through Midway.

War-trace Fork, one of the north branches of Duck river, in Bedford county, above Shelbyville.

Washington, a county in East Tennessee, bounded on the north by Sullivan, on the east by Carter, on the west by Greene, and on the south by North Carolina. Length from north to south 35 miles; breadth from east to west about 22. Its principal streams are the Nolachucky and branches. It contains the towns of Jonesboro', the seat of justice, and Leesburg. The southern part of the county is very mountainous, and parts of it are hilly, rather too much so, for advantageous cultivation. In the mountainous parts, are *coves,* of land of good quality, but of small extent. The Greasy Cove is the largest, being six or seven miles long, and varying in width from a half to two miles; and there is some excellent land in Bumpass Cove, of the quality termed mulatto land. There is a chain of mountains on the south line near thirty miles wide, thinly inhabited. Those who reside in the valleys or small coves subsist chiefly by hunting the game of the forrest, deer, bear, &c. Inexhaustable quantities of iron ore of good quality are found in this county, mixed with the dirt. And most of that used at Embree's furnace, requires no smelting or pounding, the pieces being sufficiently small, and are prepared by washing off the yellow dirt attached to them. Brown paints, plaster of paris, yellow ochre and red ochre abound in this county. It also contains two chalybeate springs.

Wheat and corn are the staples. Cotton is seldom raised, owing to the early frosts. Bacon is an article of export and is wagoned to Augusta in Georgia. Shoe thread, tow linen, feathers, bees' wax and ginseng are purchased by the resident merchants and hauled to Baltimore. Iron castings, nails, flour and whiskey are transported to Huntsville, Ala. The iron is principally from Carter. Mills are numerous, few famiiles having to go more than three miles to mill. Embree's iron works are the only establishments of the kind in the county. Washington college is situated in this county, but it has in some measure declined from its former standing, owing to rival institutions. About three miles and a half from Jones-

WAY 275

boro' on the Abingdon road, stands the first hewed log house built in the state. It was erected about 54 years ago. Washington county was erected in 1777 by the state of North Carolina, and was represented in the convention that formed the constitution of Tennessee, by John Tipton, Samuel Handly, Leroy Taylor, Landon Carter and James Stuart. Population in 1820, 9,557; in 1830, 10,995. Cent. lat. 36° 11' N., lon. 5° 33' W.

Washington, the seat of justice of Rhea county, situated on the west bank of Tennessee river, below the mouth of Clear creek. It was established in 1809, and incorporated in 1819. In 1833, it contained about 400 inhabitants, two lawyers, two doctors, one clergyman, two churches, one academy, one school, five stores, two taverns, three carpenters, one cabinet maker, one hatter, one tailor, two shoemakers, two saddlers, two blacksmiths, two tanners, two bricklayers, one wagon maker and two cotton gins. It is about 100 miles below Knoxville, 130 E. S. E. from Nashville, and 606 S. W. by W. from Washington City. Lat. 35° 38' N., lon. 7° 48', W.[293]

Washington Furnace, a post office in Montgomery county, established in 1833.[294]

Watauga River, a south branch of Holston. It rises in Ashe county, N. C., and flows S. W. through Carter, in this state, via Elizabethton, and joins the S. branch on the line of Washington and Sullivan, between Jonesboro', and Blountsville. Watauga signifies the River of Islands.

Wayne, a county in Middle Tennessee, erected in 1817. It is bounded on the south by Lauderdale county, Ala., on the north by Perry and Hickman, on the east by Lawrence, and on the west by Hardin. It is 28 miles long and 22½ wide. It lies encircled by the great bend of Tennessee river, which touches its north west corner. The principal branches of the Tennessee in this county, are Shoal and Cypress creeks on the south, and Second, Reinses, Swift, Camp and White Oak

---

[293] Washington, a small town and ferry on the Tennessee River in Rhea County, has been superceded by Dayton as the county seat.

[294] Discontinued as a post office.

creek on the west. Population in 1820, 2,439; in 1830, 6,013. Seat of justice, Waynesboro'; and there is a post office at Carrolsville. Cent. lat. 35° 14' N., lon. 10° 50' W.

Waynesboro', a post town and the seat of justice of Wayne county, situated on Green river, a south branch of Buffaloe. It is 31 miles E. from Savannah, 101 S. W. from Nashville, and 810 W. S. W. from Washington City, in lat. 35° 11' N., 10° 53' W.

Weakley, a county in West Tennessee, erected in 1823. It is bounded on the east by Henry, on the south by Gibson and Carroll, on the west by Obion, and on the north by Kentucky. It is 26 miles long from north to south, and 24 wide, from east to west, containing an area of 625 square miles. The surface is level and the soil fertile. In 1829 it was estimated that at least 350,000 acres, more than half of the county had been located. The county is drained by the Obion river and branches. The number of taxable free polls in 1828, was 471 whites, and 274 slaves; and tax was received for 179,967 acres of land. Population in 1830, 4,796. Seat of justice, Dresden, and the only village in the county. Cent. lat. 36° 15' N., lon. 11° 45' W.

Weakley's Creek, a western branch of Richland creek in Giles county, north west of Pulaski.

Wear's Cove, a post office in Sevier county, established in 1833.[995]

Well's Creek, in Stewart county. Near the head of this creek is an ancient fortification. The fort is 80 or a 100 feet square, and the walls twelve feet high. It rises near Humphreys county line, and joins the Cumberland at Well's Island, below Grice's creek.[996]

Wesley, a post town in Haywood county, laid off on the land of Samuel P. Ashe, Esq., at the junction of the road, within three miles of Hatchee river. The first sale of lots in

---

[995] Discontinued; the community is known as Wear Valley, postal service through Sevierville.

[996] Near Cumberland City, Stewart County.

this town was Nov. 20, 1829. It is 30 miles N. W. from Bolivar, 15 E. from Covington, 31 from Randolph, 13 from Brownsville, 18 N. from Sommerville, 45 N. E. from Memphis, 18 from Estanaula, 35 south of west from Jackson, and 180 W. S. W. from Nashville.[397]

West Fork of Stone's river, a considerable stream in Rutherford county. It receives Overall's creek on the west, and joins the East Fork at the town of Jefferson.

West's Fork, a west branch of Cany Fork, in White county.

West Sandy, a branch of Big Sandy, in Henry county.

Western District. This includes the whole territory purchased of the Chickasaw Indians at the treaty held at Doak's, in 1818, by General Jackson and Governor Shelby; bounded as follows, to wit: "beginning on the Tennessee river about 35 miles by water, below Col. George Colbert's ferry, where the thirty fifth degree of north latitude strikes the same; thence due west with the said degree of north latitude (being the line between Tennessee and Mississippi states) to where it cuts the Mississippi river at or near the Chickasaw Bluff, then up the said Mississippi river to the mouth of the Ohio; thence up the Ohio river to the mouth of Tennessee river; thence up the Tennessee river to the place of beginning." A small part on the north, falls into Kentucky, and is divided into four counties, to wit: Graves, Calloway, Hickman and McCracken. The price given for the whole territory, including the above mentioned counties, and fourteen counties and three half counties in Tennessee, was three hundred thousand dollars, payable in fifteen annual instalments. The settlement of the District began in 1819. The first county organized was Shelby. The act establishing it, passed in 1819, and it was organized, and Memphis laid off in 1820. Hardin and Perry counties, half of which lie in the District, were established at the same time. Henry, Carroll, Madison and Henderson, were established in 1821. Jackson was the first town established in these four counties. It was first called Alexandria, but was soon changed to Jackson. Paris was laid off in a thick

[397] Discontinued; at or near the present Stanton, Haywood County.

forest in the year 1823, and the first improvements were made in June of that year. Weakley, Obion, Gibson, Haywood, Tipton, Fayette, Hardeman and McNairy counties, were erected in 1823, and courts organized in 1824. At the special session of the legislature in 1822, the District, together with the counties of Lawrence and Wayne, and those parts of Hardin and Perry lying on the east side of Tennessee river, were formed into the ninth congressional District, and Col. Adam R. Alexander, in 1823 was elected the first representative. By the census of 1830, the District, exclusive of the four counties in Kentucky and those parts of Hardin, Perry and Humphreys, which lie west of Tennessee river, the population was 99,000, to wit: Carroll, 9,378; Dyer, 1,904; Fayette, 8,654; Gibson, 5,801; Hardeman, 11,628; Haywood, 5,356; Henry, 12,230; Henderson, 8,741; Madison, 11,750; McNairy, 5,697; Shelby, 5,652; Tipton, 5,317, and Weakley, 4,796. The principal rivers in the District, besides the Tennessee and Mississippi, are Sandy, Reelfoot, Obion, Forked Deer, Big Hatchee, Loosa Hatchee and Wolf. In this work, *'West Tennessee'* means *Western District.*

Wheaton's Creek, a south west branch of the south fork of Forked Deer, in the north west corner of Haywood county, between Turkey and Tisdale's creeks, in the first range.

White, a county in Middle Tennessee, erected in 1806. It is bounded on the north by Jackson and Overton, on the south east by Bledsoe; north west by Smith, north east by Overton, Fentress and Morgan, and south west by Warren (or the Caney Fork of Cumberland.) Length, 40 miles; mean width, 19; area, 750 square miles. It is drained by the eastern branches of the Caney Fork. This county contains many natural curiosities, for descriptions of which, *see* 'Arch and Big Bone Caves', 'Falling Water,' 'Calf-Killer,' 'Taylor's Creek,' &c. In 1820, White contained a population of 8,701, and in 1830, 9,967. Seat of justice, Sparta; cen. lat. 36° N., lon. 8° 30' W.

White Oak, a post office in Humphreys county, 136 miles

west from Nashville.[398]

White Oak Creek, an eastern branch of the Tennessee river, on the line of Humphreys and Stewart counties. The most of it lies in Stewart.

White Oak Creek, a west branch of the big south fork of Cumberland river, in Fentress county. It rises near Jamestown and flows an east direction, north of the road to Jacksboro', and has its junction a few miles below the confluence of New river.[399]

White Oak Creek, a west branch of Caney Fork, in White county.

White Oak Creek, a west branch of the Tennessee. It rises in M'Nairy and Henderson, and running east receives Mud creek on the south, and joins the river above Doe creek, about half way between Lee's Bluff and Indian Island, in Hardin county.

White Oak Creek, an east branch of Tennessee, in the north west corner of Wayne county, at the east bend of the river.

White's Creek, a north branch of Holston river, at Knoxville, in Knox county.

White's Creek, a north branch of Cumberland, in Davidson county, below Nashville.

White's Creek, a north west branch of Tennessee, on the line between Roane and Rhea counties.

White-house, a post office in Williamson county, established in 1833.[400]

White Plains, a post office in Jackson county, 64 miles N. of E. from Nashville.[401]

Whiting, a post office in Madison county, 150 miles W. S. W. from Nashville.[402]

Wild-cat Creek, a branch of Calf-killer, in White county.

---

[398] Discontinued; the community is in Houston County (established in 1871).

[399] Its mouth is in Scott County (established in 1849).

[400] Discontinued; there is a White House, town and post office, on the line between Sumner and Robertson counties.

[401-402] Discontinued as a post office.

Williams', a post office in Montgomery county, 38 miles N. W. from Nashville.[403]

Williamsburg, The former seat of justice of Jackson county, at Fort Blount, on the left bank of Cumberland river, 70 miles N. of E. from Nashville.[404]

Williamsport, a post town in Maury county, established on the land of Edward Williams, on the south side of Duck river, in 1819. It is 38 miles S. from Nashville, and 12 S. W. from Columbia. Incorporated in 1831.

Williamson, a county in Middle Tennessee, erected in 1799, and reduced to its constitutional limits in 1807. It is bounded on the north by Davidson, south by Bedford and Maury, or the chain of hills dividing the waters of Cumberland and Tennessee; on the east by Rutherford, and west by Hickman and Dickson. Its principal streams are the Big and Little Harpeth rivers, which flow from south east to north west. It contains the towns of Franklin, the seat of justice, Versailles and Nolensville, and there are post offices at Evan's X Roads, Hardeman's X Roads, Good Spring and Messina. Williamson is one of the best farming counties in Middle Tennessee, and contains much wealth as well as an enterprising population. A good McAdamized turnpike road has lately been completed between Franklin and Nashville. Population in 1820, 20,640; in 1830, 26,608.

Willingham's, a post office in Weakley county, 152 miles N. of W. from Nashville.[405]

Wilson, a county in Middle Tennessee, bounded on the north by the Cumberland river or Sumner county, on the north east by Smith, on the south east by Warren, on the south by Rutherford and on the west by Davidson. Wilson was erected in 1799, in 1801 its bounds were extended south; and in 1815, a part was attached to Rutherford, and its bounds circumscribed to about its constitutional area, 625 square

---

[403] Discontinued as a post office.

[404] Little remains of Williamsburg or of Fort Blount. The county seat of Jackson County is Gainesboro.

[405] Discontinued as a post office.

miles. It is drained by branches of the Cany Fork and Cumberland; the principal of which are Smith's Fork, Hickman, Mulherin, Round Lick, Cedar Spring, Barton's and Cedar Lick creeks. It contains the towns of Lebanon, the seat of justice, Statesville and Cainsville. Wilson is a populous county, and contains a great deal of good farming land. It is remarkable for its extensive cedar groves. There is scarcely a farmer in the county who has not more or less cedar growing on or contiguous to his lands. Population in 1820 was 18,730; in 1830, 25,477; making an increase in ten years of 6,747.

Wilson's Creek, a north branch of Duck river, in Bedford county, between Spring creek and North Fork.[406]

Wilson's, a post office in Anderson county, 189 miles N. of E. from Nashville.[407]

Winchester, a post town and the seat of justice of Franklin county, situated on the Boiling Fork of Elk river. It was established in 1810, and incorporated in 1813. In 1833 it contained about 700 inhabitants, seven lawyers, four doctors, one presbyterian, one methodist, and one baptist church, one male and one female academy, eleven stores, four taverns, six carpenters, four cabinet makers, four brick layers, two hatters, twelve tailors, four shoe makers, fourteen blacksmiths, one silversmith, three carriage and wagon maker's shops, (eighteen hands) three turners, one copper smiths' shops, two painters, two tanyards, (eight hands) two saddlers' shops, (six hands) and three groceries. It is 60 miles S. S. E. from Murfreesboro', 95 from Nashville and 684 W. S. W. from Washington City; lat. 35° 16' N., lon. 9° 6' W.

Winton, a town established in 1827, at the Big Spring in the county of Maury, on a tract of land granted to General Winn.

Winton, a town established in 1831, in Gibson county, on the land of Benjamin P. Tyson.

---

[406] Wilson Creek, near Chapel Hill, is in Marshall County (established in 1836).

[407] Discontinued as a post office.

Witcher's X Roads, a post office in Smith county, established in 1833.[408]

Wolf River, an east branch of the Mississippi. It rises in the state of Mississippi, and flowing nearly a west course through Fayette, joins the river at Memphis, in Shelby county. In the S. E. corner of Fayette, it passes the town of Lagrange, a handsome village containing about sixty families. The river is declared navigable as high up as the North Fork.

Wolf River, the name of a post office in Hardeman county, 240 miles S. W. by W. from Nashville.[409]

Wolf River, a branch of Obid's river. It rises in the Cumberland mountains, N. E. of Jamestown, in Fentress county, near the new Monticello road. It then flows west and crossing the old Monticello road, receives Ratten's Fork on the north, then turns south; crosses Pile's turnpike, flows N. W. parallel with Doubletop mountain, enters Overton, receives the Cany Fork on the north, and joins Obid's river N. E. of Monroe. This stream is subject to sudden rises and falls, and is too rapid and rocky for navigation.

Woodbourne, a post office in Knox county, late 'Woods.'[410]

Woodholm, a post office in Carroll county, 130 miles W. from Nashville, late 'Wood's Store.'[411]

Wood's Ferry, a post office in Greene county, 250 miles E. from Nashville.[412]

Woodsville, a town established in Greene county, in 1829, on Nolachucky river. Proprietors, Woods and James.

Wood Lake, on the north line of Obion county, near the Mississippi river. A marshy swamp extends south into Dyer.

Wyman's Creek, a north branch of Duck river in the N. W. corner of Maury county.

Wynnsborough, a town established in 1819, on the land of Thomas Wynn, below the mouth of Leatherwood creek, on the east bank of the Tennessee river, in Stewart County.

[408-412] Discontinued as a post office.

X

Y

Yellow Creek, a post office in Montgomery county 56 miles N. of W. from Nashville.[113]

Yellow Creek, a south branch of Cumberland river. It rises in Dickson, and joins the river in Montgomery county below Palmyra.

Yellow Creek, a north branch of White Oak creek, east of Jamestown in Fentress county.

Yellow Mountain, north of the Nolachucky, on the line between North Carolina and Tennessee, at the south corner of Carter county.

Z

---

[113] The community is now in Houston County (established in 1871), postal service through Erin and Cumberland City.

APPENDIX

A list of Lawyers in the State of Tennessee, with their places of residence.

Athens.
Return J. Meigs,
Alex. D. Keys,
Asbury M. Coffey,
James F. Bradford,
Victor M. Campbell,
T. N. Vandyke,
John W. Brazeale.

Blountsville.
John Rhea,
William K. Blair,
James D. Rhea,
John Netherland,

Brownsville.
Jas. W. Strother,
William H. Loving,
Ed. Richmond,

Bolivar.
Roger Barton, *Atty. Gen.*
Edward R. Belcher,
David Fentress,
Valentine D. Barry,
Pendleton Gaines,
Austin Miller,
Wiliam C. Dunlap,

Clinton.
Harding,

Charlotte.
John Montgomery,
John C. Collier,
Valentine S. Allen,
Will. H. Dortch,

Centerville.
H. R. Nixon, *Atty. Gen.*
James M. Howry,

Columbia.
Ed. Dillahaunty, *Atty. Gen.*
William P. Martin,
Wm. E. Gillespie,
Robert L. Cobbs,
Allen Brown,
Jonas E. Thomas,
Terry H. Cahal,
Rich. C. Whitsides,
Gid. J. Pillow,
Saml. D. Frierson,
Charles W. Webber,
Jas. A. Thomas,
A. O. P. Nicholson,
James K. Polk.

Clarksville.
Wm. K. Turner, *Atty. Gen.*
Mort. Ab. Martin,
Herbert S. Kimble,
W. B. Johnson,
Geo. Boyd,
A. M. Clayton,
N. H. Allen,
Wm. Overton,
R. J. Rivers,
J. H. Quarles,
J. B. Reynolds,
Jos. Johnson,
Cave Johnson,
F. W. Huling,

Carthage.
A. W. Overton,
William Owen,
William Hart,
William M'Clain,
J. G. Park,
O. B. Hubbard,
Robert Allen, jr.
D. A. J. Crenshaw,
W. B. Campbell,
A. Ferguson,

Covington.
Nathan C. Ross,
Robert Greene,
G. D. Searcy,
Addison H. White,
Phil. B. Glenn,
Thomas Crutcher,

Dandridge.
Robert H. Hynd,

John H. Carson,
Bynam Jarnagin,

Dover.
Alfred H. Powel,

Dyersburg.
Mark Mitchell,

Dresden.
A. G. Bondurant,
John A. Gardner,
William Fitzgerald,

Elizabethton.
Thos. A. R. Nelson, *Atty. General.*
Alfred W. Taylor,
Thomas D. Love,
Christian C. Nave,

Fayetteville.
James Fulton,
Saml. W. Cormack,
Wm. M. Inge,
William T. Ross,
Davis Eastland,
John R. Wilson,
Geo. A. Wilson,
Arch. Yell,
Wm. D. Thompson,

Franklin.
Richard Alexander,
Rob. C. Foster,
Peter N. Smith,
John Marshall,
H. Marshall,

John Donelson,
R. L. Andrews,
Wm. Hadly,
Thomas Sconce,
David Campbell,

Gainesboro'.
James T. Quarles,
Thomas Smith,

Gallatin.
John J. White,
William Trousdale,
John H. Turner,
David M. Saunders,
Wm. M. Blackmore,
Joseph C. Guild,
George A. Baskerville,
Balie Peyton,
Thomas Barry,
George W. Parker,
Josiah W. Baldridge,
John R. Chenault,
Axtianex A. Mills,
C. P. M'Daniel,

Greenville.
James W. Wyly,
A. H. Wyly,
Geo. T. Gillespie,
Alfred Russell,
Robert J. M'Kinney,

Huntingdon.
John M'Kernon,
Jesse Benton,
Thomas J. Jennings,

Jacksboro'.
David Richardson,
John E. Wheeler,

Jasper.
Wm. J. Standifer,
D. W. Campbell,
George W. Wood,
James H. Wilkinson,

Jamestown.
John M. Clemens,
William Richardson,

Jonesboro'.
Thomas Emerson,
John Kennedy,
Jas. V. Anderson,
Mark T. Anderson,
Seth W. Lucky,
Nathaniel Kelsey,
Thomas D. Greer,
John Blair,
William K. Blair,
Robert Maclin,
Samuel Lowry,

Jackson.
A. B. Bradford, *Atty. Gen.*
A. L. Martin,
Wm. Stodert,
William B. Miller,
Robert Hughes,
Milton Brown,
Micajah Autry,
Henry Strange,
John Read,
A. Huntsman,

Jackson.
P. M. Miller,
    Hodge,
J. W. Cloud,
R. B. M'Cleland,

Knoxville.
John R. Nelson, *Atty. Gen.*
Spencer Jarnagin,
Ebenezer Alexander,
Hugh Brown,
Hugh L. White,
Thos. L. Williams,
John Williams,
Rob. M. Anderson,
Wm. C. Mynatt,
Sam. B. Boyd,
Geo. W. Churchwell,
Samuel R. Rogers,
Reuben B. Rogers,
Saml. B. Kennedy,
James Hare,
Caleb Putnam,
Wm. B. A. Ramsey,
R. G. Dunlap,

Kingston.
James M'Campbell,
John Y. Smith,
Thos. N. Clark, Jr.,
Henry S. Purris,
John A. Hooke,
Hugh L. Brazeale,

Lawrenceburg.
William C. Davis,
Y. G. Porter,
    Royal,

Lebanon.
Saml. Yerger, *Atty. Gen.*
John Hall,
Rob. M. Burton
Rob. L. Caruthers,
John S. Topp,
Wm. L. Martin,
Wm. L. Sypert,
D. A. J. Crenshaw,
John H. Dew,

Lexington.
Christopher H. Williams,
James M. White,
Wm. P. Withers,
Micajah Bullock,
Daniel Wilson,

Livingston.
Jacob Dillon,
Alvah Cullom,
Ed. Cullom,
J. Totten,
Benj. Gabbert,
    Copps,

Maryville.
Jacob F. Foute,
    Wilkinson,

Madisonville.
James A. Coffin,
Bradley Kimbrough,
John O. Conner,
Iredel D. Wright,

Montgomery.
James A. Dabney,

Murfreesboro'
Samuel Anderson,
David W. Dickinson,
Andrew J. Hoover,
Charles Ready,
William Brady,
E. W. Keeble,
John Bruce,
J. P. Burrus,
Sam. Rucker,
S. D. Rowan,

M'Minnville.
Andrew J. Marchbanks,
John B. Forrester,
Nap. B. Beard,
J. Thompson,
Brum. L. Ridley,

Nashville.
Jas. Collinsworth, *U.S. Atty.*
And. Hays, *Atty. Gen.*
Geo. S. Yerger, *Reporter.*
Felix Grundy,
Ephraim H. Foster,
Francis B. Fogg,
James P. Grundy,
William T. Brown,
David B. Craighhead,
Thomas B. Craighead,
Jacob S. Yerger,
Godfrey M. Fogg,
Washington Barrow,
Samuel Watson,
Leonard P. Cheatham,
William Thompson,
Thomas Washington,
William Washington,

Wm. E. Anderson,
James P. Clark,
Thomas H. Fletcher,
Edwin Ewing,
James Rucks,
Dixon Allen,
Alfred Balch,
Geo. S. Childress,
John Childress,
John R. Wharton,
James T. Holman,
Valerius P. Winchester,
Charles D. Shrewsberry,
J. W. Perkins,
Sam. H. Laughlin,
Thomas Hoge,
Eastin Morris,
John M. Hays,
John Trimble,
Charles Scott,

Newport.
Dewit M'Nutt,
Jas. A. Marshall,

Paris.
Geo. W. Terrel, *Atty. Gen.*
James M'Means,
Andrew M'Campbell,
Arc. Wynns,
Henry A. Garret,
John R. Grundy,
James Jones,
Wm. R. Harris,
Wm. M. Brown,
John H. Dunlap,

Paris.
Dudly S. Jennings,
Berry Gillespie,

Pikeville.
James A. Whitesides,

Perryville.
Jared S. Allen,
Wm. F. Dougherty,
James G. Hyde,

Pulaski.
Aaron V. Brown,
James M'Combs,
J. H. Rivers,
Wm. C. Flournoy,
Wm. H. Field,
D. C. Topp,
A. Wright,
A. F. Goff,
J. J. Davenport,
E. J. Shields,
John W. Goode,
G. Washington,

Purdy.
Joseph Young,
Maclin Cross,

Rutledge.
John Cocke,
James Lafferty,
David Barton,
Pryor Lea,

Rogersville.
John A. M'Kinny,
Peter Parsons,

Michl. McCann,
Sterling Cock,
Dicks Alexander,
William O. Winston,
Orville Bradley,

Reynoldsburg.
Thos. B. Hudson,
Stephen C. Pavatt,

Raleigh and Memphis.
Robert C. M'Alpin,
Robertson Topp,
Wm. H. Hurst,
Seth Wheatly,
Chas. C. Lewis,
B. Jones,
Shelton Watson,
J. D. Martin,

Sevierville.
James P. H. Porter,
Felix Auley,
Ignatius Riggin,
Isaac A. Miller,

Shelbyville.
J. E. Frierson, *Atty. Gen.*
William Gilchrist,
Wm. B. Sutton,

Savannah.
Orville Harrison,
James Scott,
Nathaniel Casey,
A. M. Hardin, *Atty. Gen.*

Springfield.
Thornton H. Cooke,

Sparta.
Nathan Haggard,
David Ames,
A. B. Lane,
Saml. Turney,
John H. Anderson,
Richard Nelson,

Sommerville.
John Brown,
William Davis,
Granville Lewis,
Bennet H. Henderson,
John Blackwell,
West H. Humphreys,

Tazewell.
John M. Brabson,
James B. Robinson,
Gray Garrett,

Trenton.
J. H. Dyer, *Atty. Gen.*

James L. Totten,
James Moore,
R. P. Raines,
John Parker,
J. A. Taliafero,
Felix Parker,

Troy.
Jas. L. Daviess,
Charles M'Alister,
A. O. W. Totten,

Washington.
Thos. J. Campbell,

Waynesboro'.
Thomas F. Edward,
C. J. Nickson,

Winchester.
Jacob C. Isaacs,
James Campbell,
Hop. L. Turney,
John Goodwin,
Micah. Taul,
Osborn D. Herndon,
Stephen Adams,

GOVERNORS OF TENNESSEE.

William Blount, Territorial, appointed	1790
John Sevier, State, elected	1796
Archibald Roane do do	1801
John Sevier,	1803
Willie Blount,	1809
Joseph M'Minn,	1815
William Carroll,	1821
Samuel Houston,	1827
William Hall, Speaker of the Senate, part of	1829
William Carroll elected.	1829

APPENDIX 293

GOVERNMENT, 1834.

William Carroll, Governor, salary $2000
Samuel G. Smith, Secretary of State, salary } $750
and perquisites.
Miller Francis, Treasurer of East Tennessee.
Thomas Crutcher, Treasurer of Middle Tennessee.
James T. Caruthers, Treasurer of West Tennessee.

JUDICIARY.

Supreme Court.

	Salary.
John Catron, Chief Justice,	$1800
Robert Whyte, Judge,	1800
Jacob Peck, do	1800
Nathan Greene, do	1800

Court of Chancery.

William A. Cook, Chancellor,	1500
William B. Reese, do	1500

Judges of the Circuit Court—salaries $1300 each.

Samuel Powell,	James C. Mitchell,
Edward Scott,	Thomas Stuart,
John W. Cooke,	Joshua Haskell,
Charles F. Keith,	Abraham Caruthers,
Lunsford M. Bramlet,	Parry W. Humphreys,
William B. Turley,	

Supreme Court, when and where held, and clerks.

Towns.	When Held.	Clerks.
Jackson,	2nd Mon. February,	J. H. Talbot,
Nashville,	1st Mon. March,	Randal M'Gavock,
Centerville,	1 do June,	James M. Howry,
Jonesboro'	3 do June,	
Knoxville,	2 do July,	Hugh Brown,
Sparta,	2 do December,	Trent. C. Conner.

Chancery Courts, when and where held, and Clerks.

Towns.	When Held.	Clerks.
Rogersville,	1 Mon. May & Nov.	Dicks Alexander,
Greenville,	2 " May & Nov.	Geo. T. Gillespie,
Knoxville,	3 " April & Octo.	Wm. B. A. Ramsy,
Madisonville,	4 " May & Nov.	
Kingston,	2 " June & Decr.	Thos. N. Clark, jr.
Carthage,	2 " July & Jan.	John G. Park,
M'Minnville,	2 " June & Dec.	Joseph Morford,
Franklin,	1 " May & Nov.	Benj. Litton,
Columbia,	1 " March & Sept.	Wm. E. Gillespie,
Charlotte,	3 " June & Decr.	Will. H. Dortch,
Jackson,	4 " March & Sept.	Henry Strange,
Paris,	3 " March & Sept.	A. M'Campbell,
Bolivar,	2 " Mar. & Sept.	E. P. Gaines.

Counties.	County Courts. Mondays	Cir. Courts. Mondays
Anderson,	2 Jan. April, July, Oct.	4 Feb. Aug.
Bledsoe,	4 Feb. May, Aug. Nov.	4 Mar. Sept.
Blount,	4 Mar. June, Sept. Dec.	1 af 4 Fe. Au.
Bedford,	1 Feb. May, Aug. Nov.	1 June, Dec.
Cocke,	4 Feb. May, Aug. Nov.	2 Jan. July,
Carter,	2 Feb. May, Aug. Nov.	3 Mar. Sept.
Claiborne,	4 Feb. May, Aug. Nov.	3 April, Oct.
Campbell,	2 Mar. June, Sept. Dec.	4 April, Oct.
Carroll,	2 Mar. June, Sept. Dec.	1 Jan. July,
Davidson,	3 Jan. April, July, Oct.	4 May, Nov.
Dickson,	1 Jan. April, July, Oct.	1 Mar. Sept.
Dyer,	3 Mar. June, Sept. Dec.	1 May, Nov.
Fentress,	4 Jan. April, July, Oct.	4 Feb. Aug.
Fayette,	2 Jan. April, July, Oct.	2 June, Dec.
Franklin,	4 Feb. May, Aug. Nov.	2 Jan. July,
Greene,	4 Jan. April, July, Oct.	1 Mar. Sept.
Giles,	3 Feb. May, Aug. Nov.	1 Feb. Aug.
Gibson,	2 Mar. June, Sept. Dec.	4 April, Oct.

APPENDIX 295

Counties.	County Courts. Mondays	Cir. Courts. Mondays
Grainger,	3 Feb. May, Aug. Nov.	2 April, Oct.
Hamilton,	2 Mar. June, Sept. Dec.	2 April, Oct.
Hawkins,	4 Feb. May, Aug. Nov.	1 April, Oct.
Hickman,	2 Jan. April, July, Oct.	2 Mar. Sept.
Humphreys,	4 Jan. April, July, Oct.	3 Mar. Sept.
Hardeman,	1 Jan. April, July, Oct.	4 May, Nov.
Hardin,	3 Mar. June, Sept. Dec.	2 May, Nov.
Haywood,	2 Mar. June, Sept. Dec.	1 Jan. July,
Henry,	4 Mar. June, Sept. Dec.	4 May, Nov.
Henderson,	2 Feb. May, Aug. Nov.	2 April, Oct.
Jefferson,	2 Mar. June, Sept. Dec.	3 Jan. July,
Jackson,	2 Feb. May, Aug. Nov.	3 Mar. Sept.
Knox,	1 Jan. April, July, Oct.	2 Feb. Aug.
Lincoln,	3 Jan. April, July, Oct.	3 Mar. Sept.
Lawrence,	1 Jan. April, July, Oct.	4 Feb. Aug.
Marion,	3 Feb. May, Aug. Nov.	3 April, Oct.
M'Minn,	1 Mar. June, Sept. Dec.	2 April, Oct.
Monroe,	3 Mar. June, Sept. Dec.	2 May, Nov.
Morgan,	3 Jan. April, July, Oct.	1 Mar. Sept.
Maury,	2 Mar. June, Sept. Dec.	3 April, Oct.
Montgomery,	3 Jan. April, July, Oct.	3 Feb. Aug.
Madison,	1 Feb. May, Aug. Nov.	3 Jan. July
M'Nairy,	4 Mar. June, Sept. Dec.	3 May, Nov.
Obion,	1 Jan. April, July, Oct.	2 May, Nov.
Overton,	5 Jan. April, July, Oct.	1 Mar. Sept.
Perry,	3 Jan. April, July, Oct.	1 April, Oct.
Roane,	4 Jan. April, July, Oct.	2 Mar. Sept.
Rhea,	1 Feb. May, Aug. Nov.	4 Mar. Sept.
Rutherford,	3 Feb. May, Aug. Oct.	1 April, Oct.
Robertson,	2 Feb. May, Aug. Nov.	2 April, Oct.
Sullivan,	3 Feb. May, Aug. Nov.	4 Mar. Sept.
Sevier,	1 Mar. June, Sep. Dec.	4 Jan. July
Shelby,	3 Jan. April, July, Oct.	3 June, Dec.
Smith,	4 Feb. May, Aug. Nov.	2 April, Oct.
Sumner,	2 Feb. May, Aug. Nov.	2 Mar. Sept.

Counties.	County Courts. Mondays.	Cir. Courts. Mondays.
Stewart,	1 Feb. May, Aug. Nov.	4 Mar. Sept.
Tipton,	1 Mar. June, Sep. Dec.	4 June, Dec.
Washington,	2 Jan. April, July, Oct.	2 Mar. Sept.
Warren,	1 Jan. April, July, Oct.	4 Jan. July
White,	2 Jan. April, July, Oct.	3 May, Nov.
Wilson,	4 Mar. June, Sept. Dec.	4 April, Oct.
Williamson,	1 Jan. April, July, Oct.	1 Feb. Aug.
Wayne,	2 Mar. June, Sept. Dec.	1 May, Nov.
Weakley,	2 Jan. April, July, Oct.	3 May, Nov.

Federal Court.

John M'Lean, Circuit Judge.

Morgan W. Brown, District Judge.

The trial term of the Circuit court of the U. S. is held at Nashville on the 1st Monday in September, and at Knoxville on the 2nd Monday in October. The return term of the Circuit court at Nashville, is on the 1st Monday in March. The District court of the U. States is held at Nashville on the 4th Mondays of May and November; at Knoxville on the 3rd Monday in April, and 2nd Monday in October.

N. A. McNairy, Clerk of the Western District.
Samuel B. Marshall, Marshal   do   do
Wm. C. Mynatt, Clerk of the Eastern District.
Wm. Lyon, Marshal,   do   do

Senators and Representatives in Congress from Tennessee.

Senators	In	Out
Joseph Anderson,	1797	1815
William Blount,	1796	1797
George W. Campbell,	1811	1814
	1815	1818
William Cocke,	1796	1797
	1799	1805
John H. Eaton,	1818	1829
Felix Grundy,	1829	1839
Andrew Jackson,	1797	1798
	1823	1825
Daniel Smith,	1798	1799
	1805	1809
Jesse Wharton,	1814	1815
Hugh L. White,	1815	1835
Jenkin Whitesides,	1809	1811
John Williams,	1815	1823

Representatives.	In	Out
Adam R. Alexander,	1823	1827
Robert Allen,	1819	1827
Thomas D. Arnold,	1831	1833
John Bell,	1827	1835
John Blair,	1823	1835
Wm. G. Blount,	1815	1819
John H. Bowen,	1813	1815
Henry H. Bryan,	1819	1823
Samuel Bunch,	1833	1834
George W. Campbell,	1803	1809
Newton Cannon,	1814	1817
	1819	1823
Wm. C. C. Claiborne	1797	1801
Thomas Claiborne,	1817	1819
John Cocke,	1819	1827

Senators and Representatives in Congress from Tennessee.

Representatives.	In	Out
David Crockett,	1827	1831
	1833	1835
Robert Desha,	1827	1831
William Dickson,	1801	1807
William C. Dunlap,	1833	1835
William Fitzgerald,	1831	1833
John B. Forrester,	1833	1835
Felix Grundy,	1811	1814
William Hall,	1831	1833
Thomas K. Harris,	1813	1815
Bennet H. Henderson,	1815	1817
Samuel Hogg,	1817	1819
Samuel Houston,	1823	1827
Parry W. Humphreys,	1813	1815
Jacob C. Isaacs,	1823	1833
Wm. M. Inge,	1833	1835
Andrew Jackson,	1796	1797
Cave Johnson,	1829	1835
Francis Jones,	1817	1823
Pryor Lea,	1827	1831
Luke Lee,	1833	1835
John H. Marable,	1825	1829
George W. L. Marr,	1817	1819
Pleasant M. Miller,	1809	1811
James C. Mitchell,	1825	1829
James K. Polk,	1825	1835
Samuel Powell	1815	1817
Balie Peyton,	1833	1835
James B. Reynolds,	1815	1817
	1823	1825
John Rhea,	1803	1815
	1817	1823
James T. Sanford,	1823	1825
John Sevier,	1811	1815

Senators and Representatives in Congress from Tennessee.

Representatives.	In	Out
James Standefer,	1823	1825
	1829	1835
Isaac Thomas,	1815	1817
Robert Weakley,	1809	1811
Jesse Wharton,	1807	1809
James White,	1792	1794

EXECUTIVE DEPARTMENT OF THE U.S.

The twelfth Presidential term of four years began on the 4th of March 1833; and will expire, with the 24th Congress, on the 3rd of March 1837.

		Salary
ANDREW JACKSON, Ten.	President,	$25,000
Martin Van Buren, N. Y.	V. President,	5,000

The following are the principal officers in the executive department of the government, who all hold their offices at the will of the President.

Department of State.

		Salary
Louis McLane,	Secretary,	$6,000
Daniel Brent,	Chief Clerk,	2,000
J. D. Craig,	Super. of the Pat Office,	1,500
Alexander McIntire,	Clerk,	1,000

Treasury Department.

		Salary
R. B. Taney,	Secretary,	$6,000
Asbury Dickins,	Chief Clerk,	2,000
Joseph Anderson,	First Comptroller,	3,500
James B. Thornton,	Second Comptroller,	3,000
Richard Harrison,	First Auditor,	3,000
William B. Lewis,	Second Auditor,	3,000
Peter Hagner,	Third Auditor,	3,000
Amos Kendal,	Fourth Auditor,	3,000
Stephen Pleasonton,	Fifth Auditor,	3,000
John Campbell,	Treasurer,	3,000
Thomas L. Smith,	Register,	3,000
Virgil Maxey,	Solicitor of the Treasury,	3,500

General Land Office.

| Elijah Hayward, | Commissioner, | 3,000 |

War Department.

		Salary
Lewis Cass,	Secretary,	$6,000
John Robb,	Chief Clerk,	2,000
L. L. Van Kleeck,	Clerk in the Req. Bar.	1,600
James L. Edwards,	Pr. Clk. in the Pen. Bur.	1,600
Elbert Herring,	Com. of Indian Affairs,	3,000
C. Irvine,	Com. of Gen. of Purchases,	3,000
Nathan Towson,	Paymaster General,	2,500
Joseph Lovell,	Surgeon General,	2,500

Navy Department.

		Salary
Levi Woodbury,	Secretary,	$6,000
John Boyle,	Chief Clerk,	2,000

Board of Navy Commissioners.

		Salary
John Rogers,	Com. and Pres. of the Board,	$3,500
Charles Stewart,	Commissioner,	3,500
Charles Morris,	do	3,500
Charles W. Goldsborough,	Secretary,	2,000
William G. Ridgely,	Chief Clerk,	1,600

General Post Office.

		Salary
William T. Barry,	Post-Master General	$6,000
C. K. Gardner,	Asst. P. M. Gen. 1st Divis.	2,500
Selah R. Hobble,	Asst. do 2d Divis.	2,500
Obadiah B. Brown,	Chief Clerk,	1,700
B. F. Butler,	Attorney General	3,500

STAGE ROUTES IN TENNESSEE.

1. From Nashville to Tuscumbia.

Good Spring	12	
Franklin,	6	18
Spring Hill	12	30
Columbia,	12	42
Mount Pleasant	10	52
Lawrenceburg	23	75
Florence	46	121
Tuscumbia	4	125

2. From Nashville to Huntsville, Ala. via Murfreesboro'.

To Mount View	11	
Murfreesboro'	22	33
Shelbyville	26	59
Lynchburg	14	73
Fayetteville	13	86
Hazle Green	16	102
Meridianville	7	109
Huntsville	8	117

3. From Nashville to Huntsville via Columbia and Pulaski.

To Columbia as in No. 1.	42	
Pulaski	33	75
Elkton	15	90
Huntsville	30	120

4. From Nashville to Memphis.

To Chestnut Grove	18	
Charlotte	22	40
Reynoldsburg	38	78
Huntingdon	31	109
Jackson	38	175
Bolivar	28	147
Middleburg	7	182
Sommerville	16	198
Morning Sun	21	219
Raleigh	12	131
Memphis	3	239

5. From Nashville to Mills Point, Ken.

To Reynoldsburg, as in No. 4	78	
Paris	30	108
Cullen	14	122
Dresden	9	131
Troy	29	160
Mill's Point,	19	179

6. From Blountsville to Huntsville, Ala. via Knoxville and M'Minnville.

To Kingsport	18	
Surgoinesville,	17	33
Rogersville	10	43
Bean's Station	18	61
Rutledge	9	70
Blain's X Roads	12	82
Knoxville	21	103
Campbell's Station	16	119
Kingston	25	144
Sparta	62	206

APPENDIX 303

M'Minnville	25	231
Winchester	42	272
Salem	10	283
New Market, Ala.	17	300
Huntsville	17	317

7. From Knoxville to Nashville, via Sparta and Murfreesboro'.

Campbell's Station	16	
Kingston	25	41
Sparta,	62	103
M'Minnville	25	128
Danville	22	150
Readyville	8	158
Murfreesboro'	12	170
Jefferson	10	180
Mount View	12	192
NASHVILLE	11	203

8. From Knoxville to Nashville, via Sparta and Lebanon.

To Sparta, as in No. 7		103
Allen's Ferry	18	121
Liberty	17	138
Alexandria	8	145
Lebanon	16	161
NASHVILLE	31	192

9. From Shorn's X Roads to Knoxville.

To Elizabethtown,	34	
Jonesboro'	18	52
Greenville,	24	76
Wood's Ferry	10	86
Newport,	12	98
Dandridge	15	113
New Market,	14	127
Knoxville	20	147

10. From Knoxville to Huntsville, Ala.

To Maryville	17	
Madisonville	11	28
Athens	14	42
Washington	23	65
Pikeville	23	88
Mount Airy,	14	102
Delphi	10	112
Jasper	21	133
Bellefonte, Ala.	32	165
Woodsville	21	186
Huntsville	30	216

11. From Knoxville to Spring Place, Geo.

Campbell's Station	14	
New Philadelphia	20	34
Athens	20	54
Calhoun	15	69
Spring Place, Geo.	25	94

12. From Asheville, N. C. to Nashville.

To Warm Springs	36	
Newport, Ten.	25	61
Dandridge	15	66
New Market	14	80
Knoxville	20	100
NASHVILLE, as in No. 8.	192	292

13. From Sparta to Glasgow, Ken.

To Milledgville	10	
Gainesboro'	30	40
M'Leansville	17	57
Tompkinsville, Ken.	12	69
Glasgow	26	95

14. From Sparta to Gallatin.

To Milledgeville	10	
Mount Richardson	10	28
Carthage	15	43
Dixon's Springs	10	53
Hartsville	6	59
Cairo,	14	73
Gallatin	5	78

15. From Jackson to Memphis.

To Denmark	12	
Brownsville	16	28
Durhamville	15	43
Covington	7	50
Randolph	16	66
Memphis	34	100

16. From Asheville, N. C. to Bean's Station.

To Warm Springs	36	
Greenville, Ten.	27	63
Cheek's X Roads	24	87
Bean's Station	12	99

17. From Warm Springs, N.C. to Huntsville.

To Newport, Ten.	25	
Sevierville	30	55
Marysville	30	85
Huntsville, as in No. 10.	190	284

18. From Florence, Ala. to Memphis

To Savannah	49	
Purdy	17	66
Bolivar	28	94
Memphis, as in No. 4	64	158

19. From Louisville to Nashville.

West Point,	21	
Elizabethtown,	22	43
Monfordsville,	27	70
Three Forks,	15	85
Dripping Spring,	10	95
Smith's Grove,	3	98
Bowlinggreen,	13	111
Franklin,	20	131
Tyree's Springs, T.	21	152
Haysboro',	15	167
Nashville,	6	173

20. From Frankfort, Ky., to Nashville.

Lawrenceburg,	12	
Salvisa,	9	21
Harrodsburg,	9	30
Perryville,	10	40
Lebanon,	19	59
New Market,	6	65
Allentown,	9	74

Campbellsville,	3	77
Greensburg,	12	89
Monroe,	13	102
Glasgow,	20	122
Scottsville,	23	145
Gallatin, T.,	37	182
Hendersonville,	10	192
Nashville,	15	207

21. From Lexington to Nashville.

Nicholasville,	13	
Shakertown,	12	25
Harrodsburg,	7	32
Perryville,	10	42
Lebanon,	19	61
New Market,	6	67
Allenton,	9	76
Campbellsville,	3	79
Greensburg,	12	91
Monroe,	13	104
Glasgow,	20	124
Scottsville,	23	147
Gallatin, T.	37	184
Nashville,	25	209

22. From Bowlinggreen to Nashville.

South Union,	14	
Russellville,	14	28
Adairsville	12	40
Springfield, T.,	11	51
Nashville	25	76

23. From Hopkinsville to Nashville.

Oak Grove,	12	
Clarksville, T.,	13	25
Lowe's	25	50
Nashville,	21	71

24. From Nashville to Shawneetown, Ill.

Springfield, T.	25	
Adairsville, Ky.	11	36
Russellville,	12	48
Greenville,	34	82
Madisonville,	23	105
Carla,	18	123
Morganfield,	20	143
Shawneetown,	15	158

25. From Nashville to Smithland.

Lowe's	21	
Clarksville,	25	46
Oak Grove,	13	59
Hopkinsville,	12	71
Oakland,	10	81
Princeton,	16	97
Salem,	29	126
Smithland,	15	141

STEAM BOAT ROUTES.

New Orleans to Florence, Al.		
M'h of Ohio river,		1005
Trinity, Ill.,	4	1009
America,	6	1015
Belgrade,	28	1043
Mouth of Ten. or Paducah, Ky.	6	1049
Duval's Ferry, T.,	37	1036
Ford's Ferry, T.,	29	1115
Petersville,	5	1120
Reynoldsburg,	36	1156
Duck River,	18	1174
Perryville,	24	1198
Carrollsville,	27	1225
Coffee	26	1251
Savannah,	9	1260
Waterloo, Al.,	25	1285
Bear creek,	12	1297
Colbert's Ferry,	14	1311
Florence	24	1335

New Orleans to Nashville, T.		
Mouth of Ohio,		1005
America, Ill.	10	1015
Belgrade,	28	1043
Paducah, Ky.	6	1049
Smithland,	6	1055
Eddyville,	55	1105
Canton,	20	1125
Dover, Ten.,	30	1155
Palmyra,	31	1186
Red River,	6	1192
Harpeth river,	20	1212
Nashville,	40	1252

INDEX

Abingdon, 103.
Acre, John, 120.
Adamsville, 103.
Aiken, John A., 60.
Alexander, Adam R., 53, 55, 69, 95, 278.
Alexander, Daniel, 103.
Alexander, William, 46, 48.
Alexandria, 103.
Allen, Robert, 49, 51, 53, 69, 95.
Allen, William, 21.
Allison, David, 27.
Alpin's Fork, 103.
Amoee District, 125.
Amoee River, 103.
Anderson, Joseph M., 27, 35, 36, 37, 40, 41, 43, 46, 53, 54.
Anderson, William E., 47, 57, 63.
Anderson County, 103.
Anderson's Creek, 104.
Anderson's Crossroads, 104.
Angelica Creek, 104.
Annsville, 104.
Arch Cave, 104-105.
Archaeological Remains in Tennessee, 104-105, 113-16, 172, 183 fn., 233, 257-58, 260, 276.
Armstrong, Hugh C., 69, 95.
Arnold, Thomas D., 63.
Arnoldam, 105.
Arrington's Creek, 105.
Ashe, Samuel P., 276.
Asylums, insane, 64, 221.
Athens, 105.
Atoka, 241 fn.

Baird, John, 30.
Baker, John, 20.
Baker, William, 17.
Baker's Creek, 107.
Baker's Fork, 107.
Balch, Alfred, 42, 46.
Balch, Rev. Hezekiah, 165.
Bald Mountain, 107.

Banks and banking, 44, 46, 47, 50-51, 52, 58, 60, 63, 64, 68, 219-20.
Baptist Church, Nashville, 216.
Barrel's Creek, 107.
Barren Creek, 107, 110 fn.
Barretsburg, 107.
Barry, Valentine D., 54.
Barton, Roger, 64.
Barton, Samuel, 212.
Barton's Creek, 107-108.
Bat Creek, 108.
Batavia, 108.
Bath Springs, 267 fn.
Batson's, 108.
Battle Creek, 108.
Bay's Mountain, 108.
Bean's Creek, 108.
Bean's Station, 108.
Bear Creek, 22, 108.
Beason's (Beoison's) Creek, 110 fn., 135 fn.
Beaver Creek, 18.
Beaver-dam Creek, 108-109.
Bedford, Thomas, 107, 109.
Bedford County, 109.
Beech Creek, 109.
Beech Grove, 109.
Beech Hill, 109.
Beech Plains, 109.
Beech River, 111.
Beechgrove, 109 fn.
Belboro', 110.
Belknap's, 110.
Bell, John, 57, 58, 63, 65.
Bellevue (Bellville), 110 fn.
Bellville, 110.
Belmont, 110.
Belmontaine (Toulon), 110, 285.
Bend Creek, 110.
Bent Creek, 110.
Beoison's Creek, 110.
Berryhill, William M., 220.
Big Barren Creek, 110.

Big Bluff Creek, 117 fn.
Big Bone Cave, 104-105.
Big Butt, 110.
Big Creek, 17, 110-111.
Big Hatchee, 111.
Big Honeycut, 111.
Big Limestone Creek, 18.
Big Muddy, 111.
Big Pigeon River, 111, 234.
Big Sandy, 249 fn.
Big Sycamore, 111.
Big War Creek, 111.
Bigby Creek, 110.
Bigbyville, 110.
Bird. See Byrd.
Birdsong Creek, 111.
Black, Joseph, 35, 116.
Black Water, 112.
Blackburn, Dr. Gideon, 218.
Blair, _____, 112 fn.
Blair, John, 35, 53, 55, 57, 58, 63, 65.
Blair's Crossroads, 112.
Blair's Ferry, 112.
Bledsoe, Abraham, 20.
Bledsoe, Isaac, 21, 22.
Bledsoe County, 112.
Bledsoe's Creek, 112-13.
Bledsoe's Lick, 21, 22, 113-16.
Blooming Grove Creek, 116.
Blount, William, 27, 28, 34, 35, 36, 37.
Blount, William G., 45, 48.
Blount, Willie, 36, 43, 44, 45, 46, 95.
Blount, Fort, 157, 280 fn.
Blount, Fort (Williamsburg), 157, 157 fn., 280, 280 fn.
Blount College, 187.
Blount County, 116-17.
Blountsville, 117.
Blue Creek, 117.
Blue Spring Creek, 117.
Bluff Creek, 117.

Boatyard, 118, 185. See also Kingsport.
Boiling Fork of Elk, 118.
Bolivar, 118.
Boone, Daniel, 17.
Boon's Creek, 118.
Boonshill (Boon's Hill), 118 fn.
Bowen, John H., 42, 45.
Bowers', 118.
Bowlinggreen, 118, 119. See also Branson's.
Boyd's Creek, 118.
Boyer's Warehouse, 161.
Bradford, Alexander B., 48.
Bradford, Benjamin, M., 55.
Bradshaw, Richard, 69, 95.
Bradshaw's Creek, 118.
Brady, William, 55.
Brainard Mission, 118-19, 254.
Bramlett, Lunsford M., 68.
Branson's (Bowlinggreen), 118, 119.
Bratton's, 119.
Brattontown (Bratton's), 119 fn.
Brazeale, Drury W., 36.
Breath, The, Indian chief, 33.
Brewer, Sterling, 51.
Brick Academy, 119.
Bridge Creek, 119.
Brimstone Creek, 119 fn.
Brookhill, 119.
Brown, Jacob, 120.
Brown, Dr. Morgan, 36, 231.
Brown, William F., 55.
Brown, William L., 46, 54.
Brownham, 119.
Brown's Cove, 119.
Brownsboro', 120.
Brownsville, 120.
Brunsonville, 120.
Brush Creek, 120 fn.
Bryan, Henry H., 49, 51.
Buchanan's Creek, 120.
Buckingham, Nathaniel B., 35, 37.
Bud Creek, 120.

Budd's Creek, 120.
Buffalo Creek, 121.
Buffalo Ironworks, 120.
Buffalo Mountain, 121.
Buffalo Port, 121.
Buffalo River, 121.
Bull Run, 121.
Bumpass' Cove, 121, 274.
Bumpass' Creek, 121.
Bunch, Samuel, 65.
Burford, David, 67.
Burges, Thomas, 130.
Burrville (Clinton), 133.
Burton, Robert M., 69, 95.
Bush Creek, 121.
Butler, 121, 145 fn.
Butler's Ferry, 121.
Byrd, William, 15.

Cade's Cove, 123.
Cabal, Terry H., 69, 95.
Cainsville, 123.
Cairo, 123.
Caldwell's Creek, 123.
Caledonia, 123.
Calf-killer River, 123-24.
Calhoun, 124.
Calhoun's Creek, 124.
Camp, J. D., 128.
Camp, John H., 57.
Camp Creek, 124.
Campbell, Rev. Aaron, 218.
Campbell, Abraham, 191.
Campbell, David, 27, 37, 190.
Campbell, George W., 38, 39, 40, 46, 48.
Campbell, John, 191.
Campbell, Thomas J., 46-47, 48, 51, 53, 56, 57, 58, 63.
Campbell, William, 22.
Campbell, William B., 64.
Campbell County, 124.
Campbell's Creek, 124.
Campbell's Station, 124-25.

Campbellsville, 186.
Canasauga, 125.
Cane Creek, 125.
Caney Creek, 125.
Caney Fork, 125-26.
Caney Spring Creek, 125.
Cannon, Newton, 46, 49, 51, 69, 95.
Canton, 126.
Cantrell, Stephen, 35
Caper's Creek, 126.
Carrick, Rev. Samuel, 31, 187.
Carroll, William, 51-52, 53, 54, 55, 57, 58, 59, 63, 64, 65, 67, 212, 221.
Carroll County, 126.
Carrollsville, 126.
Carrollton, 126.
Carson's Ironworks, 126.
Carter, Gen., 38.
Carter, Landon, 24, 36.
Carter, William B., 69, 95, 101.
Carter County, 126-27.
Carter's Valley, 17.
Carthage, 127.
Caruthers, Abraham, 68.
Caruthers, James, 58.
Caruthers, Robert L., 53, 58, 64.
Castalian Springs, 21, 116, 127.
Catawba Indians, 15.
Cathey's Creek, 127.
Catholic Church, in Nashville, 219.
Catron, John, 64.
Cave Hill, 127.
Cedar Creek, 127-28.
Cedar Grove, 128.
Cedar Lick Creek, 128.
Cedar Spring, 128.
Cedar Spring Creek, 128.
Celico, 128.
Celina, 128.
Center Hill Lake, 154 fn.
Centerville, 128.
Chalk-level, 128.
Chalmers, James R., 54.

INDEX

Chambers' Creek, 129.
Chapel Hill (Gideonsville), 129, 162 fn.
Charles, Solomon, 129.
Charleston, 129 fn.
Charlestown, 129.
Charley's Creek, 129.
Charlotte, 129.
Chattanooga (Chattonaga), 129, 141 fn.
Cheatham, Leonard P., 58.
Cheatham, Richard, 69, 95.
Cheek's Crossroads, 129.
Cherokee Creek, 129.
Cherokee Indians, 15, 16, 18, 19, 23, 25, 28, 29, 30, 31, 32, 33, 68, 119, 129, 130 fn., 143, 167, 197, 264, 267, 271.
Cherry Creek, 130.
Cherry Hill, 130.
Cherryville, 130.
Chestnut Grove (Joslin's), 130, 184.
Chestua, 130.
Chewalee, 130.
Chickamauga, 130.
Chickasaw Bluffs, 15, 33, 130.
Chickasaw Indians, 23, 28, 33, 34, 277.
Chickasaw Purchase, xi, 201.
Childress, William G., 69, 95.
Chilhowee, 130.
Chisholm's Creek, 130.
Chismburg, 130.
Chiswell (Chissel), Fort, 15, 16.
Choctaw Indians, 28.
Chota (Chote, Etchoe), 16, 130 fn.
Christian, Gilbert, ix, 17, 18.
Christian's Creek, 130-31.
Christmasville, 131.
Chuckey, 137 fn.
Chucky Bend, 131, 183.
Chunn's Store, 183.
Citico (Celico), 128 fn.

Civil Order, 131.
Clack, Spencer, 35.
Claiborne, Thomas, 45, 48.
Claiborne, William C. C., 36, 37, 38.
Claiborne County, 131-32.
Clark's Creek, 132.
Clark's Mills, 132.
Clarksville, 132.
Clear Creek (Spring Creek), 132, 255.
Clear Fork, 132-33.
Clerks, Edmund Tipton, 58.
Cleveland, Benjamin, 22.
Clifton (Carrollsville), 126 fn.
Clifty, 133.
Clifty Creek, 133.
Clinch Dale, 133.
Clinch Mountain, 17, 133.
Clinch River, 15, 20, 133.
Clinton, 104, 133.
Cloud's Creek, 133-34.
Clover Creek, 134.
Clover Hill, 134.
Clover Valley, 134.
Coal Creek, 134.
Cobb's, 134.
Cobbs, Robert L., 47, 56, 69, 95.
Cocke, John, 35, 36, 43, 49, 51, 53.
Cocke, Sterling, 47.
Cocke, William, 25, 30, 35, 36, 37, 42, 46.
Cocke County, 134-35.
Coffee, 135.
Coffee Landing, 135 fn.
Coffin, Rev. Charles, 165, 187.
Colbert, George, 277.
Cold Spring, 135.
Coleman, Joseph, 212.
Collins' River, 135.
Columbia, 135.
Columbus, 136.
Commerce, 136.
Congressional Districts, 53-54, 64.

Congressional Representatives, list of, 297-99.
Constitution of Tennessee (1835), 70-101.
Constitutional Convention (1834), 65, 68-70.
Conway, George, 37.
Conway, Joseph, 35.
Cook, William A., 64.
Cooke, Judge, 48.
Cooke, John W., 68.
Cooke, William A., 63.
Cool Spring, 136.
Copper Ridge, 136.
Cornersville, 136.
Cotton crop, estimated for 1826, 57.
Cotton Grove, 136.
Cotton Port, 136.
Cottonwood Creek, 136.
Cove Creek, 136.
Cove Spring Creek, 136.
Covington, 136-37.
Cowan, Ned, 20.
Cowan's Post Office, 137.
Cowansville, 137.
Cowen, David, 129.
Crab Orchard, 137.
Crabbe, H., 57.
Craig, David, 116.
Craig, John, 199.
Craighead, Thomas B., 56, 63.
Cranson's Creek, 137.
Crawford, John, 35.
Crawford's Creek, 137.
Creek Indians, 26, 28, 29, 31, 33, 34, 45.
Criswell's Creek, 137.
Crockett, David, 57, 58, 65.
Crockett, Robert, 20.
Cross, Maclin, 69, 95.
Cross Plains, 137.
Crooked Creek, 137.
Crooked Fork, 137.
Crump, 135 fn.

Crutcher, Thomas, 39, 41, 58.
Cub Creek, 138.
Cullen, 138.
Cumberland College (Nashville University), 215.
Cumberland Gap, 19, 138.
Cumberland Mountains, 138, 189.
Cumberland Presbyterian Church, in Nashville, 218-19.
Cumberland River, 17, 138-39.
Cypress Creek, 139.
Cypress Inn, 139 fn.

Daddy's Creek, 141.
Dale, Adam, 191.
Dallas, 141.
Daly's, 141.
Damascus, 141.
Dance, Russell, 53, 55, 57.
Dancy's, 141.
Dancyville, 141 fn.
Dandridge, 141-42.
Danville, 142.
Davidson County, 142-43.
Davidson County Academy (Nashville University), 214-15.
Davidson's Bluff, 143.
Davidson's Creek, 143.
Davidsonville, 143.
Davis' Mill, 143.
Davisville, 143.
Decatur, 143, 163 fn.
Decker, John, 223.
Deep Spring, 144.
Defeated Creek, 143-44.
DeKalb County, 21 fn.
Delaware Indians, 22.
Delphi, 144.
Denmark, 144.
Denton, 144.
Desha, Robert, 57, 58.
Desha's Creek, 144.
Dickenson, David W., 65.
Dickson, Joseph, 41.

Dickson, William, 38.
Dickson County, 144-45.
Dillahunty, Edward, 64.
Dismuke's Ferry, 199.
Dixon's Creek, 145.
Dixon's Springs, 145.
Doak, Rev. Samuel, x.
Dodson's Creek, 145.
Doe Creek, 145, 150. *See also* Elk Creek.
Doe River, 145.
Doeville (Doe River), 145 fn.
Doherty, George, 30, 35.
Doherty, James, 36.
Donelson, Samuel, 36.
Donelson, Stokely, 31.
Donelson, 157 fn.
Dotson's Camp Ground, 242 fn.
Dougherty's (McLemoresville), 197.
Douglass, Burchett, 63, 69, 95.
Dover, 145-46.
Dowell, Rev. A. M., 219.
Drake, Joseph, 20, 21, 105, 114.
Drake's Creek, 146.
Drake's Lick, 21.
Dresden, 146.
Dry Creek, 146.
Duck River, 146.
Duck River Furnace, 147.
Dugger's Ferry, 147.
Dukedom, 147.
Dumpling Creek, 147.
Duncan's (Cold Springs), 135, 147.
Dunlap, Hugh, 56.
Dunlap, William C., 85.
Durham, Thomas, 147.
Durhamsville, 147.
Dyer County, 147.
Dyer's Creek, 147.
Dyersburg, 147.

Eagle Creek, 149.

Earl, Ralph E. W., 114.
East Fork, 149.
East Liberty, 149.
Eaton, John H., 48, 49, 57, 60.
Eaton, 149.
Eaton's Creek, 149.
Edgar, Rev. John T., 218.
Education, 40, 60.
Edward's Fork, 149.
Effingham, 149.
Egnew's Creek, 149.
Elizabethton, 149-50.
Elk Creek, 145, 150. *See also* Doe Creek.
Elk Fork, 150.
Elk River, 150.
Elkin's Branch, 150.
Elkridge, 150.
Elkton, 150, 269 fn.
Elliott's Branch, 150.
Ellis' Creek, 151.
Elsworth, John C., 119.
Ely, George, 215.
Embree, Elijah, 231.
Embree's Furnace, 274.
Embree's Ironworks, 151.
Embree's (Embrey's) River, 151.
Emmerson, Thomas, 41, 48, 49, 53.
English's Creek, 151.
Enon's Creek, 151.
Episcopal Church, in Nashville, 215-16.
Erwin, John P., 55, 56, 220.
Estanallee Creek, 151.
Estanaula, Indian town, 29, 151.
Estebrook, Mr. & Mrs., 188.
Etchoe (Chota), 16, 130 fn.
Etowah (Holt's Store, Felicity), 155 fn.
Evans, Nathaniel, 29, 30.
Evan's Crossroads, 151.
Ewing, Andrew, 211.

Factor's Fork, 153.
Fall Creek, 153.
Fallingwater, 153-54.
Fallingwater Creek, 154.
Fallingwater River, 154 fn.
Farmington, 154.
Fayette County, 154.
Fayetteville, 154-55.
Felecity (Holt's Store, Etowah), 155.
Fentress, James, 46, 48, 51, 53, 156.
Fentress County, 155-56.
Ferguson, Patrick, 22.
Firey-Grizzard Creek, 156.
Fitzgerald, William, 63.
Five Mile Creek, 156.
Flat Creek, 156.
Flat Lick, 20.
Fleming's, 156.
Fletcher, Thomas H., 53, 63, 200.
Fletcher's Creek, 156.
Flinn's Creek, 156.
Flynn's Lick, 156 fn.
Fool Warrior, Cherokee chief, 143.
Ford, James, 31, 32, 35.
Fork of the River (Mecklenburg), 201 fn.
Forked Deer River, 156-57.
Fort, William, 35.
Foster, Ephraim H., 58.
Foster, Robert C., 39, 45, 48, 55, 65, 69, 95, 221.
Fountain Creek, 157.
Fountain Head, 157.
Fountain of Health, 157.
Fourth Creek, 157.
Fox Creek, 157.
Fracker, Michael, 191.
Franklin, Benjamin, 26.
Franklin, 158.
Franklin (Frankland), State of, 24, 25, 26, 184.
Franklin County, 157-58.
Frazer, John, 143-44.

Frazier, Samuel, 35.
French Broad River, 15, 158-59.
French Lick, 20, 22, 159, 211, 212, 223.
Frierson, Erwin, 58.
Fulton, James, 69.
Fulton, 159.

Gaines, E. P., 53, 161.
Gainesboro', 161.
Gallatin, 150, 161.
Garrett, Gray, 69, 95.
Garrett's Factory, 161.
Garrison Creek, 161.
Gate's (Pleasant View), 235.
General Assembly, sessions of, 35-60, 63-65, 67-68.
German's Creek, 162.
Gibbs, George W., 220.
Gibson, 162.
Gideonsville, 162.
Giles County, 162.
Gilleland, John, 224.
Gillespie's Fort, 18.
Gillespy, James, 69, 95.
Gillum's, 162-63.
Glass, Samuel, 116.
Glazebrook's, 163.
Globe Creek, 163.
Goodfield, 163.
Goodman's (Cool Spring), 138.
Goose Creek, 163.
Gordon, Boling, 69, 95.
Governors of Tennessee, list of, 292.
Graham, Daniel, 46, 48, 49, 54, 63.
Graham (Piney River), 234 fn.
Grainger County, 163.
Grant, ———, 143-44.
Grant, James, 16.
Grantsboro', 163.
Grassy Creek, 163.
Graves, Daniel, 163.

Gravesville, 163.
Gray, James, 69, 95.
Gray, Thomas, 36.
Greasy Cove, 274.
Great Island Town, 18.
Great Kenhawa River, 17.
Green, James I., 69.
Green, Nathan, 57, 64.
Green Garden, 164.
Green River, 164.
Green Valley, 164.
Greenaway, James, 116.
Greene, Nathaniel, 23.
Greene County, 164.
Greeneville, 164.
Greeneville College, 165.
Green's Lick Creek, 164.
Green-tree Grove, 164.
Greer's Fork, 165.
Grey's Creek, 164.
Grice's Creek, 165.
Grundy, Felix, 43, 45, 60.
Guess, John, 35.
Guin's Creek, 165.

Hagan, _____, 268.
Haggard, 167.
Hainsville, 167.
Half Pone, 167.
Hall, Francis, 36.
Hall, William, 57, 58, 59, 63.
Hamilton, James, 215.
Hamilton, John C., 36, 54.
Hamilton, John W., 68.
Hamilton, Joseph, 27.
Hamilton County, 167-68.
Hamlet, 168.
Hanna's, 168.
Hardeman, Thomas, 142.
Hardeman County, 169.
Hardeman's Crossroads, 169.
Hardin, James, 168.
Hardin County, 168-69.
Hardin's Creek, 168, 169.

Hardinsville, 168, 169.
Harmony (Quincy), 239.
Harpeth, 170.
Harpeth River, 169-70.
Harris, Alfred M., 47.
Harris, Thomas K., 45.
Harrisburg (Cherryville), 130.
Hart, James, 170.
Hartfield, 170.
Hartsville, 110, 141 fn.
Haskill, Joshua, 52.
Haskinsville, 170.
Hatchee, 170.
Hawkins, Benjamin, 27.
Hawkins County, 17, 170-71.
Hayes' Creek, 171.
Haynes', 171.
Haysboro', 170.
Haywood, John, 48, 55.
Haywood County, 171-72.
Heard, Stephen, 37.
Heaton's Station, 18.
Henderson, Bennet H., 46.
Henderson, Richard, 17.
Henderson, Thomas, 35, 43.
Henderson and Company, 17.
Henderson County, 172.
Hendersonville, 172.
Hend's Creek, 172.
Hend's Ridge, 172.
Henning, 159 fn.
Henry County, 172.
Hermitage, The, 172-73.
Hess, Nelson I., 69, 95.
Hess, William R., 46.
Hester, Ferrill, 173.
Hesterville, 173.
Hickman County, 173.
Hickman's Creek, 173.
Hickory Creek, 173.
High Peak, 173.
Hightower's Store, 173.
Hilham, 173.
Hill, H. R. W., 221.
Hill, Isaac, 69, 95.

Hill, John, 18.
Hill, William K., 58, 63, 67, 69, 96, 101.
Hill's Creek, 174.
Hillsboro', 174.
Hilly Creek, 174.
Hiwassee (Jolly's) Island, 183 fn.
Hiwassee lands, 5-51.
Hiwassee River, 174.
Hobson, Nicholas, 60, 64, 220.
Hodges, Calloway, 69, 95.
Hodges, James, 236.
Hogg, Dr. Samuel, 48.
Holiday, John, 21.
Holly (Hilly) Creek, 174 fn.
Holston, Treaty of, 31.
Holston River, 15, 17, 18, 20, 29, 174, 254.
Holston Seminary, 174, 224.
Holt's Store (Felicity, Etowah), 155, 174.
Honey Creek, 175.
Honeycutt (Honey) Creek, 175 fn.
Hopewell, 175.
Horn, Stanley F., quoted, iii.
Horse Creek, 175.
Horton, Joshua, 17.
Hoss, Henry, 165.
Houston, James, 35, 116.
Houston, Samuel, 49, 53, 55, 57, 58.
Howry, James M., 67.
Huling, Frederick W., 63, 67.
Humphreys, Parry W., 41, 42, 45, 48, 49.
Humphreys, West H., 69, 95.
Humphreys County, 175-76.
Humphrey's Mill, 176.
Hunting Creek, 176.
Huntingdon, 176.
Huntland, 249 fn.
Hurricane, 177.
Hurricane Creek, 176, 177.
Hurt's Crossroads, 177.

Independence, 179.
Indian Camp Creek, 179.
Indian Creek, 179.
Inge, William M., 65.
Insane, Nashville hospital for, 221.
Internal Improvements, 59, 60.
Iredill, 180.
Iron Mountain, 180.
Ironworks, in 1810, 43.
Isaacs, Jacobs C., 48, 53, 55, 57, 58, 63.
Island Creek, 180.
Isom's Store, 180.

Jack's Creek, 181.
Jacksboro (Jackborough), 181 fn.
Jacksborough, 181.
Jackson, Andrew, xi, 27, 36, 37, 53, 54, 56, 142, 212.
Jackson, 181-82.
Jackson College, 182.
Jackson County, 181.
Jamestown, 155-56, 182.
Jasper, 182-83.
Jefferson, first seat of Rutherford County, 183.
Jefferson County, 183.
Jennings, Dr. Obadiah, 218.
Jenning's Creek, 183.
Johnson, Cave, 47, 58, 63, 65.
Johnson, Thomas, 35, 46.
Johnson's Creek, 183.
Johnston, Samuel, 27.
Johnsville, 183.
Jolly's Island, 183.
Jones, Francis, 46, 48, 49, 51.
Jones Creek, 184.
Jonesboro', 183-84.
Joslin's (Chestnut Grove), 130, 184.
Joyner's, 184.
Judiciary, 42-43, 45, 47, 49, 52, 54, 57, 59, 63, 393-96.
Julius' (Dugger's Ferry), 147.

Kelly, Alexander, 29, 30, 35.
Kelly, John, 69, 95.
Kelly, William, 42, 45, 48.
Kendall, Peter, 69, 95.
Kendrick's Creek, 185.
Kennedy (Keneday) William E., 56, 68.
Kentucky River, 15.
Kercheval's, 185.
Kimbrough, Bradley, 69, 95.
Kincaid, Joseph, 69, 95.
Kincannon, A. A., 69, 95.
King, Robert, 185.
King Creek, 185.
King's Creek, 185.
King's Mountain, Battle of, 22.
Kingsbury, Rev. Cyrus, 119.
Kingsport, 185.
Kingston, 185-86.
Knox, ———, 186.
Knox, Robert, 36.
Knox, William, 233.
Knox County, 186.
Knox's, 186.
Knoxville, 36, 186-87.
Knoxville *Gazette*, 28.

Lacy, Hopkins, 31, 36.
Lafayette, Marquis de, visit to Tennessee, 54-55, 56.
LaFollette, 163 fn.
LaGrange, 189.
Lake Oliver, 189.
Lancaster, Richard, 189.
Lancaster, 189.
Lapsley, Rev. Robert A., 219.
Laughlin, Samuel H., 47.
Laurel Furnace, 189.
Laurel Gap, 189.
Laurel Mountains, 189.
Lawrence, James, 190.
Lawrence County, 189-90.
Lawrenceburg, 190.

Lawyers, in Tennessee, list of, 285-91.
Lea, Luke, 40, 41, 65.
Lea, Luke, Jr., 63, 67.
Lea, Pryor, 57, 58.
Leatherwood Creek, 190.
Lebanon, 190.
Lecory, John, 36.
Ledbetter, William, 69, 95.
Lee Valley, 191.
Leesburg, 190-91.
Lewis, Joel, 35, 142.
Lewis, Seth, 35, 36.
Lewis (Pleasant Hill), 235.
Lewis', 191.
Lexington, 191.
Liberty, 191.
Lick Creek, 191-92.
Liddonsville, 192.
Lieper's Fork, 192.
Limestone (Brownsboro), 120 fn.
Limestone Creek, 192.
Linch, David, 21.
Linch, William, 21.
Lincoln County, 192.
Lindsday, Isaac, 19.
Lindsey, Isaac, 212.
Lindsley, Rev. Philip, 215.
Linseyville, 192.
Lionel, 192.
Little Barren Creek, 192.
Little Bigby Creek, 192.
Little Doe River, 192.
Little Hatchee, 192.
Little Pigeon, 192.
Little Pigeon River, 193.
Little River, 193.
Little Rock Creek, 193.
Little Sycamore Creek, 193.
Little Tennessee River, 16.
Littlefield, Edward B., 220.
Log Mountain, 193.
Lone Mountain, 193.
Long Creek, 193.
Long Island, 16, 193.

INDEX

Long Island Flats, Battle of, 18.
Look Out Mountain, 193-94.
Looney, David, 35.
Looney, Mary, x.
Looney, Peter, 194.
Looneyville, 194.
Loosa Hatchee, 194.
Lost Creek, 194.
Loudon, Fort, 15, 16.
Louisville, 194.
Louisville & Northern Stages, schedule, 223.
Love, Robert, 194.
Lovell (Campbell's Station), 125 fn.
Love's Store, 235.
Loveville, 194.
Loving, William H., 69, 95.
Lowry, James P., 58.
Lowry, John, 36, 40, 143.
Loy's Crossroads, 195.
Luton, Reed, 120.
Lynch. *See* Linch.
Lynchburg, 195.
Lynnville (Lynn Creek), 195 fn., 245 fn.
Lyon's Creek, 195.

McAdoe's Creek, 197.
MacAllis' Crossroads, 197.
McAllister's Crossroads, 197 fn.
M'Clellan, Abram, 69, 95.
McClung, Charles, 36.
McCorry, Thomas, 39, 41.
McCrory's Creek, 197.
McDowell, Charles, 22.
M'Gaughey, John, 69, 96.
McGavock, Randal, 36.
McIntosh, John, 221.
McKendree, Bishop, 217.
M'Kinney, John A., 69.
M'Kinney, Robert J., 69, 95.
McKoysville, 197.
MacLean's Mills, 197.
McLeansville, 197.
McLemore, John C., 44.
McLemoresville (Carrollton), 128.
McMillan's, 198.
McMinn, Joseph, 35, 39, 40, 41, 45, 47-48, 50, 197.
McMinnville, 197-98.
McNairy, Andrew, 36.
McNairy, Boyd, 221.
McNairy, John, 142, 212.
McNairy County, 198.
McNutt, Isaac, 36.
McReary's, 198.

Mabry, Joseph A., 69, 96.
Macay, John, 212.
Maclin, William, 34, 35, 38, 41.
Macon (Beech Plains), 109.
Madison County, 198.
Madisonville, 198, 254 fn.
Mansker, Kasper, 20, 21, 199.
Mansker's Creek, 21, 199.
Mansker's Lick, 21, 22.
Marable, John H., 55, 57.
Marion County, 199.
Marr, G. W. L., 42, 48, 69, 96.
Marrowbone, 199.
Marsh Creek, 199.
Marshall's Creek, 199.
Marshall's Ferry, 199.
Martin, Abraham, 57.
Martin, John D., 53.
Martin, William, 58.
Martin, William B., 47.
Martin's Creek, 199.
Maryville, 199-200.
Maury, Abraham, 158.
Maury County, 200.
Meadow Creek, 200.
Mecklenburg, 200-201 fn.
Meigsville, 201.
Memphis, 201.
Memphis and La Grange Railroad Company, viii

Menifee, John, 26, 35.
Meridian Creek, 201.
Mero District, 27-28, 35, 36, 40.
Methodist Church, in Nashville, 216-17.
Middle Fork, 201-202.
Middleburg, 201.
Midway, 202.
Mifflin, 202.
Miles, William, 32.
Mill Creek, 202.
Mill Fork, 202.
Milledgeville, 202.
Miller, Francis, 58.
Miller, Pleasant M., 43.
Miller's Cove, 202.
Miller's Island, 202.
Milton, 202.
Minor, Henry, 45, 46.
Mississippi River, 15, 202-205.
Mitchell, James C., 45, 55, 57.
Monroe, 205-206.
Monroe County, 205.
Montgomery, John, 32, 69, 96.
Montgomery, John A., 49.
Montgomery, William, 35.
Montgomery, 206.
Montgomery County, 206.
Montgomery's, 206.
Moody's Fork, 206.
Moore, Jacob, 103.
Moorsburg, 206.
Moorsville, 206-207.
Morgan County, 207.
Morgantown (Morganton), 207 fn.
Morris, Eastin, iii-iv, vii-ix, vi, 64, 221.
Morrison, David, 221.
Morrison's Crossroads, 207 fn.
Morristown, 207.
Morrow, Dr. William I., 69.
Moscow, 207-208.
Moss Creek, 183, 208.
Mossy Creek, 208.

Mossy Run, 208.
Mount Airy, 208.
Mount Carmel, 208.
Mount Comfort, 208.
Mount Henry, 208.
Mount Pinson, 208.
Mount Pisgah, 208.
Mount Pleasant, 208.
Mount Richardson, 209.
Mount Sterling, 209.
Mount View, 209.
Mountain Creek, 208.
Mountain View, 209 fn.
Mouth of Paintrock, 209.
Mount of Tellico, 209.
Mud Creek, 209.
Muddy Creek, 209.
Mulberry, 209.
Mulberry Creek, 209.
Mulherring's Creek, 209.
Mulloy, Thomas, 212.
Mulloy's, 209.
Murfreesboro, 48, 51, 209-10.

Nanconnah Creek, 211.
Naples, 211.
Narrimore, 211.
Nash, Francis, 212.
Nashboro, 212.
Nashoba, 211.
Nash's Bluff, 211.
Nashville, 56, 142, 211-24: site, 211; history, 211-13; list of tradespeople in 1834, 213; municipal buildings, 213-14; educational institutions, 214-15; churches, 215-19; banks, 219-20; penitentiary, 220-21; lunatic hospital, 221; waterworks, 221-22; Vauxhall Garden, 222-23; Sulphur Spring, 223; post office, 223; transportation, 223; location, 223-24.
Nashville, University of, 214-15.

Nashville Female Acedmy, 219.
Natchez (Miss.), 20.
Neal, John, 69, 96.
Nelson, Alexander M., 40, 41.
Nelson, Matthew, 46.
Nelson, Richard, 69, 96.
Nelson, Thomas A. R., 68.
Nelson's Creek, 224.
Nettle Carrier, 225.
Nevin's Crossroads, 224.
New Canton, 224.
New Hope, 224.
New Market (Newmarket), 224 fn.
New Port (Newport), 134, 135, 224-25.
New River, 17, 225.
New York, 225.
Newell, Samuel, 35.
Newman's Ridge, 224.
Newmarket *Telegraph*, 224.
Newport. *See* New Port.
Nickajack, Indian town, 32.
Nimble Creek, 225.
Nixon, Henry, 56.
Nixon's Fork, 225.
Noah's Fork, 225.
Nolachuckey, 225.
Nolensville, 225.
North Carolina land claims, law amended, 48.
North Chickamauga, 226.
North Cross Creek, 225.
North Fork, 226.

Oak Grove, 227.
Obed's (Obey's, Obids, Obies) River, 227.
Obion (Obionsville), 227 fn.
Obion County, 227.
Obion River, 227-28.
Obionsville, 227.
Ocoee (Amoee) River, 103 fn.
Oconnostota, Cherokee chief, 18.

Ohio River, 15, 17.
Oil spring (on Wolf River), 155.
"Old Salem," 249 fn.
Old Stone Fort. *See* Stone Fort.
Old Town, 228.
Old Town Creek, 228.
Oliver Springs (Oliver's), 228 fn.
Oliver's, 228.
Oporto, 228.
Oppossum Creek, 228.
Ordinance of 1787, 30.
Ore, James, 32.
Outlaw, Alexander, 35, 38.
Outlaw, William, 36.
Overall's Creek, 228.
Overton, John, 48.
Overton County, 228.
Owl Creek, 229.
Ozone, 153 fn.

Pactolus, 231.
Page's Mills, 231.
Paint Rock, 231.
Paint Rock Creek, 231.
Palmyra, 231.
Panther Creek, 231.
Paperville, 231-32, 253 fn.
Paris, 232.
Parker, Isham A., 36.
Parmantier, N. S., 215.
Parsons, Enoch, 48.
Paschal, 232.
Pea Ridge, 232.
Pearson, Jacob, 233.
Peck, Adam, 35.
Peck, Jacob, 41.
Penal System, 59-60, 63, 68.
Penitentiary, 220-21; proposed location, 252.
Percy Priest Lake, 259 fn.
Perry County, 232-33.
Perry's, 233.
Perryville, 233.
Person's Creek, 233.

Petersburg, 233.
Petersville, 233.
Peyton, Balie, 65.
Peyton, Ephraim, 143-44.
Peyton, John, 143-44.
Peyton, Thomas, 143-44.
Peyton's Creek, 233.
Philadelphia, 233.
Phillips, Joseph, 54, 56, 60.
Pickering, Timothy, 34.
Pickering, Fort, 157, 201.
Pigeon Creek, 234.
Pigeon River, 234.
Pigeon Roost, 233.
Pikeville, 234.
Pillow, Gideon J., 63.
Pinewood (Piney River), 234 fn.
Piney Creek, 234.
Piney River, 234.
Pinhook, 234.
Pinson Mounds, 208 fn.
Pistol Creek, 234.
Playball Creek, 234.
Pleasant Exchange, 234-35.
Pleasant Grove, 235.
Pleasant Hill, 235.
Pleasant Run, 235.
Pleasant Shade, 235.
Pleasant Town, 235.
Pleasant View, 235.
Plum Creek, 235.
Plum Point, 235.
Pocahontas, 235.
Point Centre, 235.
Polk, James K., 48, 51, 55, 57, 58, 63, 65.
Polk, William, 169.
Polkpatch Creek, 235.
Pond Creek, 235.
Poorvalley Creek, 236.
Poplar Cove, 155.
Poplar Creek, 236.
Poplar Grove, 236.
Population, 43, 49-50, 60-62, 65-67.

Port Royal, 236.
Porter, Thomas C., 69, 96.
Porter's Creek, 236.
Portersville, 236.
Portsville (Morganton), 207.
Post Office, in Nashville, 223.
Post Offices, in Tennessee, 104 fn.
Powell Ambrose, 236.
Powell, Samuel, 41, 46, 48, 49.
Powell's Mountain, 236.
Powell's River, 236-37.
Powell's Valley, 19, 20, 237.
Presbyterian Church, in Nashville, 217-18.
President's Island, 237.
Prestonville, 237.
Princeton, 237.
Proctor's Creek, 237.
Prud'homme, Fort, 15.
Pulaski, 237.
Purdy, John, 69, 96.
Purdy, 237-38.
Purdy's Garrison, 33.

Quincy, 239.

Raccoon Creek, 241.
Rains, John, 20.
Raleigh, 241.
Ramsey, Francis A., 35.
Ramsey, J. G. M., 201 fn.
Ramsey's (Mecklenburg), 200-201 fn.
Randolph, 241.
Raspberry, 241.
Rat Creek, 241.
Readyville, 241.
Red Bridge, 241.
Red Hill, 241-42.
Red River, 242.
Reed's Creek, 242.
Reedy Creek, 242.
Reel Foot River, 242.
Reinses (Indian) Creek, 179, 242.

INDEX

Reneau, Lewis, 56.
Renfro's Creek, 242.
Reynolds, James B., 46, 53.
Reynoldsburg, 242.
Rhea, Jane (Preston), ix.
Rhea, John, ix, 35, 36, 38, 39, 40, 43, 48, 49, 51.
Rhea, Matthew, iii-iv, ix-xi.
Rhea County, 243.
Rheatown, 243.
Rice's, 243.
Richardson, George W., 69, 96.
Richland Creek, 243.
Richland Grove, 243.
Richmond, 244.
Ridley, Bromfield L., 63.
Ridley, Henry, 69, 96.
Ridley, Moses, 221.
Riley's Creek, 244.
Roadman, William C., 69, 96.
Roane, Archibald, 27, 36, 38, 41, 48.
Roane County, 244.
Roane's Creek, 244.
Roaring Creek, 244.
Roaring River, 20, 244.
Robertson, Felix, 221.
Robertson, James, 17-18, 21, 28, 32, 57, 142, 211.
Robertson, Julius C. N., 69, 96.
Robertson, 245.
Robertson County, 244-45.
Robertson's Creek, 245.
Robertson's Fork, 245.
Robertson's Springs, 245, 260, 268. *See also* Sulphur Fork.
Robinson, Charles, 26.
Robinson's Creek, 245.
Rock Creek, 245.
Rock Island, 245.
Rockcastle (Ky.), 19.
Rockcastle Cove, 245.
Rockville, 245.
Rocky Creek, 245.

Rocky River (Calhoun's Creek), 124.
Rocky Springs, 245.
Rodgers, John, 172.
Rodgers, John B., 63.
Rogers, James, 49.
Rogers, William C., 123.
Rogers Creek, 246.
Rogersville, 246.
Rome, 246.
Roseton, 246.
Rosetta, 246.
Ross', 246.
Rotton's Fork, 246.
Roulston, George, 28, 37, 246.
Round Lick, 247.
Round Lick Creek, 246-47.
Rural Hill, 247.
Russell, ———, 20.
Russell's Creek, 247.
Russellville, 247.
Rutherford, Griffith, 31.
Rutherford, 247.
Rutherford County, 247.
Rutherford's Creek, 247.
Rutherford's Fork, 247.
Rutledge, George, 30, 35.
Rutledge, 247-48.

Sale Creek, 249.
Salem, 249.
"Salt Lick," 249 fn.
Salt Lick Creek, 249.
Sam's Creek, 249.
Sandy Creek, 249.
Sandy Hill, 249.
Sandy River, 249.
Savannah, 249-50.
Scott, Edward, 37.
Scott, James, 56, 69, 96.
Scott, Samuel, 206
Searcy, Bennet, 36, 45, 48.
Searcy, Robert, 38.
Searcy's, 250.

Selmer, 238 fn.
Senter, William T., 69, 96.
Sequatchee River, 250.
Sequatchee Valley, 250.
Sevier, John, 17-18, 22, 24, 26, 28, 29, 31, 35, 36, 38, 39, 40, 41, 43, 45.
Sevier County, 250-51.
Sevierville, 251.
Shannon, Robert, 251.
Shannonsville, 251.
Sharp, Henry, 69, 96.
Shaw, James, 212.
Shawnee Indians, 17, 28.
Shelby, Evan, 17, 18.
Shelby, Isaac, xi, 22.
Shelby, John, 18, 221.
Shelby County, 251.
Shelbyville, 251-52.
Shepherdsville, 252.
Sherman, Rev. David, 187.
Shields, John, 36.
Shippingport, 252.
Shippingsburg, 252.
Shoal Creek, 252.
Short Creek, 252.
Siloa, 252.
Silver Springs (Cedar Grove), 128, 252.
Simpson's, 252.
Sinking Cane, 252 fn.
Sinking Creek, 253.
Slavery, 63-64.
Smartt, William C., 69, 96.
Smith, Daniel, 37, 212.
Smith, Henry, 20.
Smith, James, 17, 258.
Smith, Rev. James, 69, 96.
Smith, Samuel G., 221.
Smith County, 253.
Smithfield, 253.
Smith's, 253.
Smith's Fork, 253-54.
Smithville, 253.
Snake Creek, 254.

Somerville (Sommerville), xi, 254 fn.
Sommerville, John, 220.
Sommerville, Robert M., 254.
South Cross Creek, 254.
South Fork, 254.
South West Point, 28, 185, 254.
Southwest Territory. *See* Territory of the United States South of the River Ohio.
South Western Theological Seminary of the Presbyterian Church, 200.
Sparta, 254.
Speedwell, 255.
Spencer, Thomas Sharpe, 21, 114, 255.
Spencer,'s Creek, 255.
Spencer's Hill, 255.
Spring Creek, 255.
Spring Creek Crossroads, 184.
Spring Hill, 182 fn., 255.
Springfield, 256.
Springmount, 256.
Stage Routes in Tennessee, 302-305.
Standing Rock, 256.
Standing Stone Creek, 256.
Stanford, James T., 53, 58, 63, 65.
State Line, 256.
Statesville, 256.
Station Camp Creek, 256-57.
Steam Boat Routes in Tennessee, 306.
Stein, Albert, 222.
Stephens, Abednego, 215.
Stephenson, Matthew, 69, 96.
Stewart County, 257-58.
Stewart's Creek, 257.
Stewart's Ferry, 257.
Stiffee, John, 257.
Stiffeetown, 257.
Stock Creek, 257.
Stone, Uriah, 17, 20, 258.
Stone Fort, 257-58.

INDEX 323

Stone Mountain, 259.
Stoner, Michael, 19.
Stoner's Creek, 258.
Stone's River, 17, 258.
Stony Creek, 259.
Stoph, Christopher, 21.
Straight Creek, 259.
Stuart, James, 35, 37, 38.
Stuart, Thomas, 42.
Sugar Creek, 259.
Sugar Loaf. See Bald Mountain.
Sugg's Creek, 259.
Sullivan County, 259-60.
Sulphur Creek, 260.
Sulphur Fork, 260.
Sulphur Lick Creek, 260.
Sumner County, 142, 260-61.
Surgoin's Creek, 261.
Surgoinsville, 261.
Swan Creek, 261.
Sweet-water Creek, 261.
Swift Creek, 261.
Sycamore Creek, 261.

Tacket's Creek, 263.
Tallassee, 263.
Tamotley (Tamotlee), Cherokee town, 18.
Tatum, Howel, 36, 37.
Taylor, J. P., 47.
Taylor, James P., 46, 68.
Taylor, Leroy, 30.
Taylor, Parmenas, 31.
Taylor's Creek, 263.
Tazewell, 263.
Tellico, 16, 263.
Tellico Plains, 263.
Ten-mile Stand, 265.
Tennessee, boundaries, 5; area, 5-6; geographical features, 6-7; minerals, 7-8; climate, 8; products of, 8-9; antiquities, 9; rivers of, 9-10; schools, 10; civil divisions of, 10-12; government of, 12-13; congressional districts of, 14; history of, 14-70; admitted to union, 34; population, 43, 49-50, 60-62, 65-67; governors of, 393; judiciary of, 393-96; congressional representatives from, 297-99; state routes in, 302-305; steam routes in, 306.
Tennessee Gazetteer, sources from which drawn, 3-5.
Tennessee Ironworks, 265.
Tennessee River, 15, 17, 32, 263-65.
Terrel, George W., 60.
Terril, Obadiah, 20.
Territory of the United States South of the River Ohio, 27.
Third Creek, 265.
Thomas, Isaac, 46.
Thomas, Micajah, 211.
Thompson, Gideon, 202.
Thompson's Creek, 265.
Three Forks, 265.
Tipton, Jacob, 46, 47, 48, 51.
Tipton, John, 30, 35, 40.
Tipton, Samuel, 149.
Tipton County, 265.
Tisdale's Creek, 265.
Tobacco Port (Brunsonville), 120 fn.
Todd's, 265.
Tollets Mill, 180.
Tom's Creek, 265.
Totten's Wells, 265.
Toulon, 265.
Townsend, 123 fn.
Trace Creek, 266.
Transylvania Purchase, 18.
Trenton, 266.
Trimble, James, 42.
Troost, Gerard, 215.
Trousdale, 266.
Troy, 266.
Tuckaluchee Cove, 266.
Tumbling Shoals, 266-67.

Tunnacunhe Creek, 267.
Tunnells, 267.
Turkey Creek, 267.
Turnbow's Creek, 267.
Turnersville, 267.
Turney, Peter, 31.
Tusculum, 267.
Tusculum College, 267 fn.
Two-mile Creek, 267.
Tyree, Richmond C., 268.
Tyree's Springs, 267-68.
Tyson, Benjamin P., 281.

Unica Mountains, 269.
Union, 269.
Union Seminary, 182 fn.
United States, Executive Officials of, 300-301.
Unitia, 269.
Upper Elkton, 269.
Ury, Ennis, 69, 96.

Valley Town, 271.
Van Buren, 271.
Vanwyck, A., 220.
Vass, John F., 128.
Vaughn's Creek, 271.
Vauxhall Garden, in Nashville, 222-23.
Vernon, 271.
Vinton, Stokely, 120.

Walden's (Wallen's) Ridge, 273 fn.
Walker, Joel, 58.
Walland, 202 fn.
Wallen, 273.
Wallen, Scaggs & Company, 236.
Wallen's Ridge, 273.
Walnut Grove, 273.
Walton, Isaac, 69, 96.
War of 1812, 44-45.
War Trace Creek, 273.

Ward, Edward, 46, 51.
Warm Springs, 158-59.
Warnersville, 273.
Warren County, 273.
Warrensburg, 273.
Wartburg, 206 fn.
War-trace Fork, 274.
Washington, Thomas, 47.
Washington, 275.
Washington County, 19, 28, 274-75.
Washington District, 27, 35, 36.
Washington Furnace, 275.
Watauga River, 275.
Watauga Settlement, 17.
Water Works, in Nashville, 222-23.
Waverly, 242 fn.
Wayne County, 275-76.
Waynesboro', 276.
Weakley, Robert, 35, 43, 45, 48, 53, 69, 96.
Weakley County, 276.
Weakley's Creek, 276.
Wear Valley (Wear's Cove), 276 fn.
Webster, Jonathan, 69, 96.
Weir, Samuel, 30.
Weller, Rev. George, 216.
Well's Creek, 276.
Wesley, 276-77.
West Fork, 277.
West Sandy, 277.
Western District, 277-78.
Wharton, Jesse, 37, 40, 45.
Wheaton's Creek, 278.
White, Hugh L., 36, 41, 46, 56, 58.
White, James, 31, 35, 36-37, 38, 186.
White, John J., 69, 96.
White County, 278.
White House, 279 fn.
White Oak, 278-79.
White Oak Creek, 279.

White Plains, 279.
White-house, 279 fn.
White's Creek, 279.
Whitesides, James A., 57, 60, 63, 67.
Whitesides, Jenkin, 43.
Whiting, 279.
Whitley, William, 32.
Whitson, John, 69, 96.
Whyte, Robert, 48.
Wilcox, Samuel, 236.
Wild-cat Creek, 279-80.
Wilkinson, John, 36, 47.
Williams, Daniel, 211.
Williams, Edward, 280.
Williams, James, 22.
Williams, John, 46, 54.
Williams, Nathaniel W., 42, 48, 49, 68.
Williams, Sampson, 31-32.
Williams, Thomas H., 35, 37.
Williams', 280.
Williamsburg (Fort Blount), 157, 157fn., 280, 280 fn.
Williamson County, 280.
Williamsport, 280.
Willingham's, 280.
Wilson, David, 31.
Wilson County, 280.
Wilson's 281.

Wilson's Creek, 281.
Winchester, James, 31, 35, 41.
Winchester, 281.
Winchester District, 40.
Winton, 281.
Witcher's Crossroads, 282.
Wolf River, 282.
Wommack, Carter, 18.
Wommack's Fort, 18.
Wood Lake, 282.
Woodbourne, 282.
Woodbury. See Danville.
Woodholm, 282.
Woods, Joseph, 221.
Wood's Ferry, 150, 282.
Wood's Store, 126, 282.
Woodsville, 282.
Woolfolk, Joseph, 184.
Wright, Frances, 211.
Wyman's Creek, 282.
Wynn, Thomas, 282.
Wynnsborough, 282.

Yearsly, David, 42, 46.
Yeatman Woods & Company, Nashville, 220.
Yellow Creek, 283.
Yellow Mountain, 283.
Yerger, Samuel, 65.

www.ingramcontent.com/pod-product-compliance
Lightning Source LLC
Chambersburg PA
CBHW071956220426
43662CB00009B/1148